THE SILENCER

CODE OF HONOR

VOL. 1

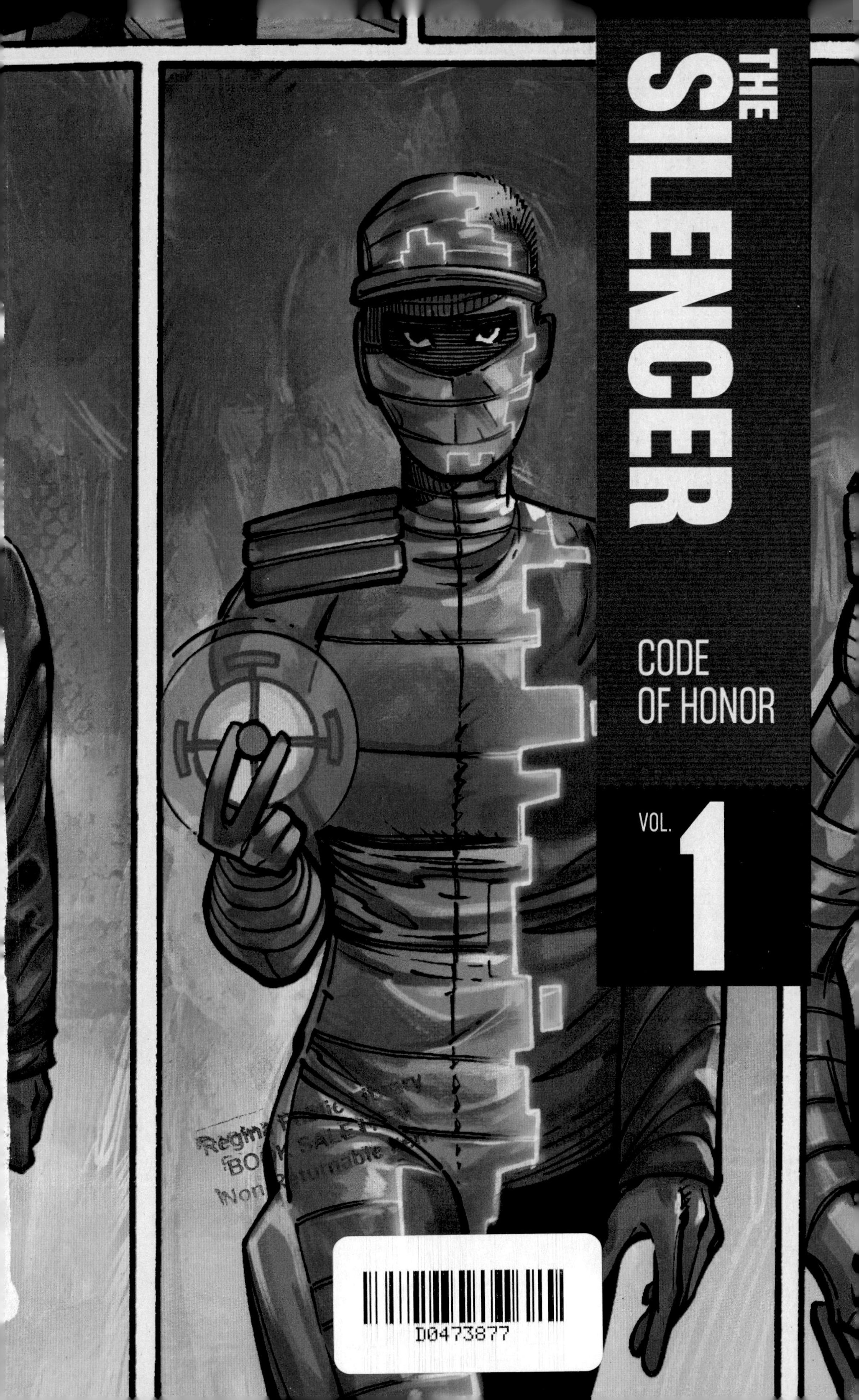

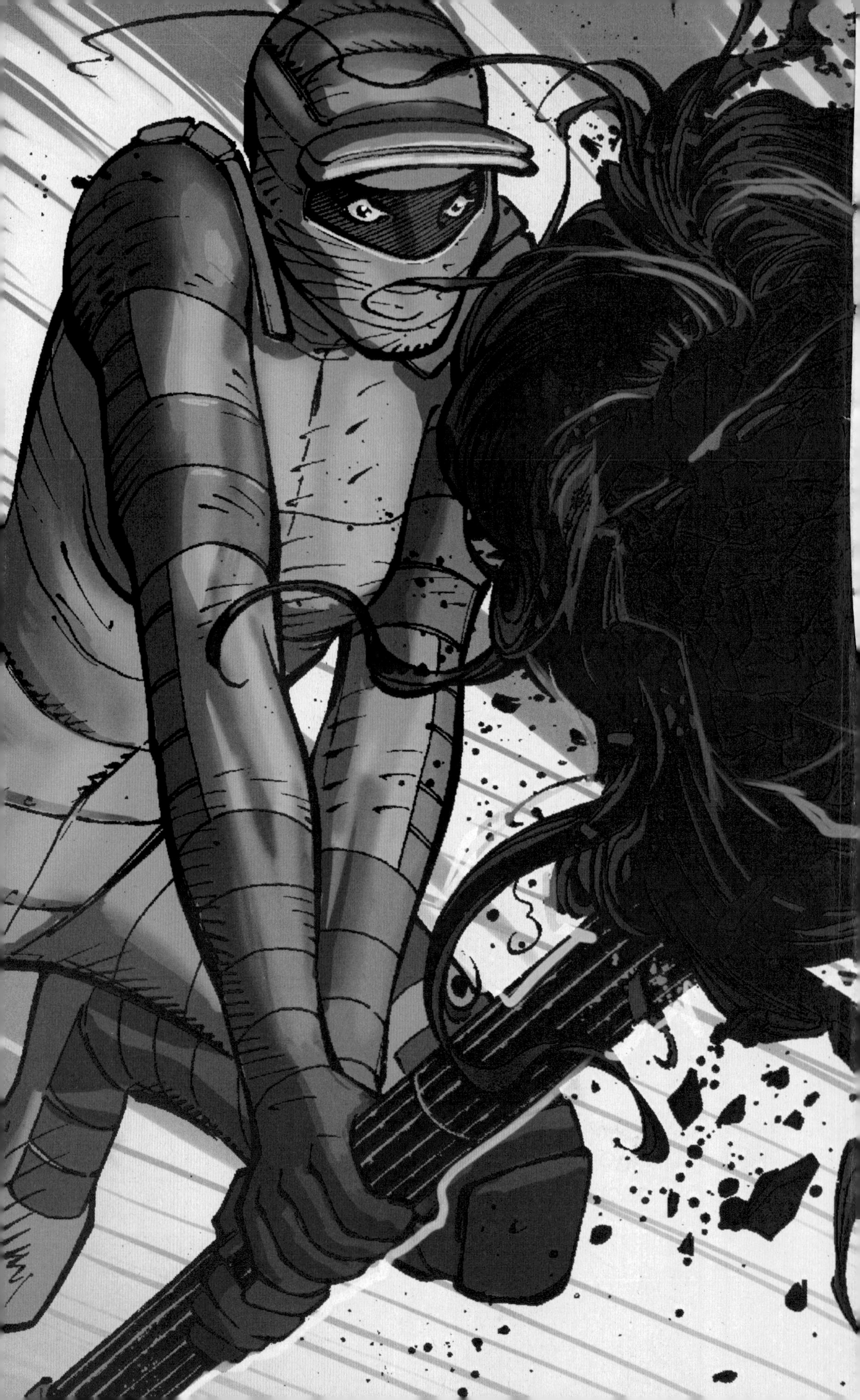

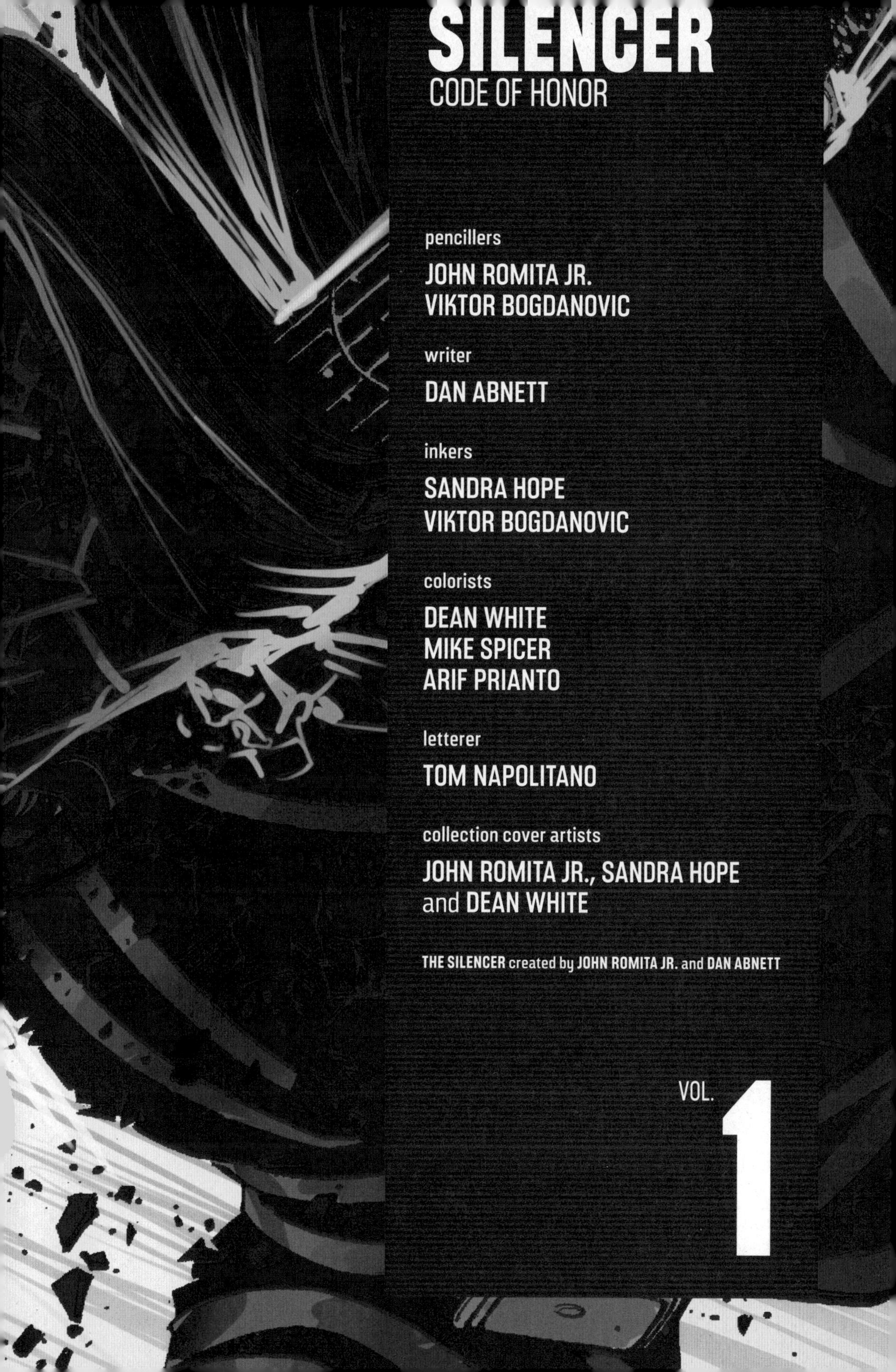

SILENCER
CODE OF HONOR

pencillers

JOHN ROMITA JR.
VIKTOR BOGDANOVIC

writer

DAN ABNETT

inkers

SANDRA HOPE
VIKTOR BOGDANOVIC

colorists

DEAN WHITE
MIKE SPICER
ARIF PRIANTO

letterer

TOM NAPOLITANO

collection cover artists

JOHN ROMITA JR., SANDRA HOPE
and **DEAN WHITE**

THE SILENCER created by **JOHN ROMITA JR.** and **DAN ABNETT**

VOL. 1

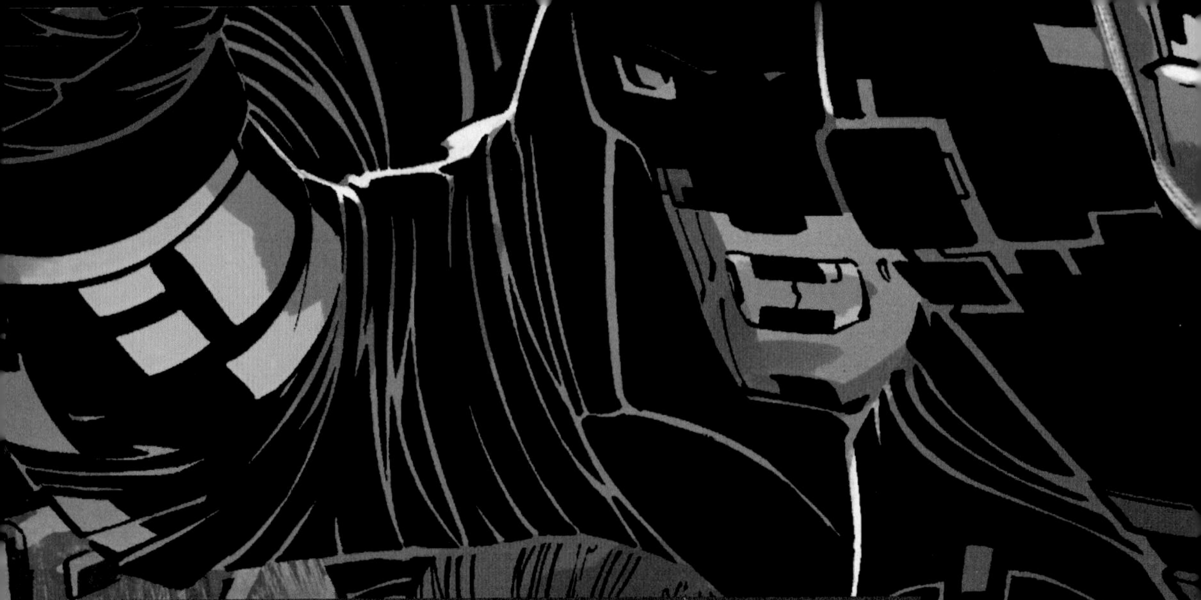

PAUL KAMINSKI Editor – Original Series
ROB LEVIN Associate Editor – Original Series
ANDREA SHEA \ ANDREW MARINO Assistant Editors – Original Series
JEB WOODARD Group Editor – Collected Editions
ROBIN WILDMAN Editor – Collected Edition
STEVE COOK Design Director – Books
MONIQUE NARBONETA Publication Design

BOB HARRAS Senior VP – Editor-in-Chief, DC Comics
PAT McCALLUM Executive Editor, DC Comics

DAN DiDIO Publisher
JIM LEE Publisher & Chief Creative Officer
AMIT DESAI Executive VP – Business & Marketing Strategy, Direct to Consumer & Global Franchise Management
BOBBIE CHASE VP & Executive Editor, Young Reader & Talent Development
MARK CHIARELLO Senior VP – Art, Design & Collected Editions
JOHN CUNNINGHAM Senior VP – Sales & Trade Marketing
BRIAR DARDEN VP – Business Affairs
ANNE DePIES Senior VP – Business Strategy, Finance & Administration
DON FALLETTI VP – Manufacturing Operations
LAWRENCE GANEM VP – Editorial Administration & Talent Relations
ALISON GILL Senior VP – Manufacturing & Operations
JASON GREENBERG VP – Business Strategy & Finance
HANK KANALZ Senior VP – Editorial Strategy & Administration
JAY KOGAN Senior VP – Legal Affairs
NICK J. NAPOLITANO VP – Manufacturing Administration
LISETTE OSTERLOH VP – Digital Marketing & Events
EDDIE SCANNELL VP – Consumer Marketing
COURTNEY SIMMONS Senior VP – Publicity & Communications
JIM (SKI) SOKOLOWSKI VP – Comic Book Specialty Sales & Trade Marketing
NANCY SPEARS VP – Mass, Book, Digital Sales & Trade Marketing
MICHELE R. WELLS VP – Content Strategy

THE SILENCER VOL. 1: CODE OF HONOR

DC Comics, 2900 West Alameda Ave., Burbank, CA 91505
Printed by Times Printing, LLC, Random Lake, WI, USA. 8/7/18. First Printing.
ISBN: 978-1-4012-8335-3

Library of Congress Cataloging-in-Publication Data is available.

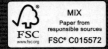

MIX
Paper from responsible sources
FSC www.fsc.org
FSC® C015572

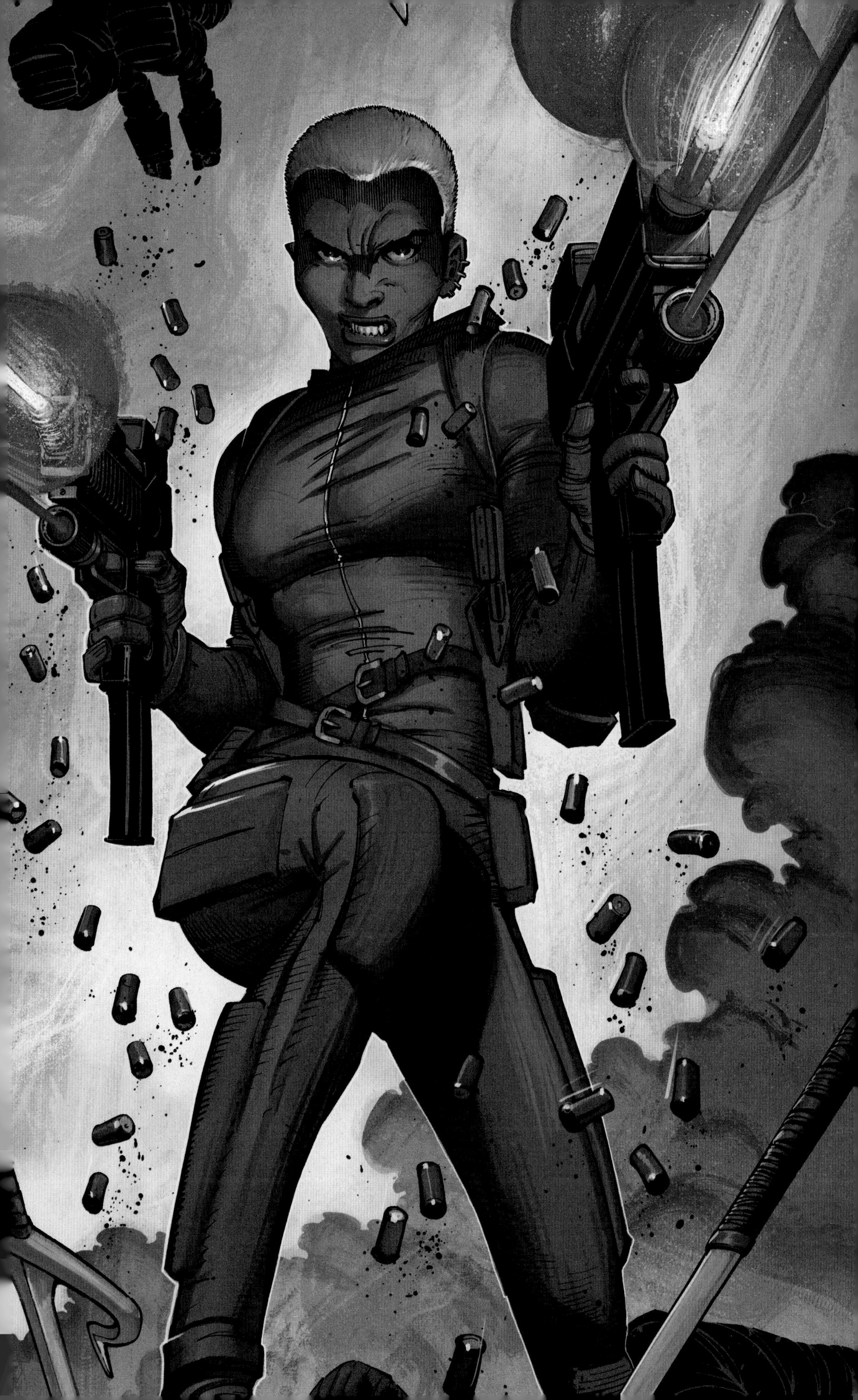

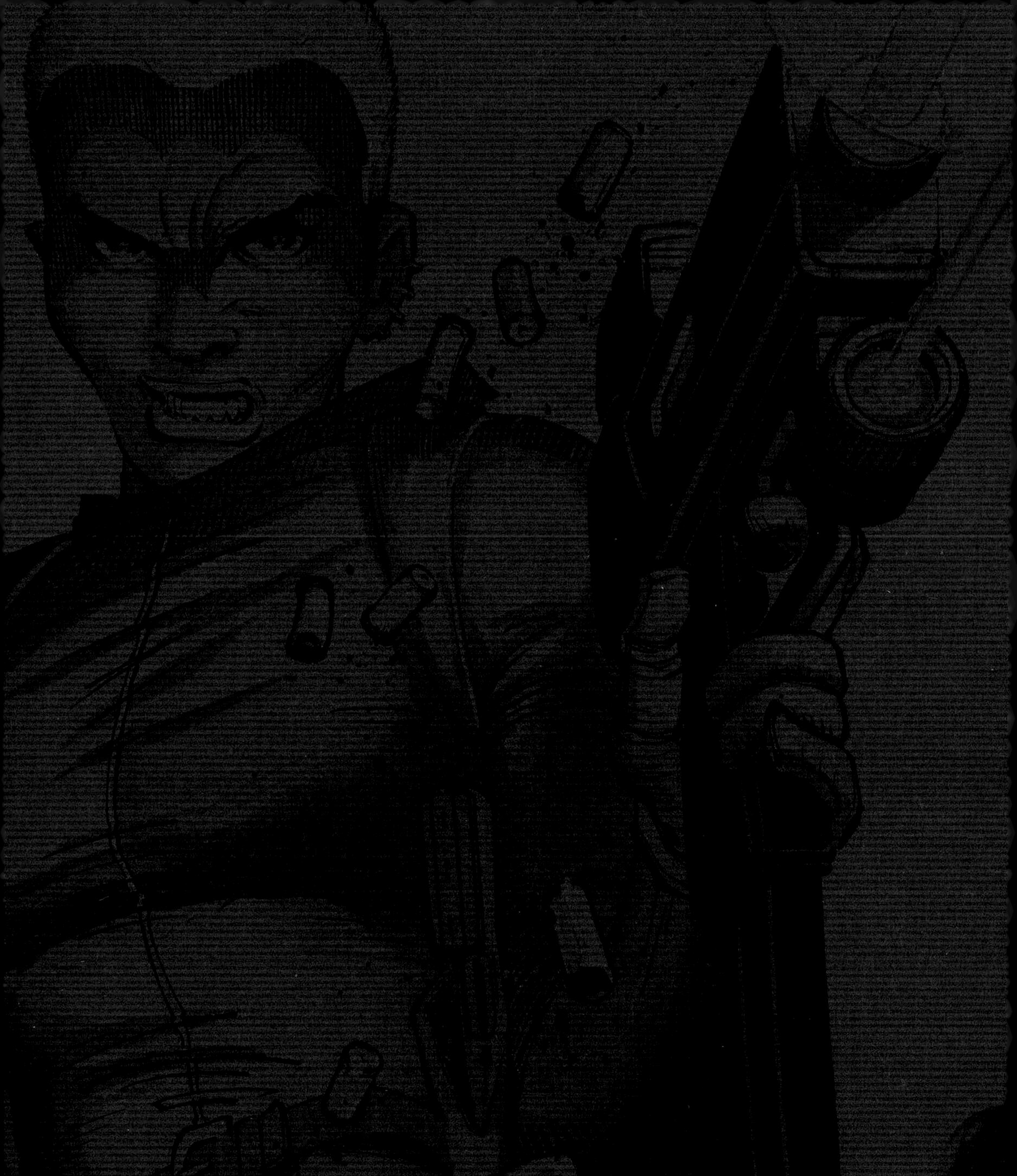

THE SILENCER
#1

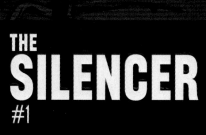

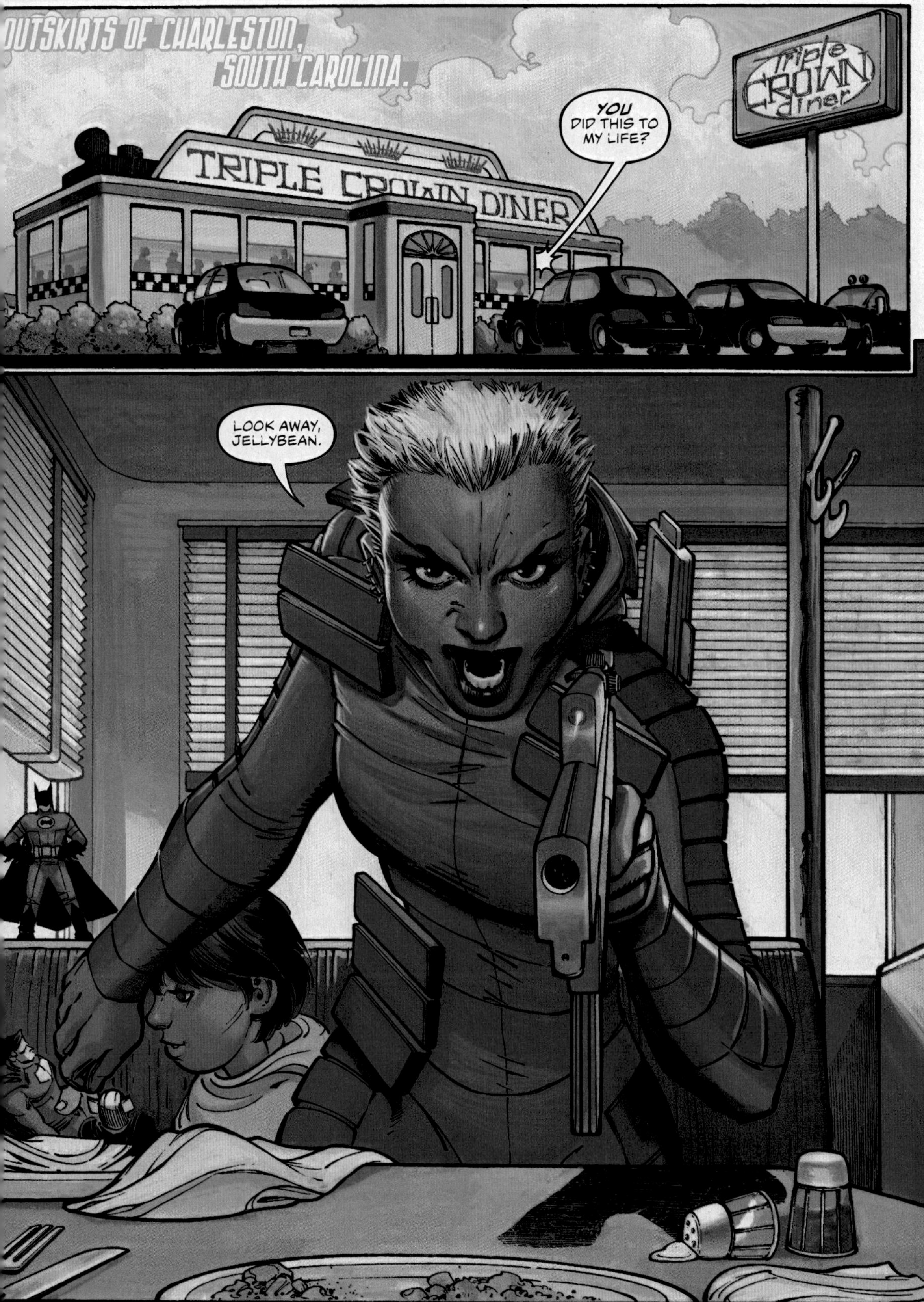
OUTSKIRTS OF CHARLESTON, SOUTH CAROLINA.
Triple CROWN diner
TRIPLE CROWN DINER
YOU DID THIS TO MY LIFE?
LOOK AWAY, JELLYBEAN.

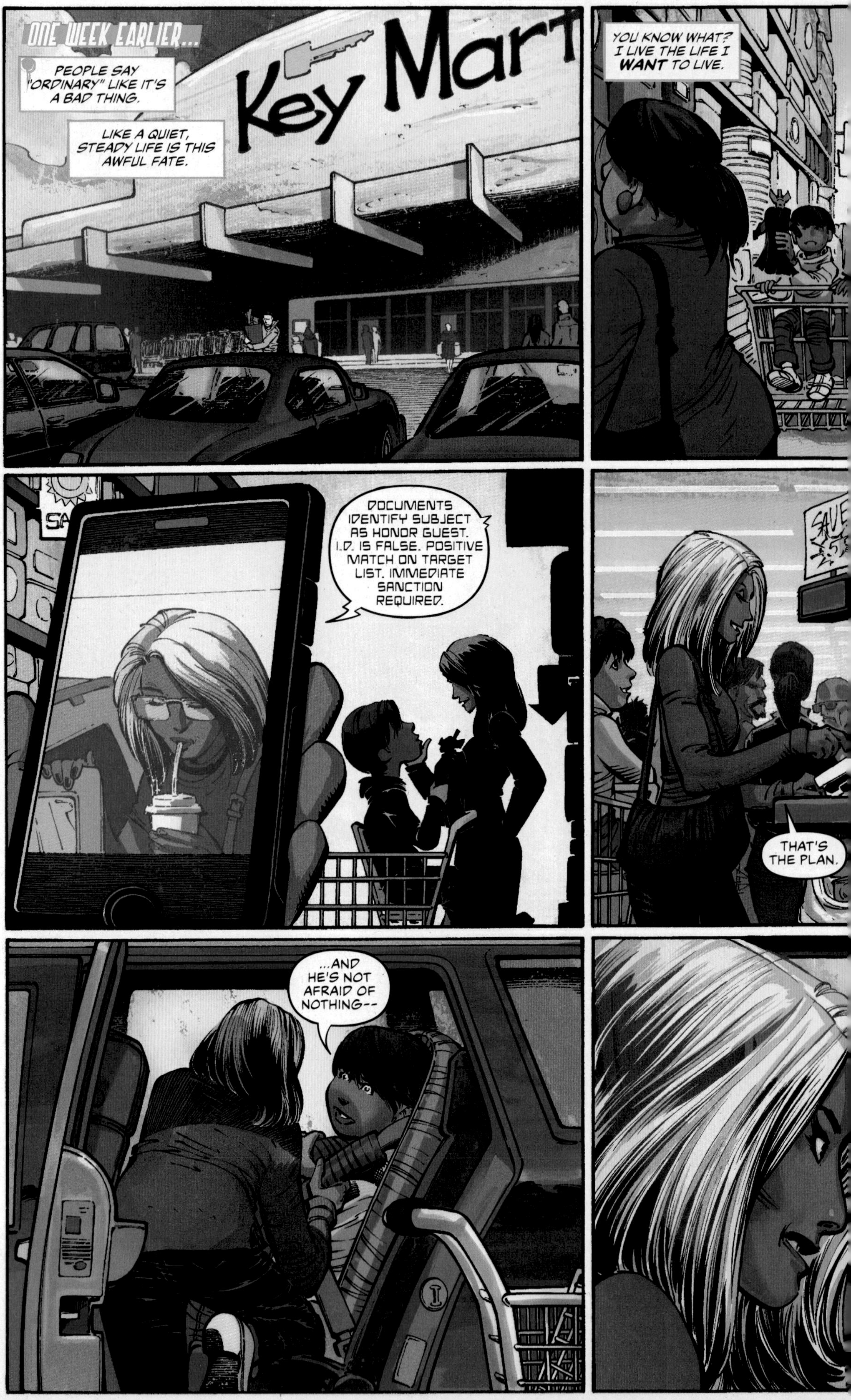
ONE WEEK EARLIER...
Key Mart
PEOPLE SAY "ORDINARY" LIKE IT'S A BAD THING.
LIKE A QUIET, STEADY LIFE IS THIS AWFUL FATE.
YOU KNOW WHAT? I LIVE THE LIFE I WANT TO LIVE.
DOCUMENTS IDENTIFY SUBJECT AS HONOR GUEST. I.D. IS FALSE. POSITIVE MATCH ON TARGET LIST. IMMEDIATE SANCTION REQUIRED.
THAT'S THE PLAN.
...AND HE'S NOT AFRAID OF NOTHING--

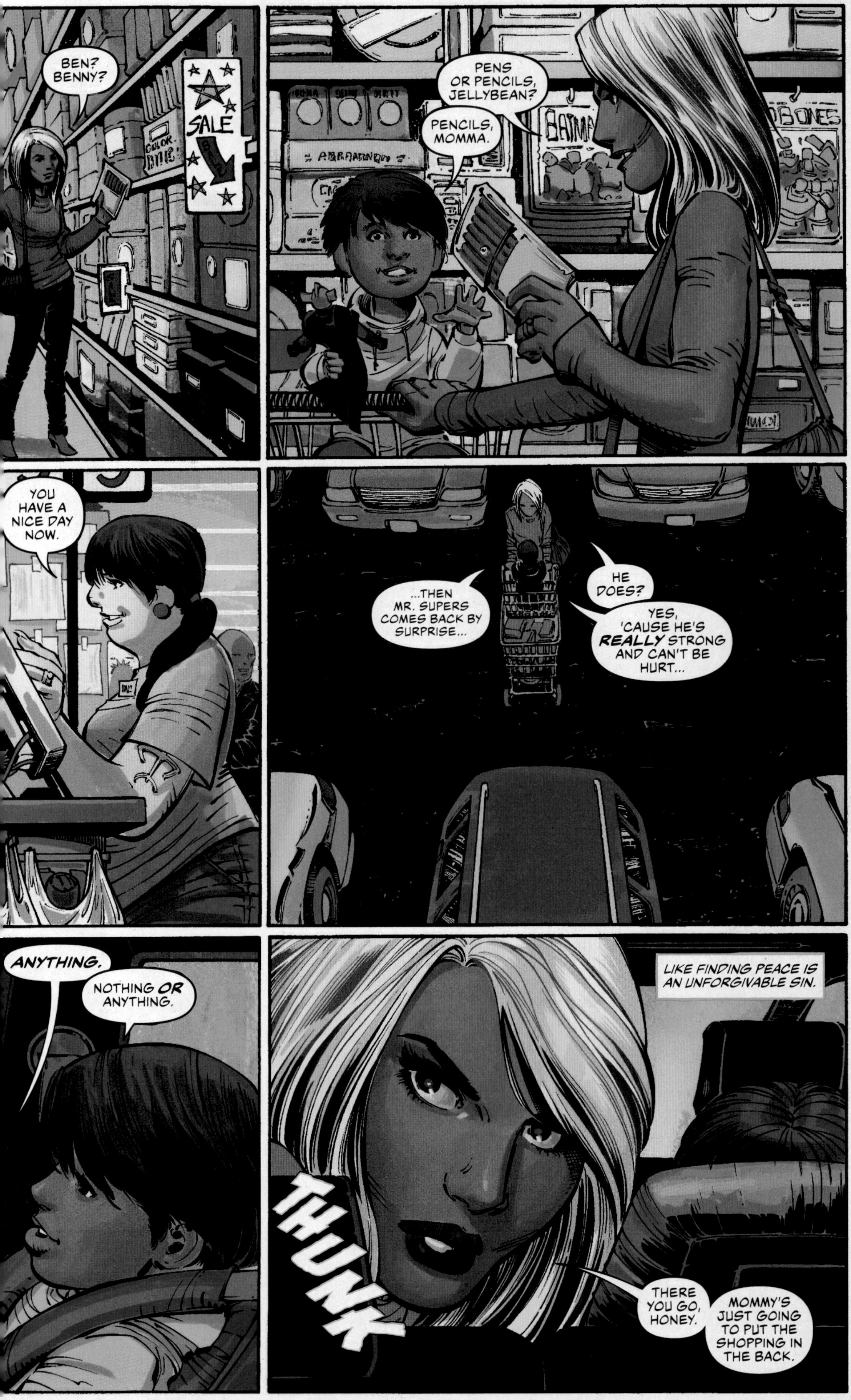
BEN? BENNY?
SALE
PENS OR PENCILS, JELLYBEAN?
PENCILS, MOMMA.
YOU HAVE A NICE DAY NOW.
...THEN MR. SUPERS COMES BACK BY SURPRISE...
HE DOES?
YES, 'CAUSE HE'S *REALLY* STRONG AND CAN'T BE HURT...
ANYTHING.
NOTHING *OR* ANYTHING.
LIKE FINDING PEACE IS AN UNFORGIVABLE SIN.
THUNK
THERE YOU GO, HONEY.
MOMMY'S JUST GOING TO PUT THE SHOPPING IN THE BACK.

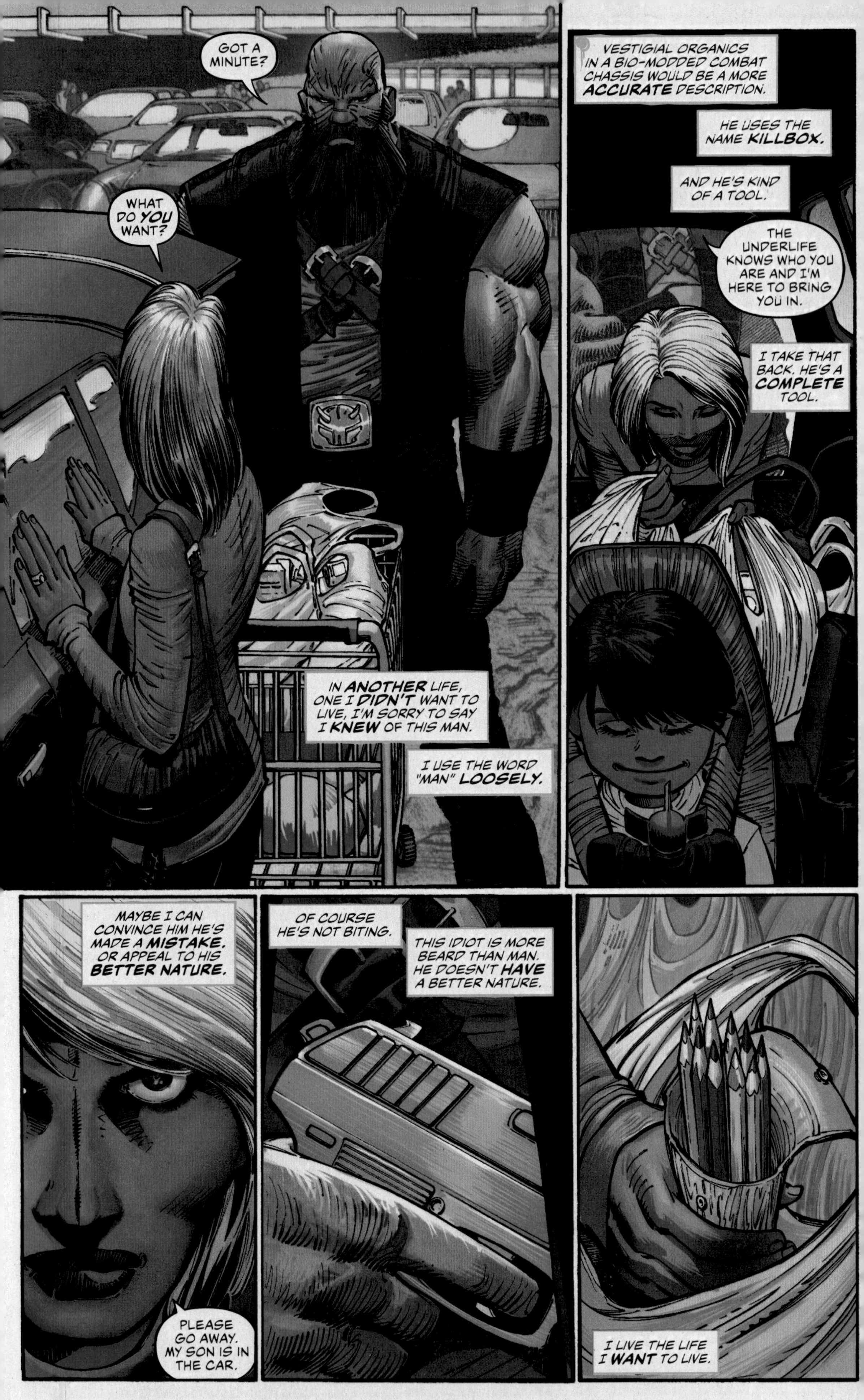
GOT A MINUTE?
WHAT DO YOU WANT?
IN ANOTHER LIFE, ONE I DIDN'T WANT TO LIVE, I'M SORRY TO SAY I KNEW OF THIS MAN.
I USE THE WORD "MAN" LOOSELY.
VESTIGIAL ORGANICS IN A BIO-MODDED COMBAT CHASSIS WOULD BE A MORE ACCURATE DESCRIPTION.
HE USES THE NAME KILLBOX.
AND HE'S KIND OF A TOOL.
THE UNDERLIFE KNOWS WHO YOU ARE AND I'M HERE TO BRING YOU IN.
I TAKE THAT BACK. HE'S A COMPLETE TOOL.
MAYBE I CAN CONVINCE HIM HE'S MADE A MISTAKE. OR APPEAL TO HIS BETTER NATURE.
PLEASE GO AWAY. MY SON IS IN THE CAR.
OF COURSE HE'S NOT BITING.
THIS IDIOT IS MORE BEARD THAN MAN. HE DOESN'T HAVE A BETTER NATURE.
I LIVE THE LIFE I WANT TO LIVE.

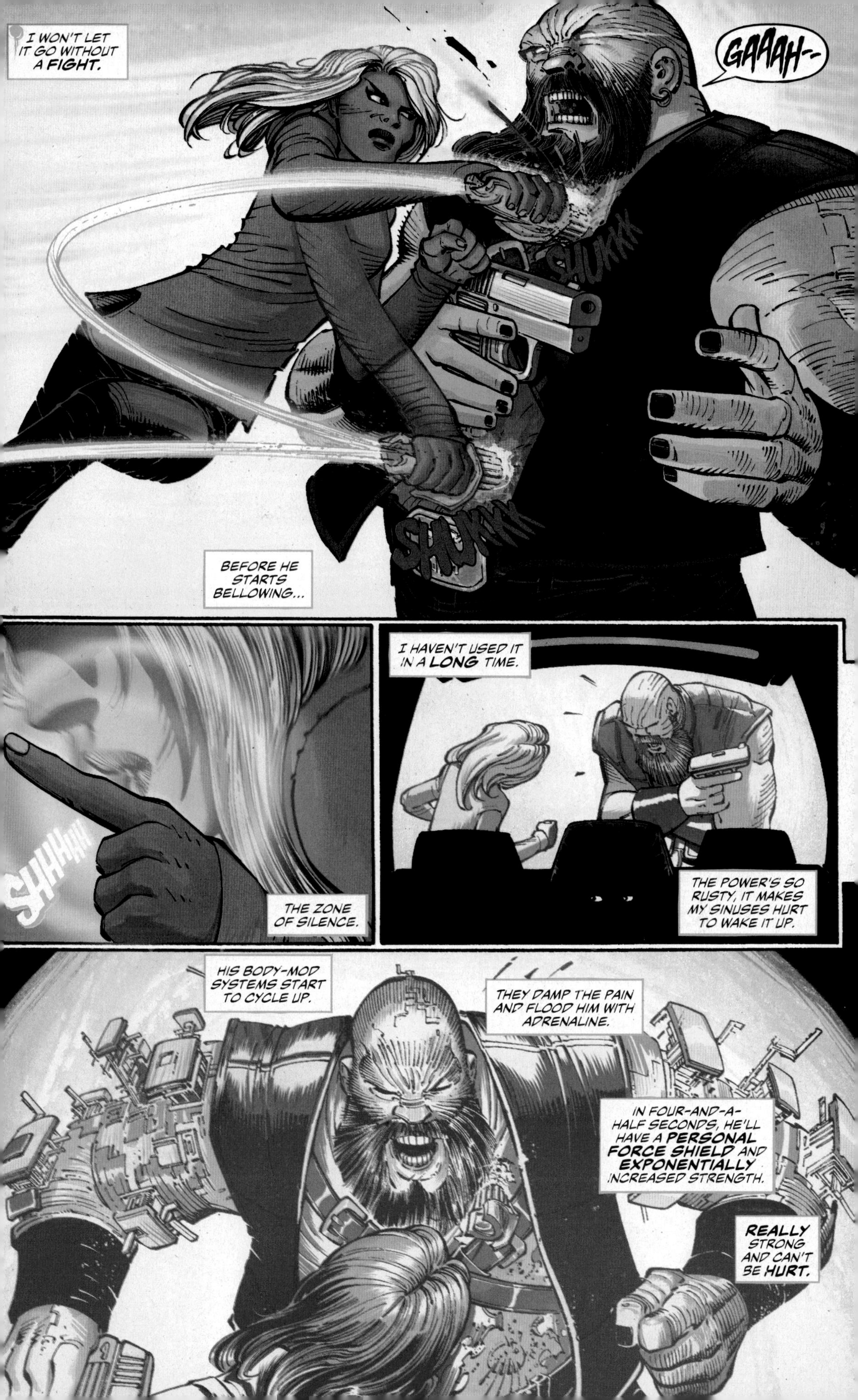

I WON'T LET IT GO WITHOUT A FIGHT.
GAAAH--
SHUKKK
SHUKKK
BEFORE HE STARTS BELLOWING...
SHHHHH
THE ZONE OF SILENCE.
I HAVEN'T USED IT IN A LONG TIME.
THE POWER'S SO RUSTY, IT MAKES MY SINUSES HURT TO WAKE IT UP.
HIS BODY-MOD SYSTEMS START TO CYCLE UP.
THEY DAMP THE PAIN AND FLOOD HIM WITH ADRENALINE.
IN FOUR-AND-A-HALF SECONDS, HE'LL HAVE A PERSONAL FORCE SHIELD AND EXPONENTIALLY INCREASED STRENGTH.
REALLY STRONG AND CAN'T BE HURT.

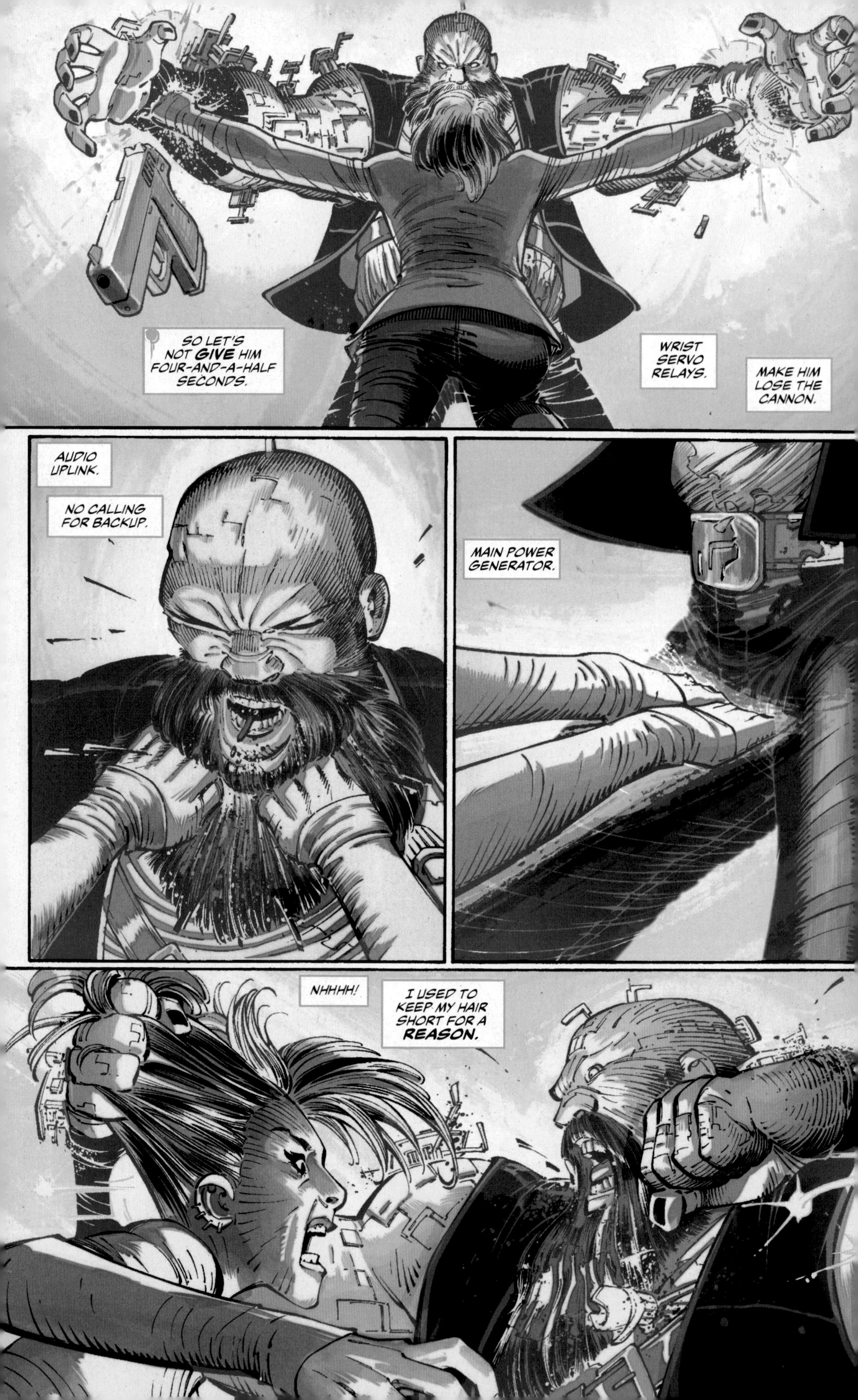
SO LET'S NOT **GIVE** HIM FOUR-AND-A-HALF SECONDS.
WRIST SERVO RELAYS.
MAKE HIM LOSE THE CANNON.
AUDIO UPLINK.
NO CALLING FOR BACKUP.
MAIN POWER GENERATOR.
NHHHH!
I USED TO KEEP MY HAIR SHORT FOR A **REASON.**

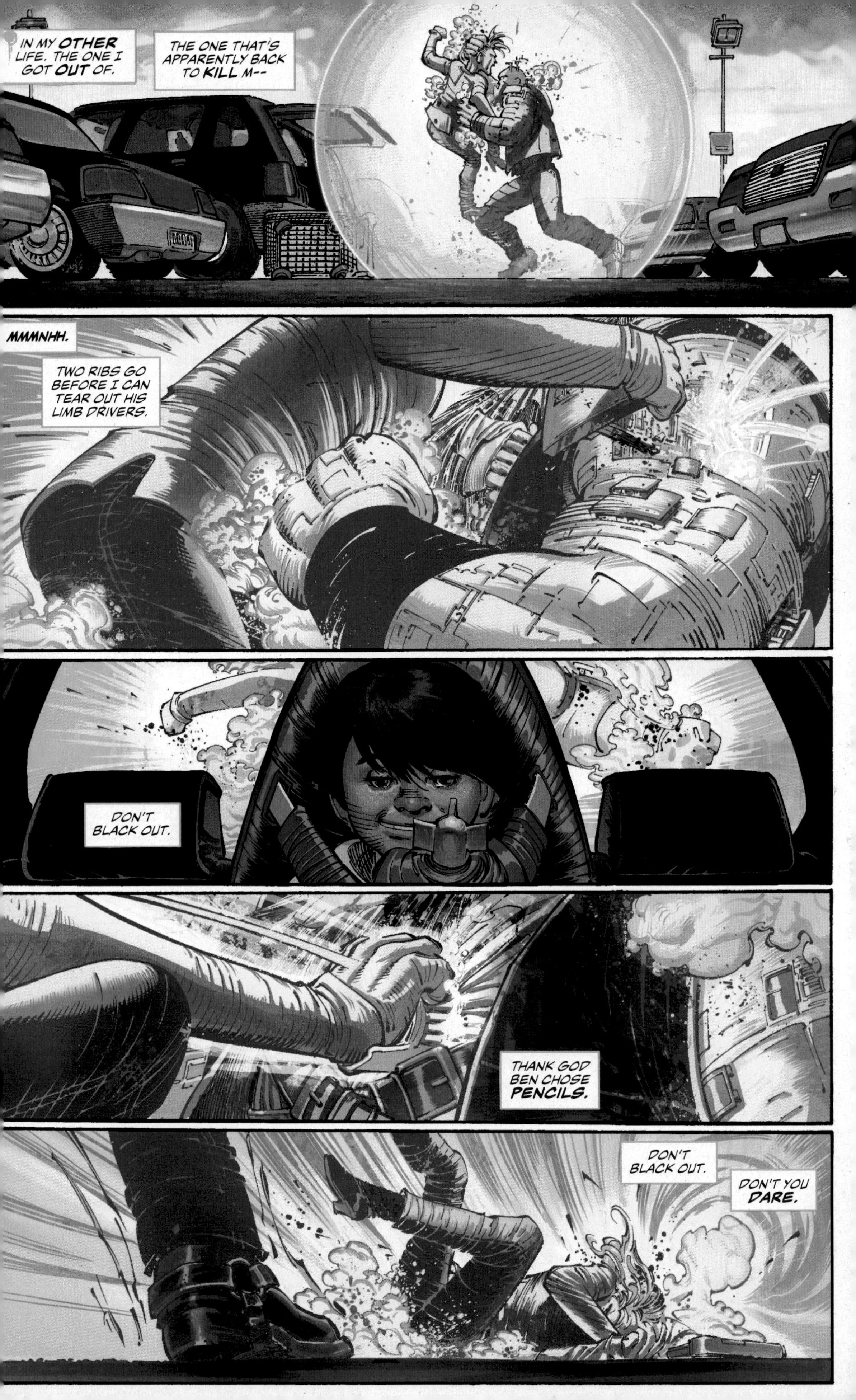
IN MY OTHER LIFE. THE ONE I GOT OUT OF.
THE ONE THAT'S APPARENTLY BACK TO KILL M--
MMMNHH.
TWO RIBS GO BEFORE I CAN TEAR OUT HIS LIMB DRIVERS.
DON'T BLACK OUT.
THANK GOD BEN CHOSE PENCILS.
DON'T BLACK OUT.
DON'T YOU DARE.

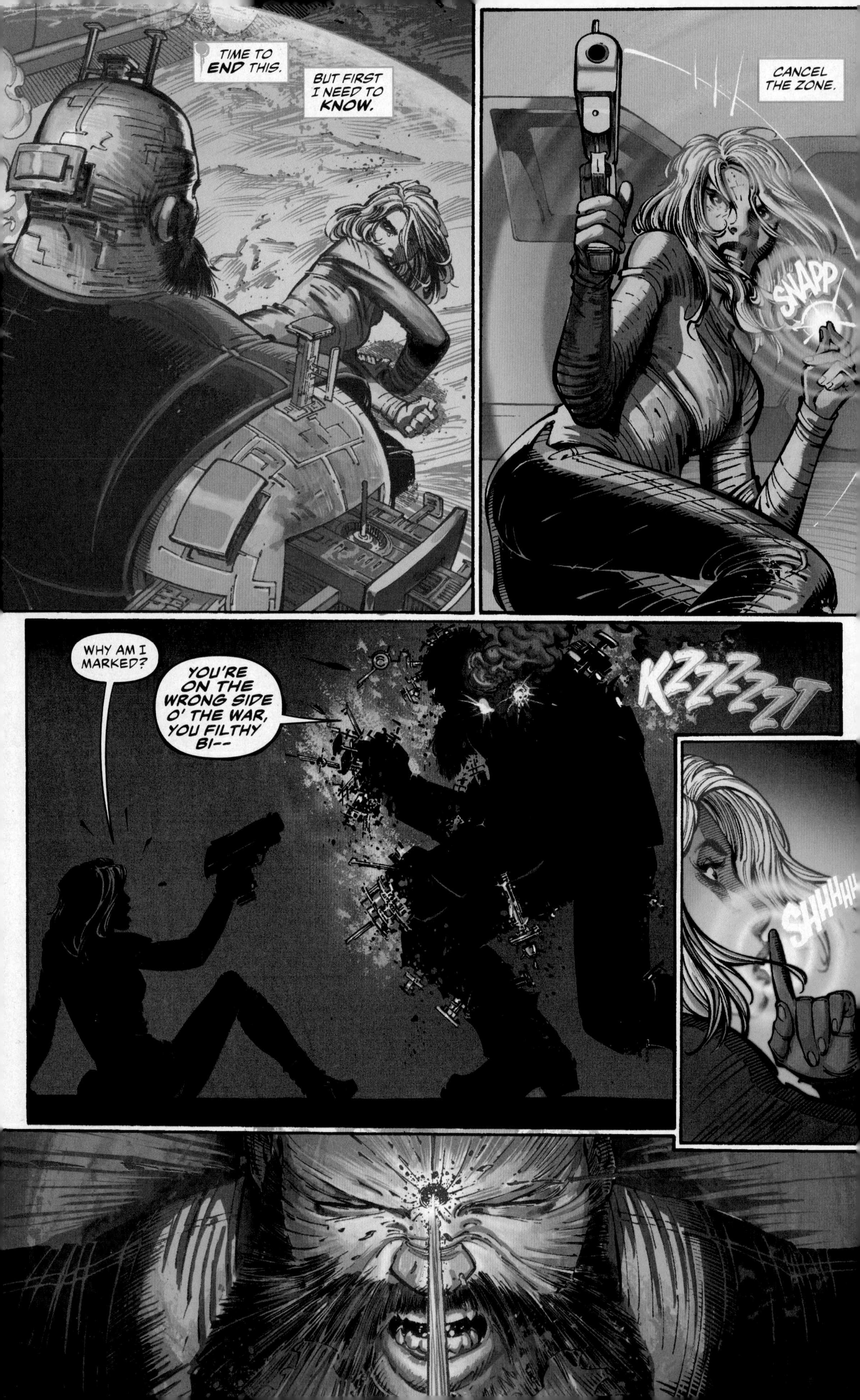
TIME TO END THIS.
BUT FIRST I NEED TO KNOW.
CANCEL THE ZONE.
SNAPP
WHY AM I MARKED?
YOU'RE ON THE WRONG SIDE O' THE WAR, YOU FILTHY BI--
KZZZZZT
SHHHH

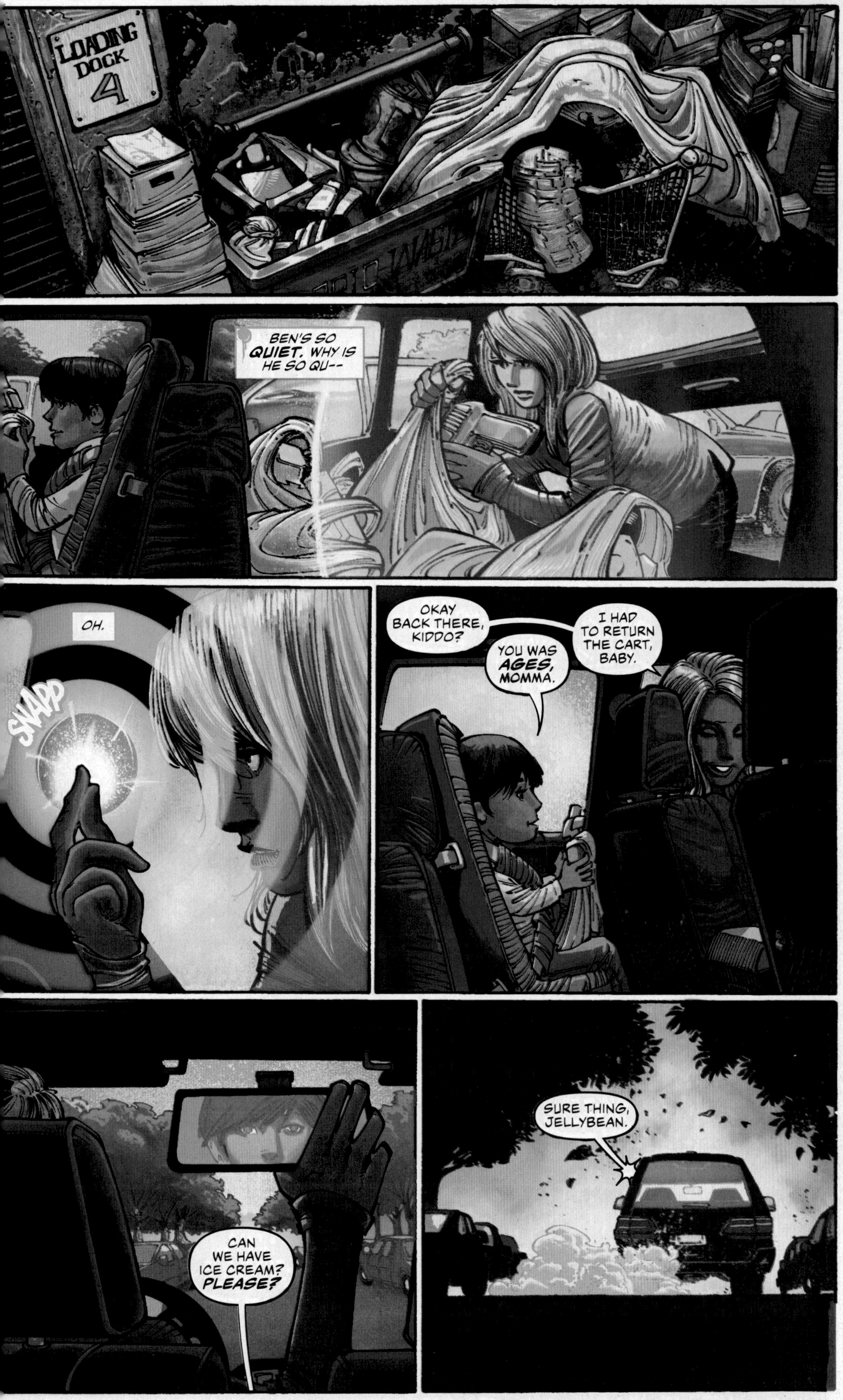
LOADING DOCK 4
BEN'S SO QUIET. WHY IS HE SO QU--
OH.
SNAPP
OKAY BACK THERE, KIDDO?
I HAD TO RETURN THE CART, BABY.
YOU WAS AGES, MOMMA.
CAN WE HAVE ICE CREAM? PLEASE?
SURE THING, JELLYBEAN.

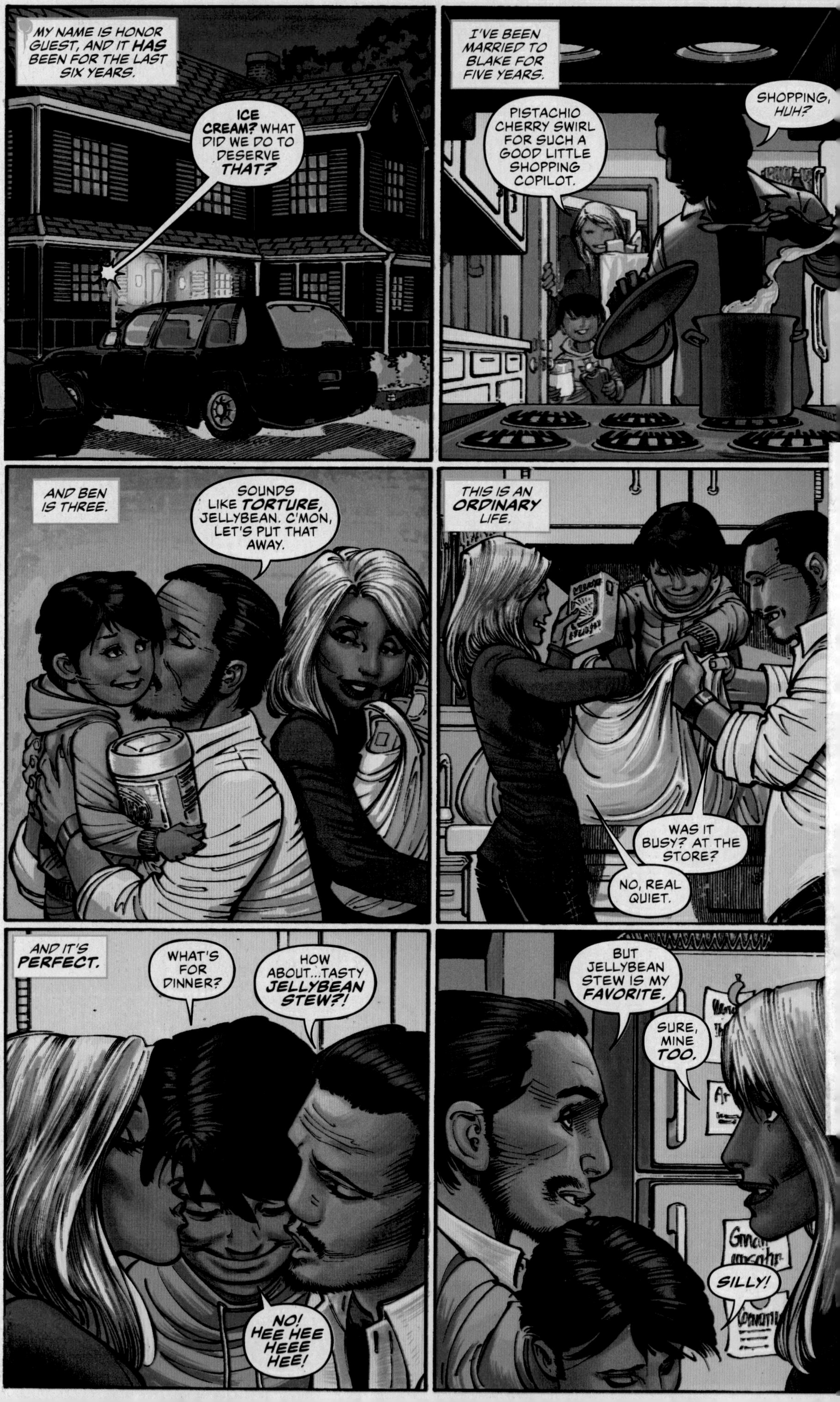
MY NAME IS HONOR GUEST, AND IT HAS BEEN FOR THE LAST SIX YEARS.
ICE CREAM? WHAT DID WE DO TO DESERVE THAT?
I'VE BEEN MARRIED TO BLAKE FOR FIVE YEARS.
PISTACHIO CHERRY SWIRL FOR SUCH A GOOD LITTLE SHOPPING COPILOT.
SHOPPING, HUH?
AND BEN IS THREE.
SOUNDS LIKE TORTURE, JELLYBEAN. C'MON, LET'S PUT THAT AWAY.
THIS IS AN ORDINARY LIFE.
WAS IT BUSY? AT THE STORE?
NO, REAL QUIET.
AND IT'S PERFECT.
WHAT'S FOR DINNER?
HOW ABOUT...TASTY JELLYBEAN STEW?!
NO! HEE HEE HEEE HEE!
BUT JELLYBEAN STEW IS MY FAVORITE.
SURE, MINE TOO.
SILLY!

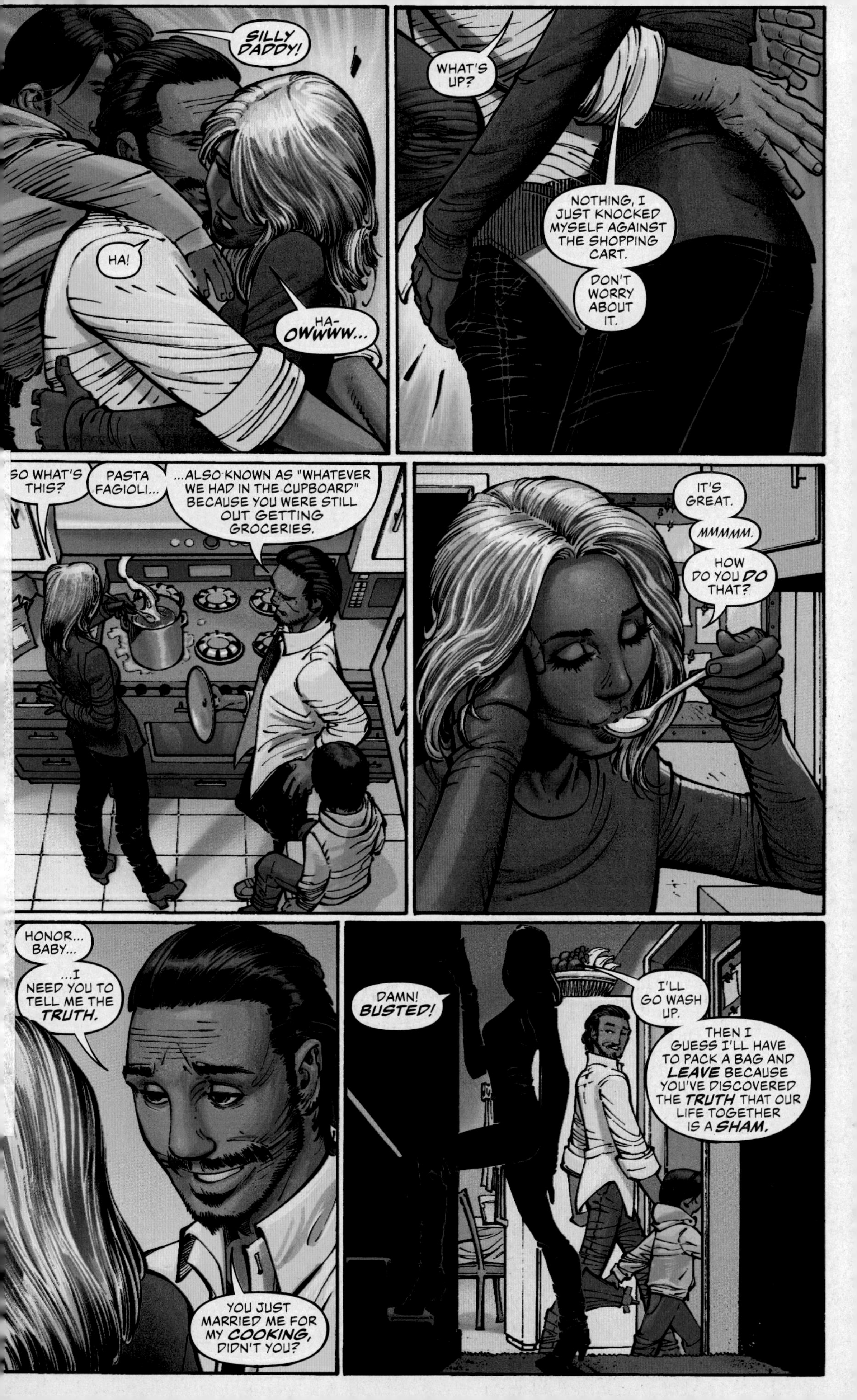
SILLY DADDY!
HA!
HA-OWWWW...
WHAT'S UP?
NOTHING, I JUST KNOCKED MYSELF AGAINST THE SHOPPING CART.
DON'T WORRY ABOUT IT.
SO WHAT'S THIS?
PASTA FAGIOLI...
...ALSO KNOWN AS "WHATEVER WE HAD IN THE CUPBOARD" BECAUSE YOU WERE STILL OUT GETTING GROCERIES.
IT'S GREAT.
MMMMM.
HOW DO YOU DO THAT?
HONOR... BABY...
...I NEED YOU TO TELL ME THE TRUTH.
YOU JUST MARRIED ME FOR MY COOKING, DIDN'T YOU?
DAMN! BUSTED!
I'LL GO WASH UP.
THEN I GUESS I'LL HAVE TO PACK A BAG AND LEAVE BECAUSE YOU'VE DISCOVERED THE TRUTH THAT OUR LIFE TOGETHER IS A SHAM.

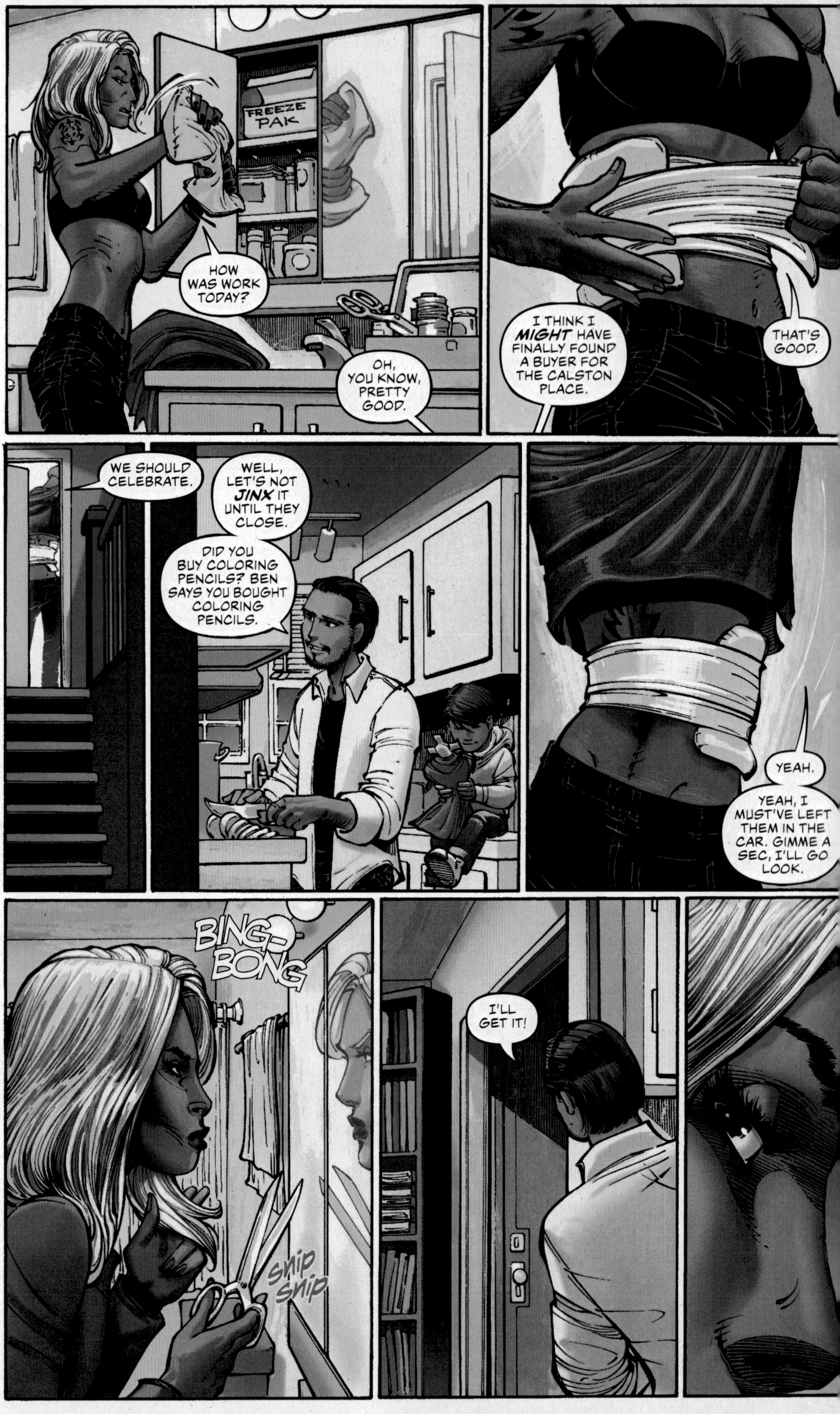

HOW WAS WORK TODAY?
OH, YOU KNOW, PRETTY GOOD.
I THINK I MIGHT HAVE FINALLY FOUND A BUYER FOR THE CALSTON PLACE.
THAT'S GOOD.
WE SHOULD CELEBRATE.
WELL, LET'S NOT JINX IT UNTIL THEY CLOSE.
DID YOU BUY COLORING PENCILS? BEN SAYS YOU BOUGHT COLORING PENCILS.
YEAH.
YEAH, I MUST'VE LEFT THEM IN THE CAR. GIMME A SEC, I'LL GO LOOK.
BING-BONG
SNIP SNIP
I'LL GET IT!
FREEZE PAK

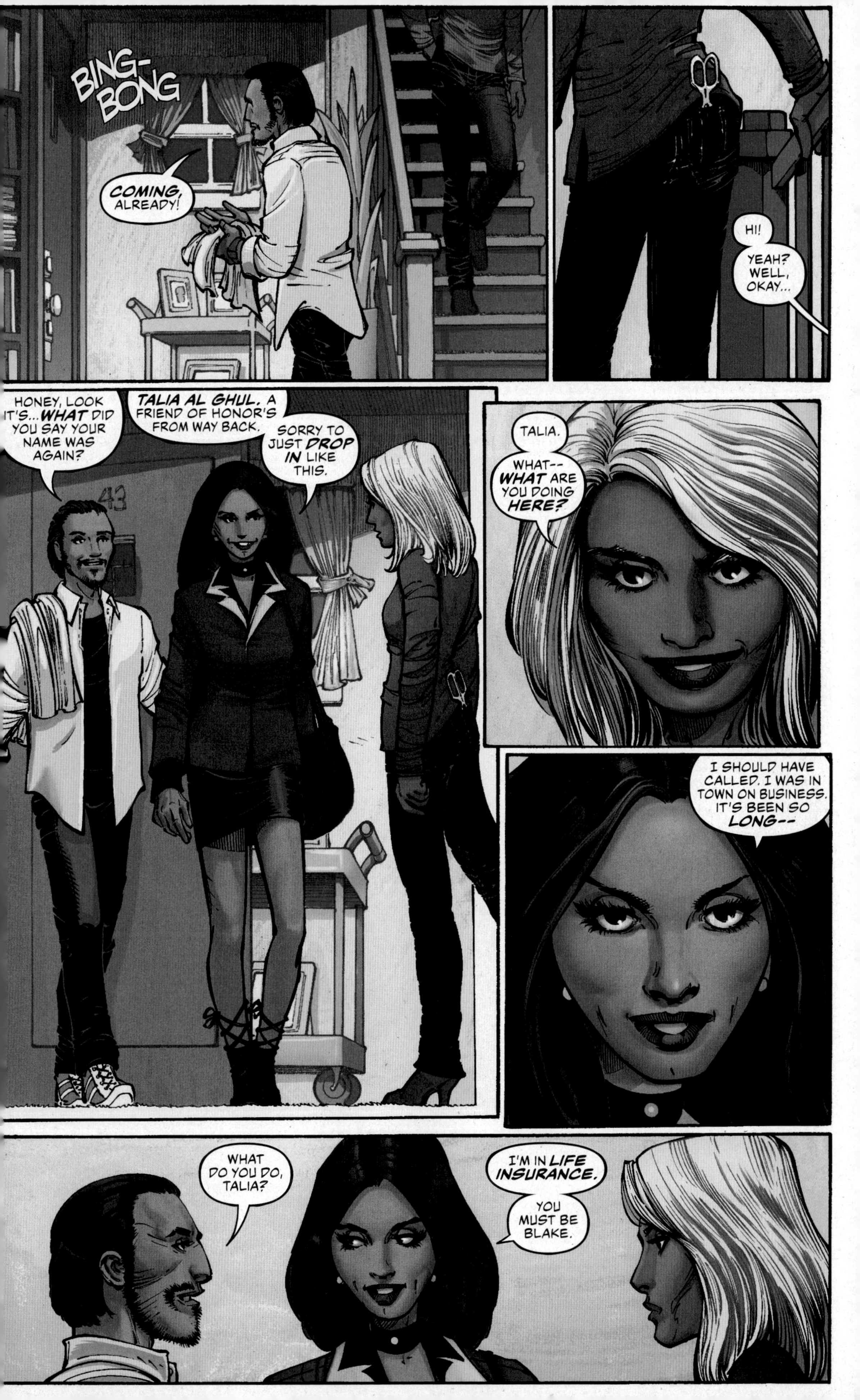
BING-BONG
COMING, ALREADY!
HI!
YEAH? WELL, OKAY...
HONEY, LOOK IT'S...WHAT DID YOU SAY YOUR NAME WAS AGAIN?
TALIA AL GHUL. A FRIEND OF HONOR'S FROM WAY BACK.
SORRY TO JUST DROP IN LIKE THIS.
TALIA.
WHAT--WHAT ARE YOU DOING HERE?
I SHOULD HAVE CALLED. I WAS IN TOWN ON BUSINESS. IT'S BEEN SO LONG--
WHAT DO YOU DO, TALIA?
I'M IN LIFE INSURANCE.
YOU MUST BE BLAKE.

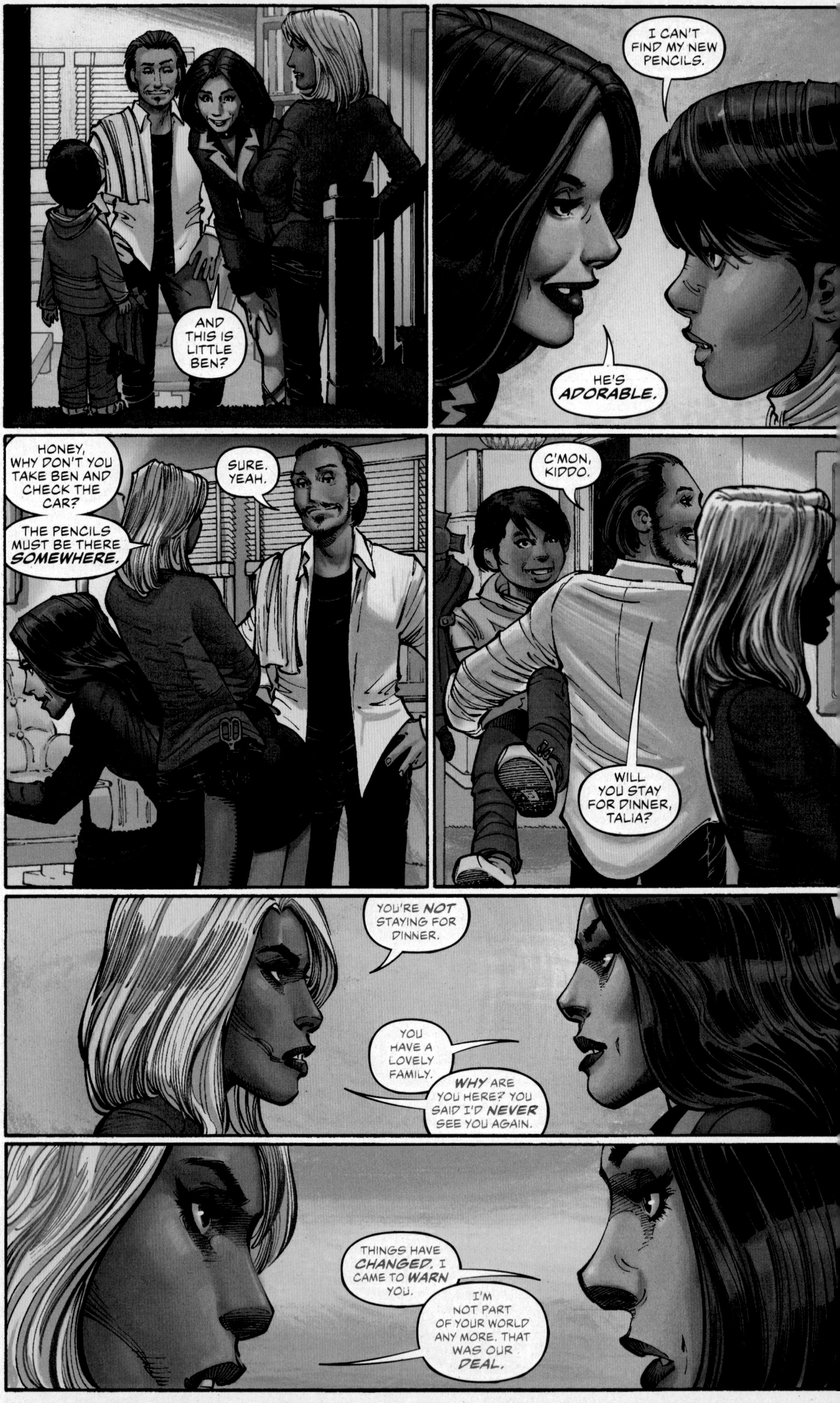
AND THIS IS LITTLE BEN?
I CAN'T FIND MY NEW PENCILS.
HE'S ADORABLE.
HONEY, WHY DON'T YOU TAKE BEN AND CHECK THE CAR?
THE PENCILS MUST BE THERE SOMEWHERE.
SURE. YEAH.
C'MON, KIDDO.
WILL YOU STAY FOR DINNER, TALIA?
YOU'RE NOT STAYING FOR DINNER.
YOU HAVE A LOVELY FAMILY.
WHY ARE YOU HERE? YOU SAID I'D NEVER SEE YOU AGAIN.
THINGS HAVE CHANGED. I CAME TO WARN YOU.
I'M NOT PART OF YOUR WORLD ANY MORE. THAT WAS OUR DEAL.

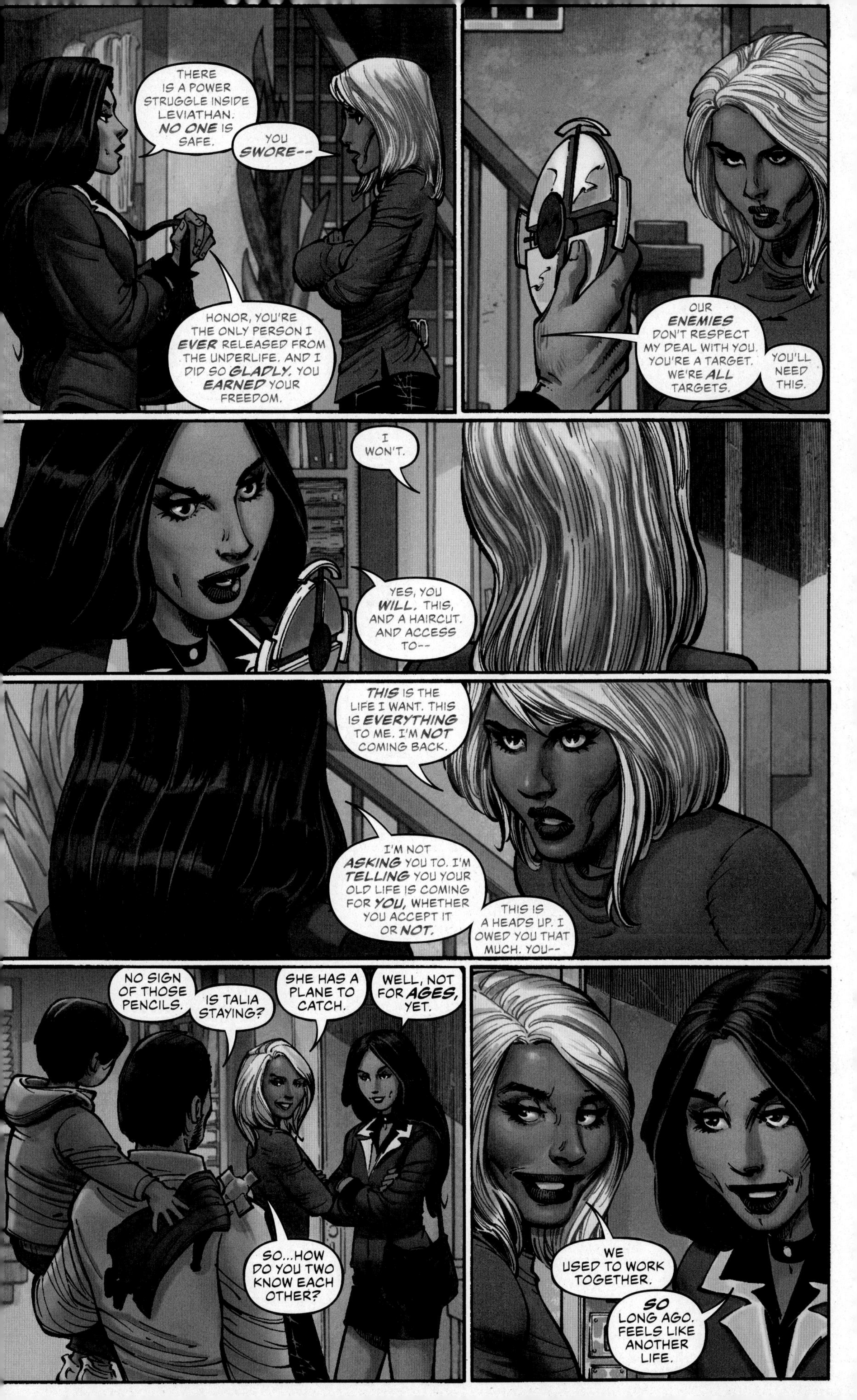
THERE IS A POWER STRUGGLE INSIDE LEVIATHAN. NO ONE IS SAFE.
YOU SWORE--
HONOR, YOU'RE THE ONLY PERSON I EVER RELEASED FROM THE UNDERLIFE. AND I DID SO GLADLY. YOU EARNED YOUR FREEDOM.
OUR ENEMIES DON'T RESPECT MY DEAL WITH YOU. YOU'RE A TARGET. WE'RE ALL TARGETS.
YOU'LL NEED THIS.
I WON'T.
YES, YOU WILL. THIS, AND A HAIRCUT. AND ACCESS TO--
THIS IS THE LIFE I WANT. THIS IS EVERYTHING TO ME. I'M NOT COMING BACK.
I'M NOT ASKING YOU TO. I'M TELLING YOU YOUR OLD LIFE IS COMING FOR YOU, WHETHER YOU ACCEPT IT OR NOT.
THIS IS A HEADS UP. I OWED YOU THAT MUCH. YOU--
NO SIGN OF THOSE PENCILS.
IS TALIA STAYING?
SHE HAS A PLANE TO CATCH.
WELL, NOT FOR AGES, YET.
SO...HOW DO YOU TWO KNOW EACH OTHER?
WE USED TO WORK TOGETHER.
SO LONG AGO. FEELS LIKE ANOTHER LIFE.

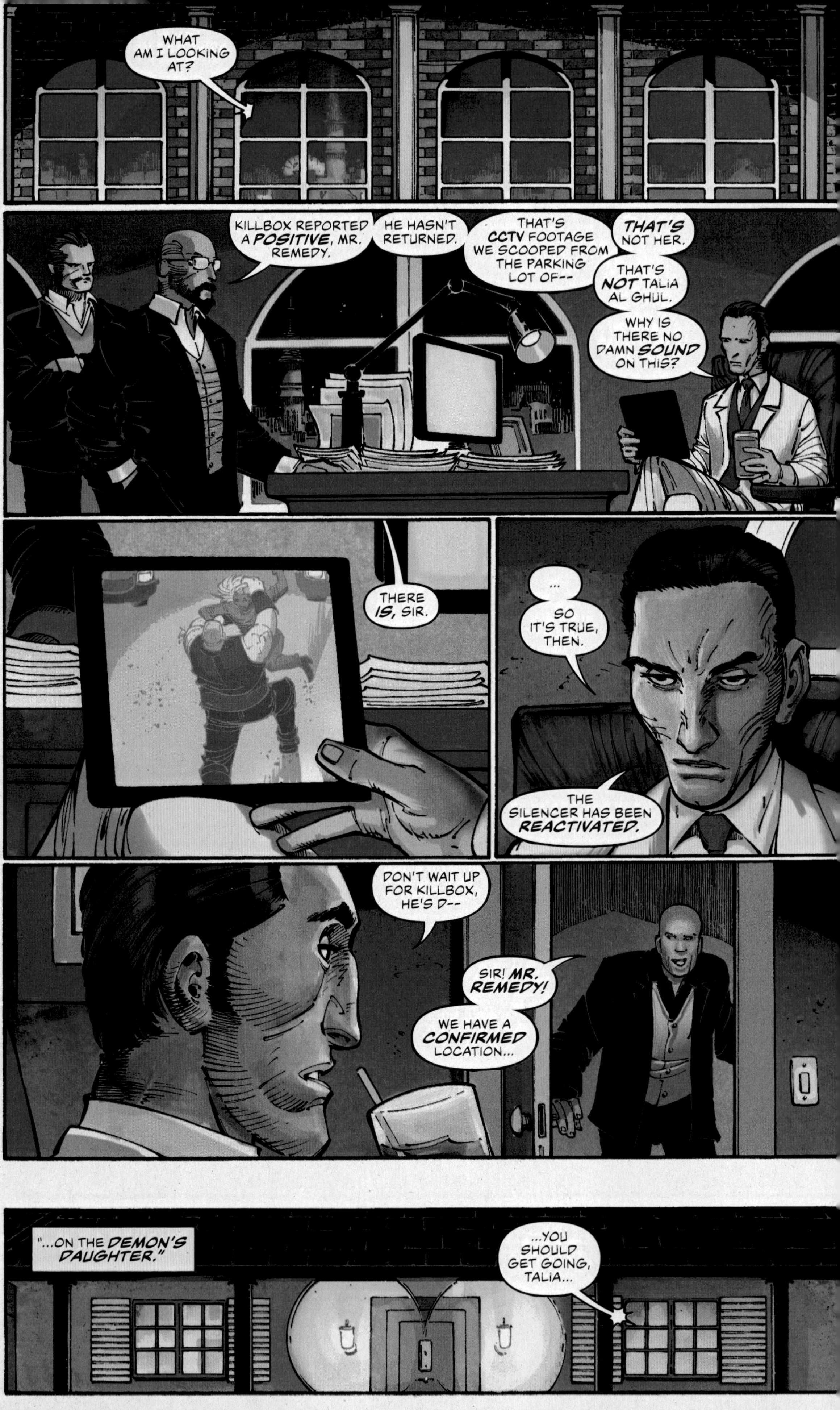
WHAT AM I LOOKING AT?
KILLBOX REPORTED A POSITIVE, MR. REMEDY.
HE HASN'T RETURNED.
THAT'S CCTV FOOTAGE WE SCOOPED FROM THE PARKING LOT OF--
THAT'S NOT HER.
THAT'S NOT TALIA AL GHUL.
WHY IS THERE NO DAMN SOUND ON THIS?
THERE IS, SIR.
...
SO IT'S TRUE, THEN.
THE SILENCER HAS BEEN REACTIVATED.
DON'T WAIT UP FOR KILLBOX, HE'S D--
SIR! MR. REMEDY!
WE HAVE A CONFIRMED LOCATION...
"...ON THE DEMON'S DAUGHTER."
...YOU SHOULD GET GOING, TALIA...

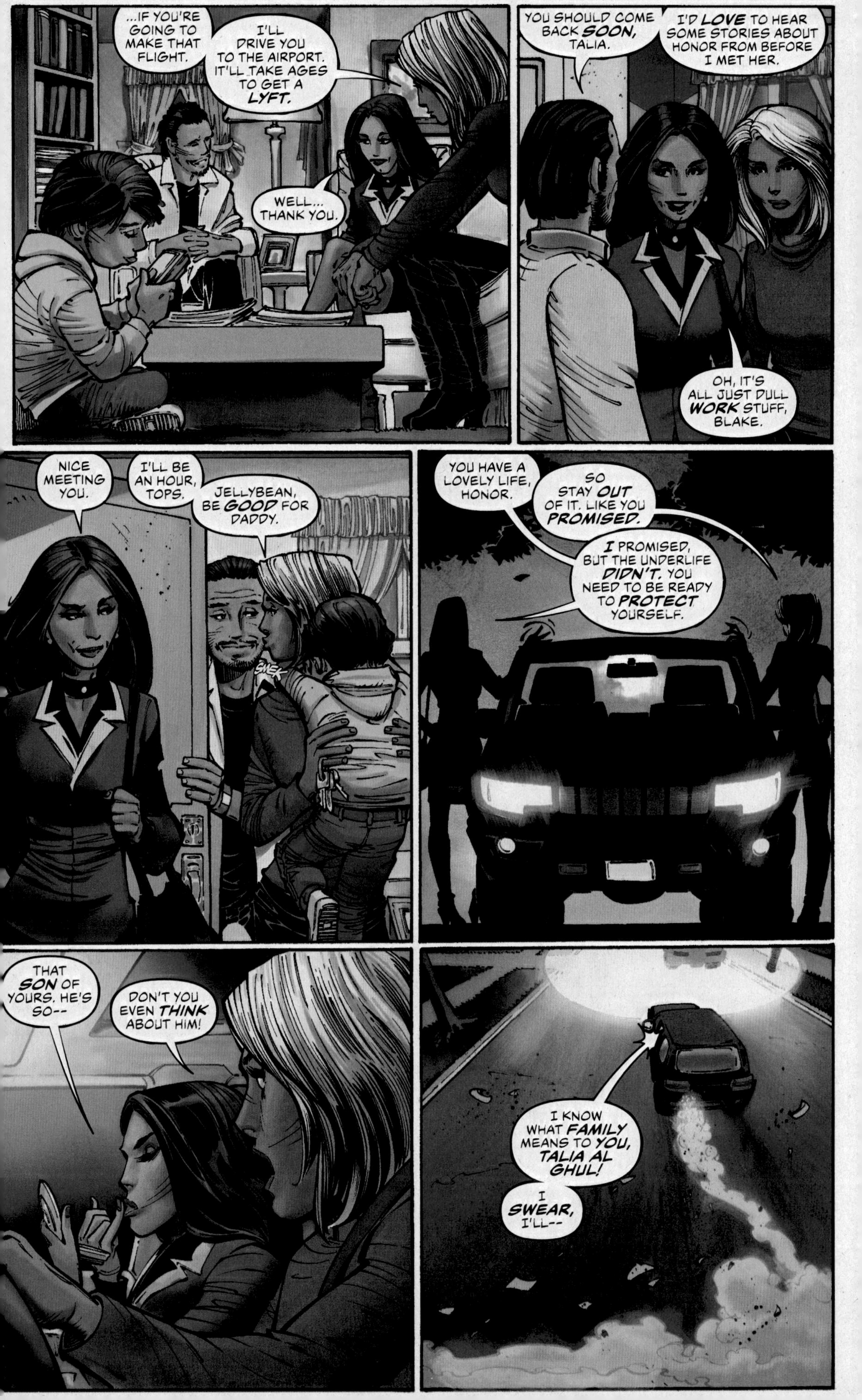
...IF YOU'RE GOING TO MAKE THAT FLIGHT.
I'LL DRIVE YOU TO THE AIRPORT. IT'LL TAKE AGES TO GET A LYFT.
WELL... THANK YOU.
YOU SHOULD COME BACK SOON, TALIA.
I'D LOVE TO HEAR SOME STORIES ABOUT HONOR FROM BEFORE I MET HER.
OH, IT'S ALL JUST DULL WORK STUFF, BLAKE.
NICE MEETING YOU.
I'LL BE AN HOUR, TOPS.
JELLYBEAN, BE GOOD FOR DADDY.
SMEK
YOU HAVE A LOVELY LIFE, HONOR.
SO STAY OUT OF IT. LIKE YOU PROMISED.
I PROMISED, BUT THE UNDERLIFE DIDN'T. YOU NEED TO BE READY TO PROTECT YOURSELF.
THAT SON OF YOURS. HE'S SO--
DON'T YOU EVEN THINK ABOUT HIM!
I KNOW WHAT FAMILY MEANS TO YOU, TALIA AL GHUL!
I SWEAR, I'LL--

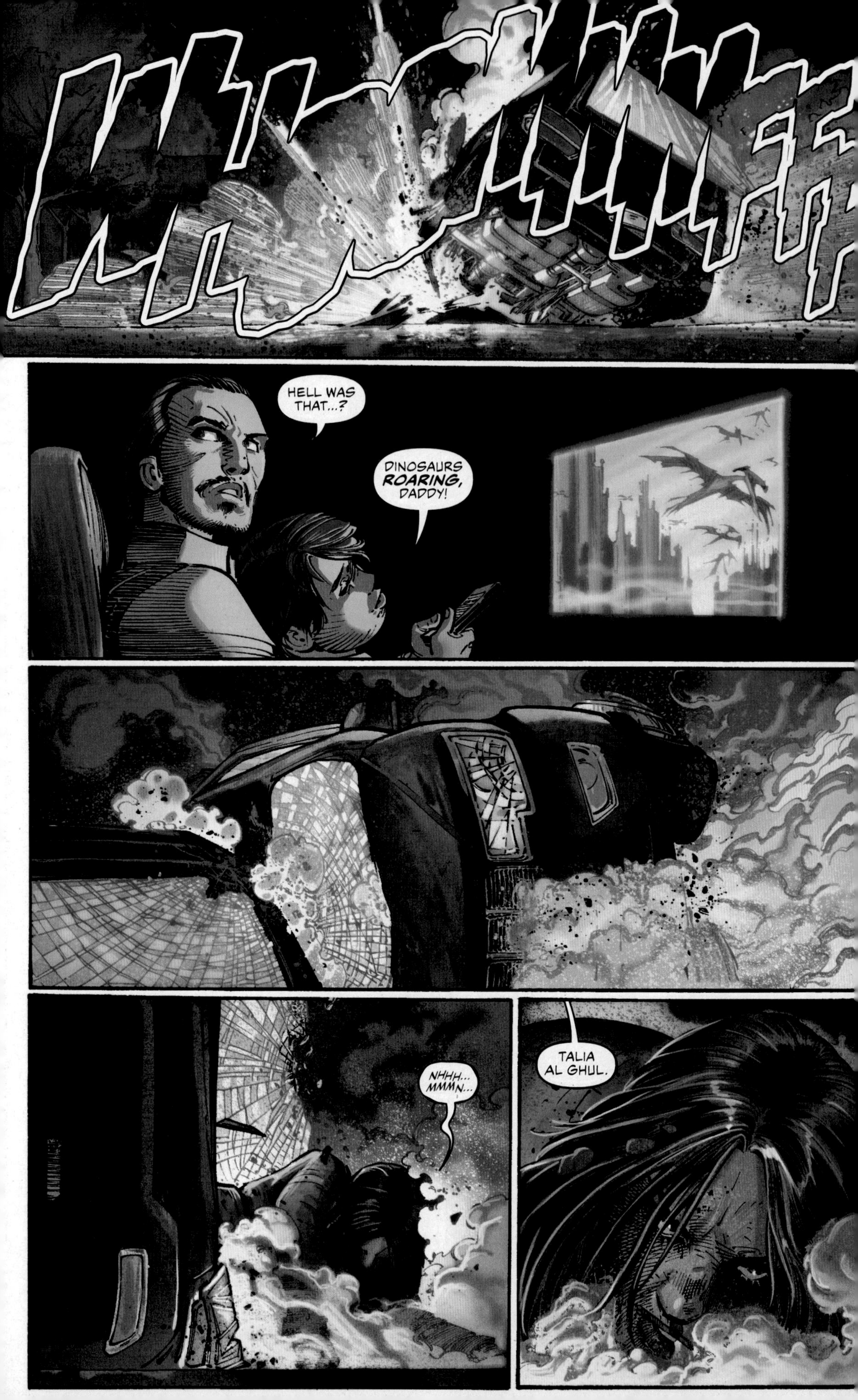

HELL WAS THAT...?
DINOSAURS ROARING, DADDY!
NHHH... MMMN...
TALIA AL GHUL.

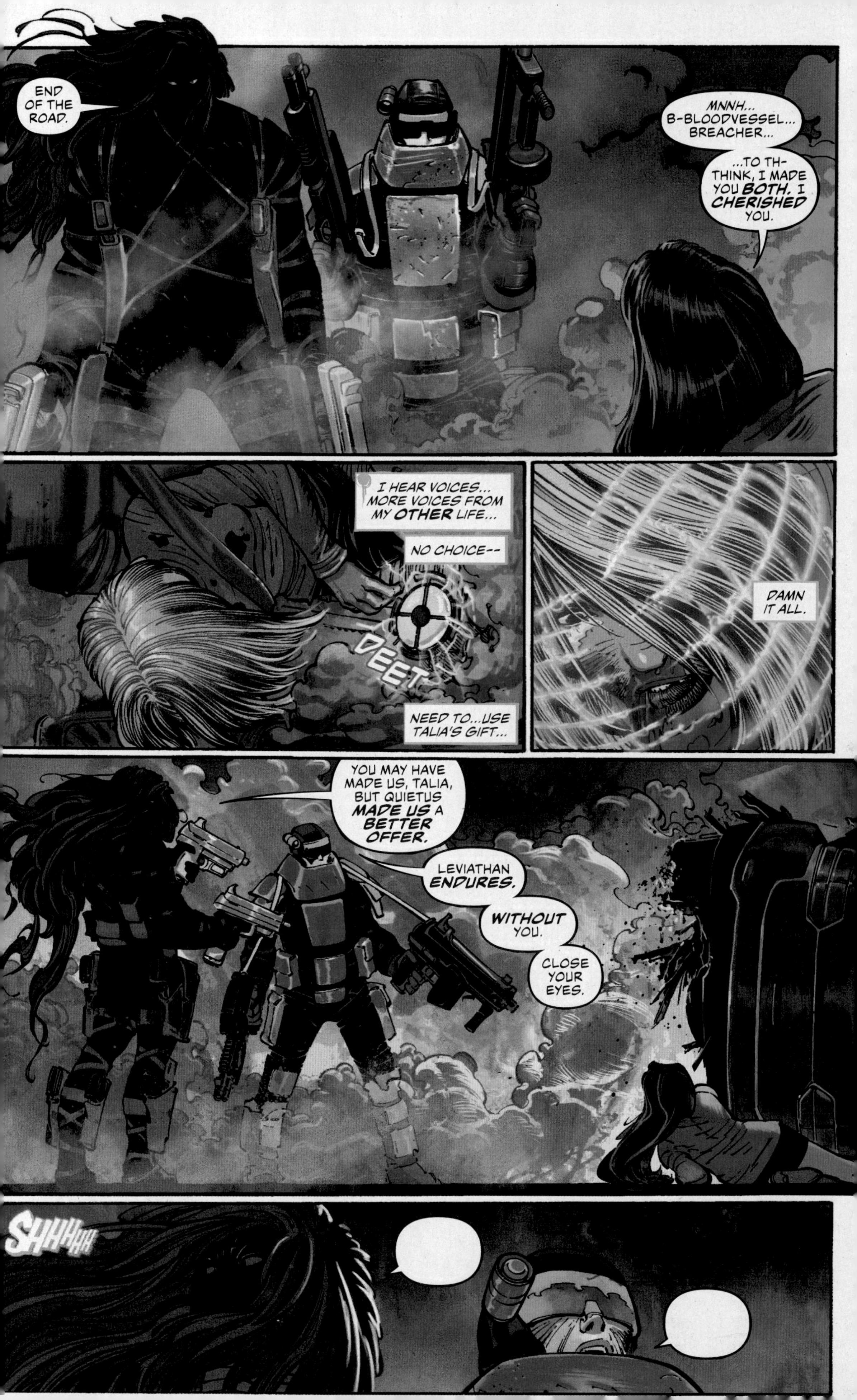
END OF THE ROAD.
MNNH... B-BLOODVESSEL... BREACHER...
...TO TH-THINK, I MADE YOU BOTH. I CHERISHED YOU.
I HEAR VOICES... MORE VOICES FROM MY OTHER LIFE...
NO CHOICE--
DEET
NEED TO...USE TALIA'S GIFT...
DAMN IT ALL.
YOU MAY HAVE MADE US, TALIA, BUT QUIETUS MADE US A BETTER OFFER.
LEVIATHAN ENDURES.
WITHOUT YOU.
CLOSE YOUR EYES.
SHHHHH

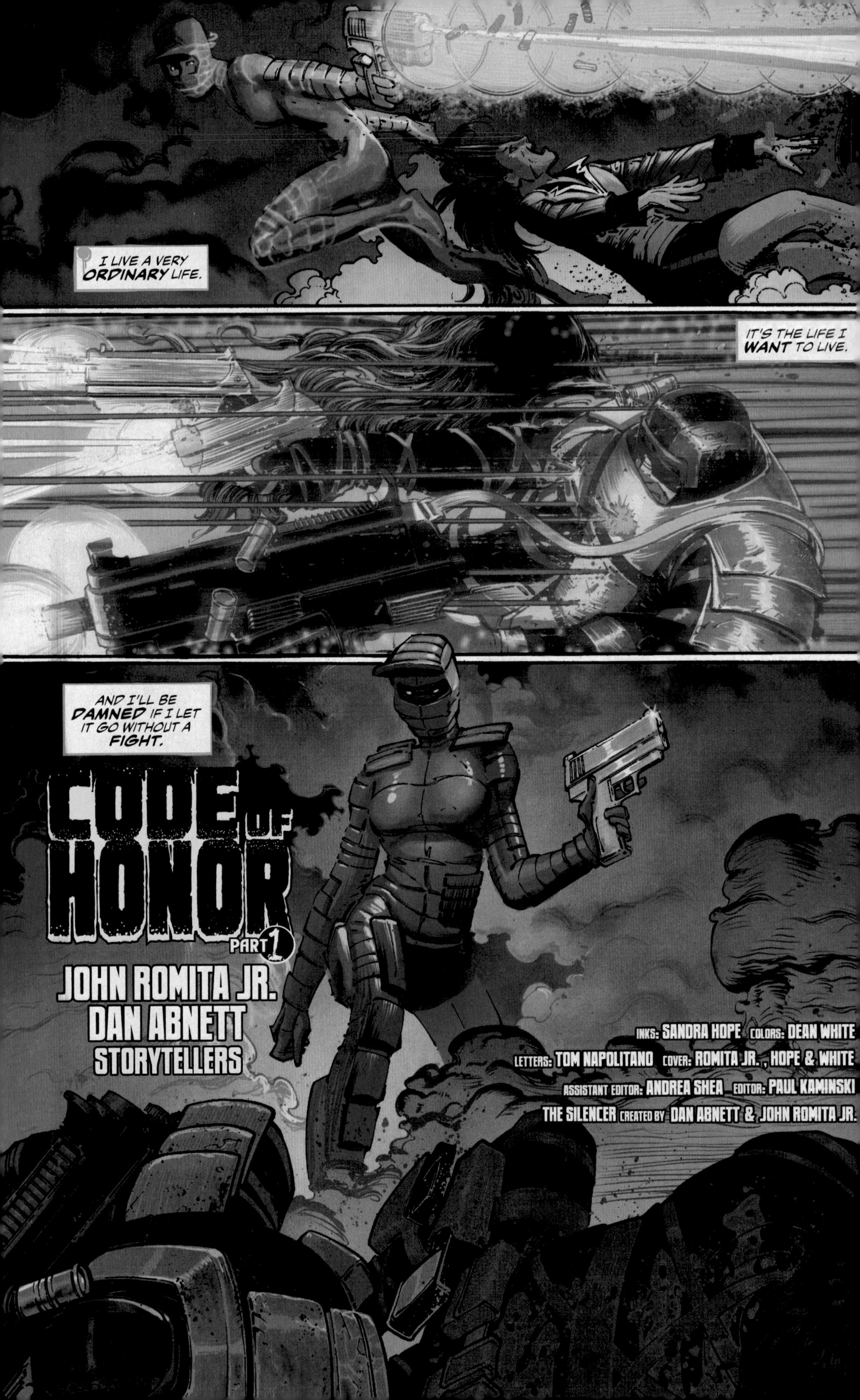
I LIVE A VERY ORDINARY LIFE.
IT'S THE LIFE I WANT TO LIVE.
AND I'LL BE DAMNED IF I LET IT GO WITHOUT A FIGHT.
CODE OF HONOR
PART 1
JOHN ROMITA JR.
DAN ABNETT
STORYTELLERS
INKS: SANDRA HOPE COLORS: DEAN WHITE
LETTERS: TOM NAPOLITANO COVER: ROMITA JR., HOPE & WHITE
ASSISTANT EDITOR: ANDREA SHEA EDITOR: PAUL KAMINSKI
THE SILENCER CREATED BY DAN ABNETT & JOHN ROMITA JR.

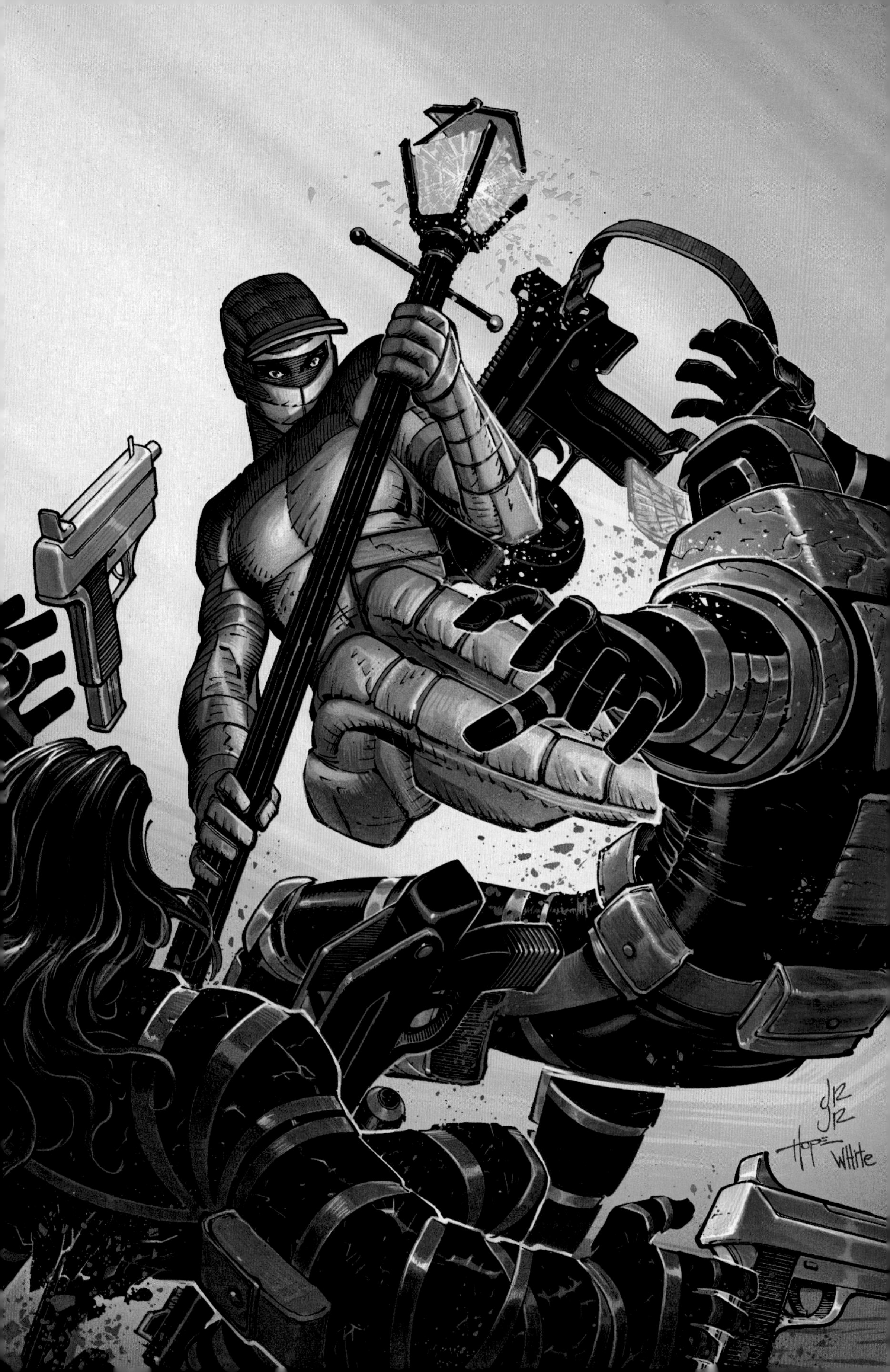
JR JR
Hope
White

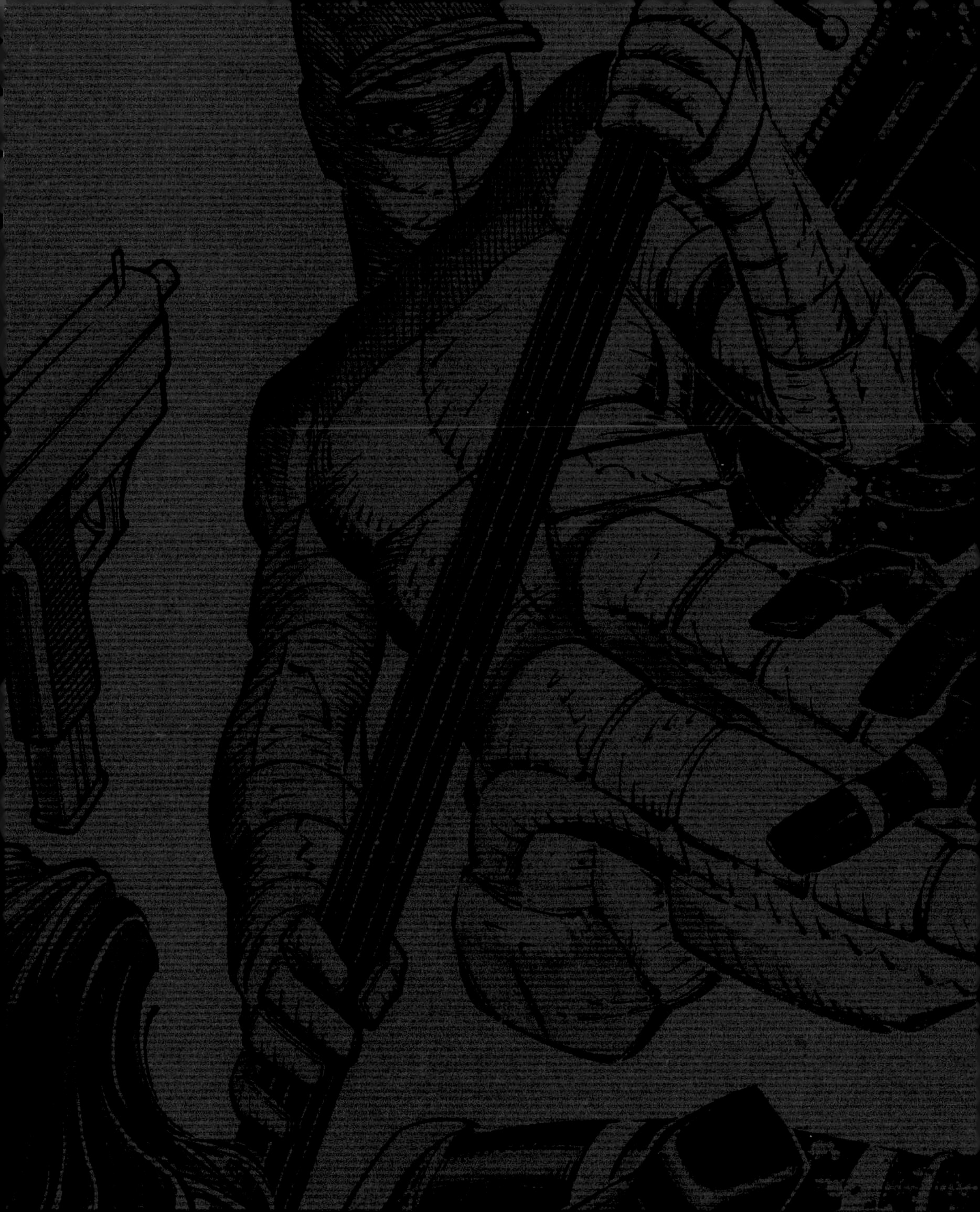

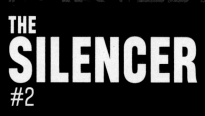

THE SILENCER
#2

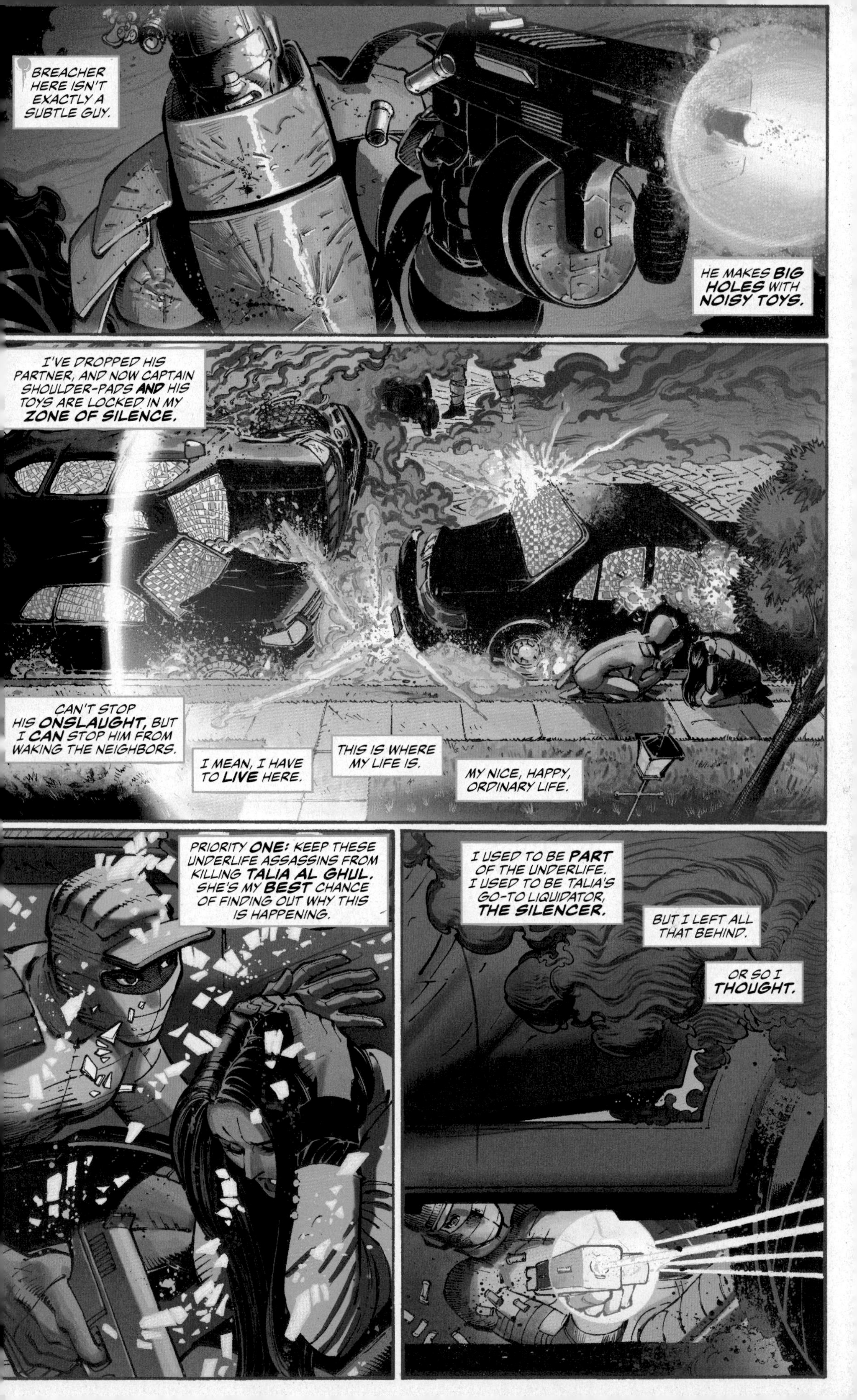
BREACHER HERE ISN'T EXACTLY A SUBTLE GUY.
HE MAKES BIG HOLES WITH NOISY TOYS.
I'VE DROPPED HIS PARTNER, AND NOW CAPTAIN SHOULDER-PADS AND HIS TOYS ARE LOCKED IN MY ZONE OF SILENCE.
CAN'T STOP HIS ONSLAUGHT, BUT I CAN STOP HIM FROM WAKING THE NEIGHBORS.
I MEAN, I HAVE TO LIVE HERE.
THIS IS WHERE MY LIFE IS.
MY NICE, HAPPY, ORDINARY LIFE.
PRIORITY ONE: KEEP THESE UNDERLIFE ASSASSINS FROM KILLING TALIA AL GHUL. SHE'S MY BEST CHANCE OF FINDING OUT WHY THIS IS HAPPENING.
I USED TO BE PART OF THE UNDERLIFE. I USED TO BE TALIA'S GO-TO LIQUIDATOR, THE SILENCER.
BUT I LEFT ALL THAT BEHIND.
OR SO I THOUGHT.

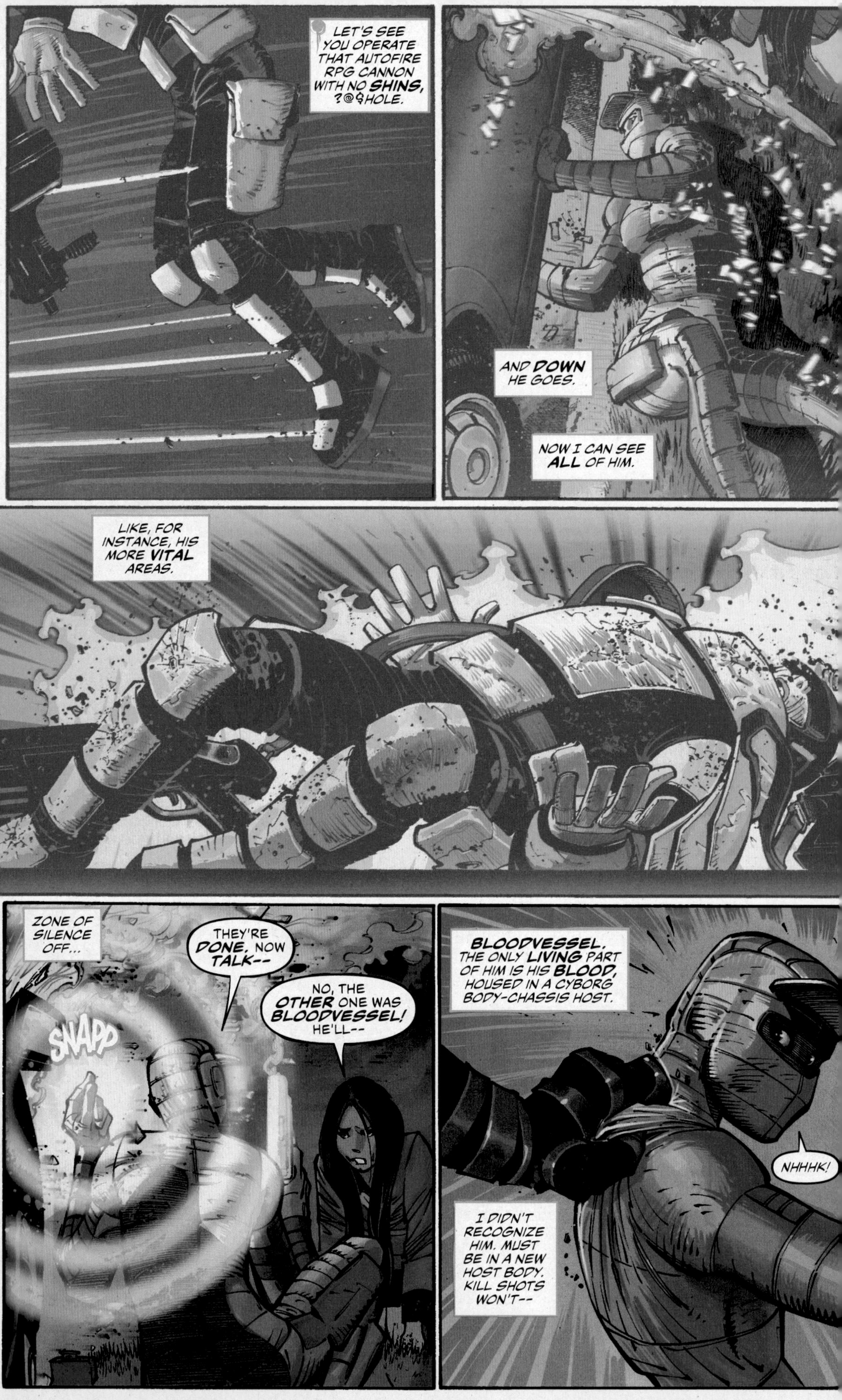
LET'S SEE YOU OPERATE THAT AUTOFIRE RPG CANNON WITH NO SHINS, ?@$HOLE.
AND DOWN HE GOES.
NOW I CAN SEE ALL OF HIM.
LIKE, FOR INSTANCE, HIS MORE VITAL AREAS.
ZONE OF SILENCE OFF...
THEY'RE DONE. NOW TALK--
NO, THE OTHER ONE WAS BLOODVESSEL! HE'LL--
SNAPP
BLOODVESSEL. THE ONLY LIVING PART OF HIM IS HIS BLOOD, HOUSED IN A CYBORG BODY-CHASSIS HOST.
NHHHK!
I DIDN'T RECOGNIZE HIM. MUST BE IN A NEW HOST BODY. KILL SHOTS WON'T--

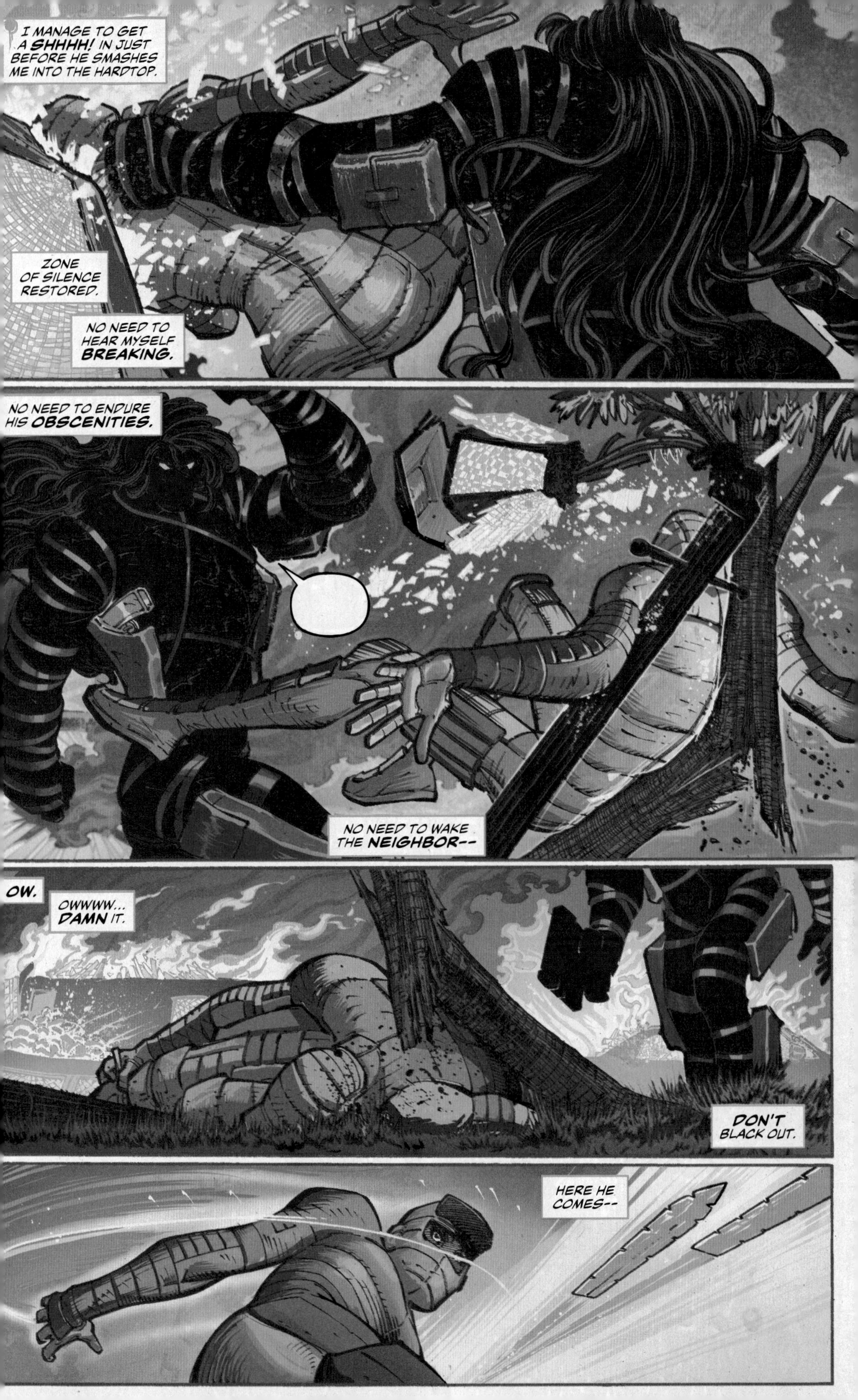
I MANAGE TO GET A SHHHH! IN JUST BEFORE HE SMASHES ME INTO THE HARDTOP.
ZONE OF SILENCE RESTORED.
NO NEED TO HEAR MYSELF BREAKING.
NO NEED TO ENDURE HIS OBSCENITIES.
NO NEED TO WAKE THE NEIGHBOR--
OW.
OWWWW... DAMN IT.
DON'T BLACK OUT.
HERE HE COMES--

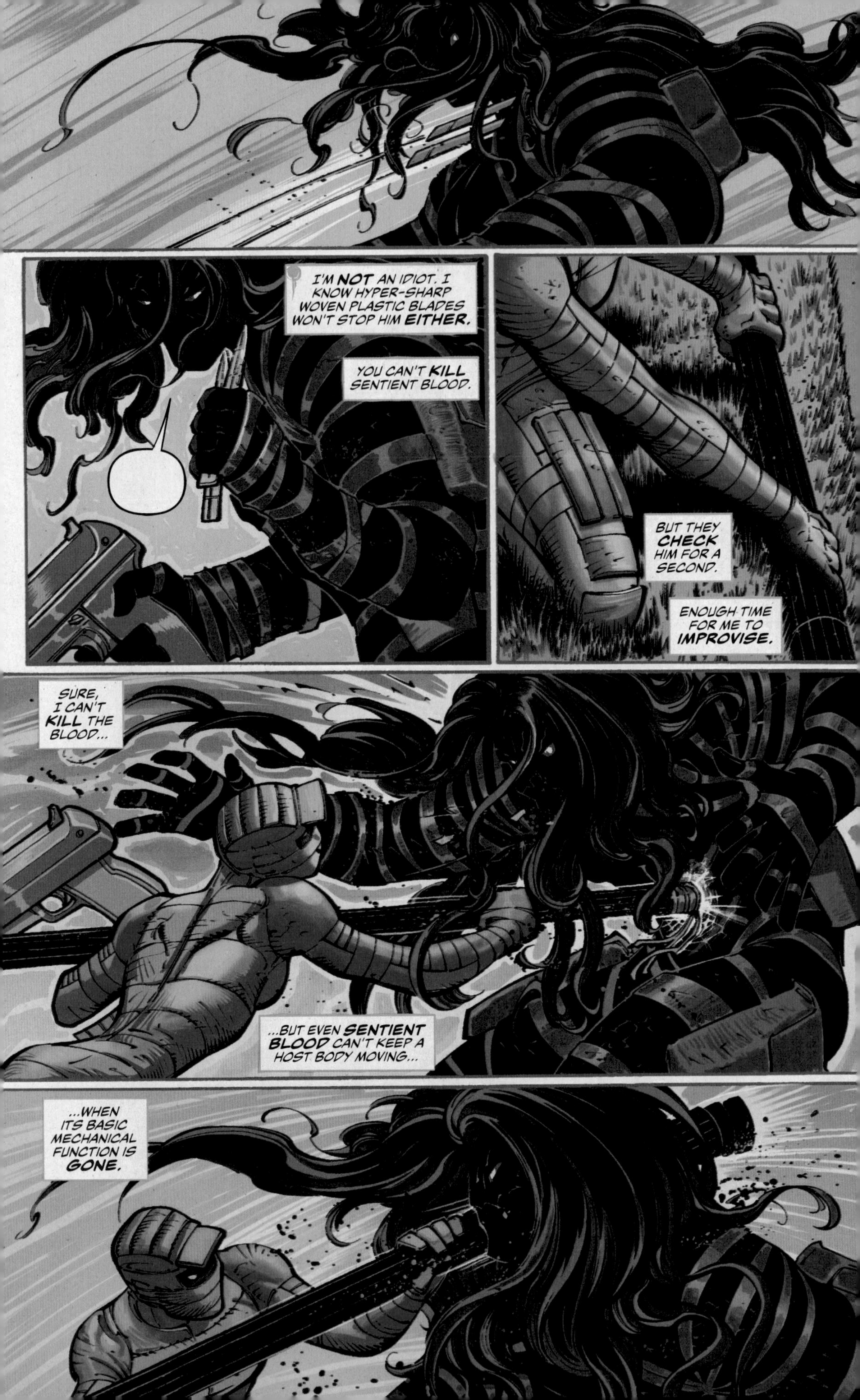
I'M NOT AN IDIOT. I KNOW HYPER-SHARP WOVEN PLASTIC BLADES WON'T STOP HIM EITHER.
YOU CAN'T KILL SENTIENT BLOOD.
BUT THEY CHECK HIM FOR A SECOND.
ENOUGH TIME FOR ME TO IMPROVISE.
SURE, I CAN'T KILL THE BLOOD...
...BUT EVEN SENTIENT BLOOD CAN'T KEEP A HOST BODY MOVING...
...WHEN ITS BASIC MECHANICAL FUNCTION IS GONE.

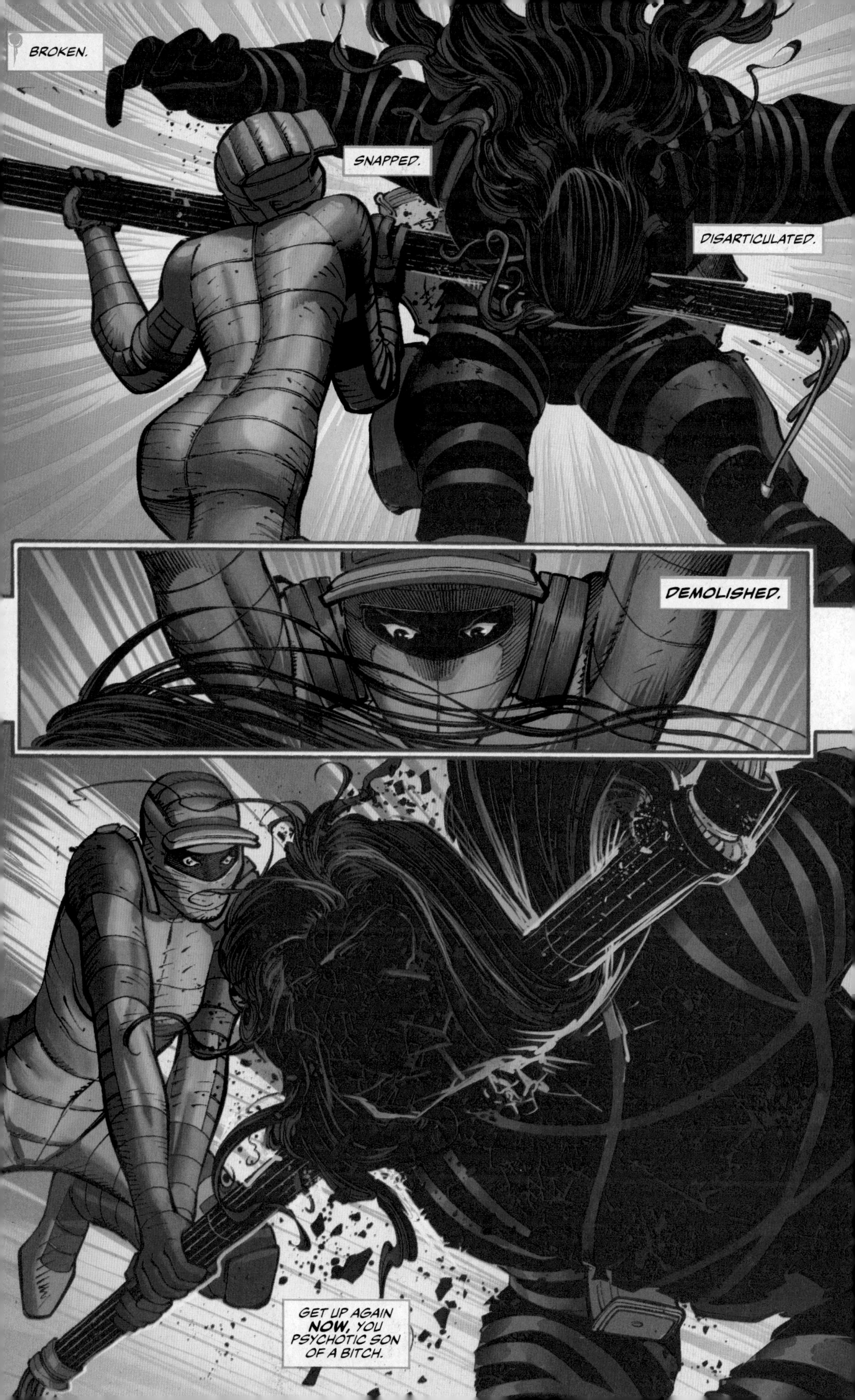
BROKEN.
SNAPPED.
DISARTICULATED.
DEMOLISHED.
GET UP AGAIN **NOW,** YOU PSYCHOTIC SON OF A BITCH.

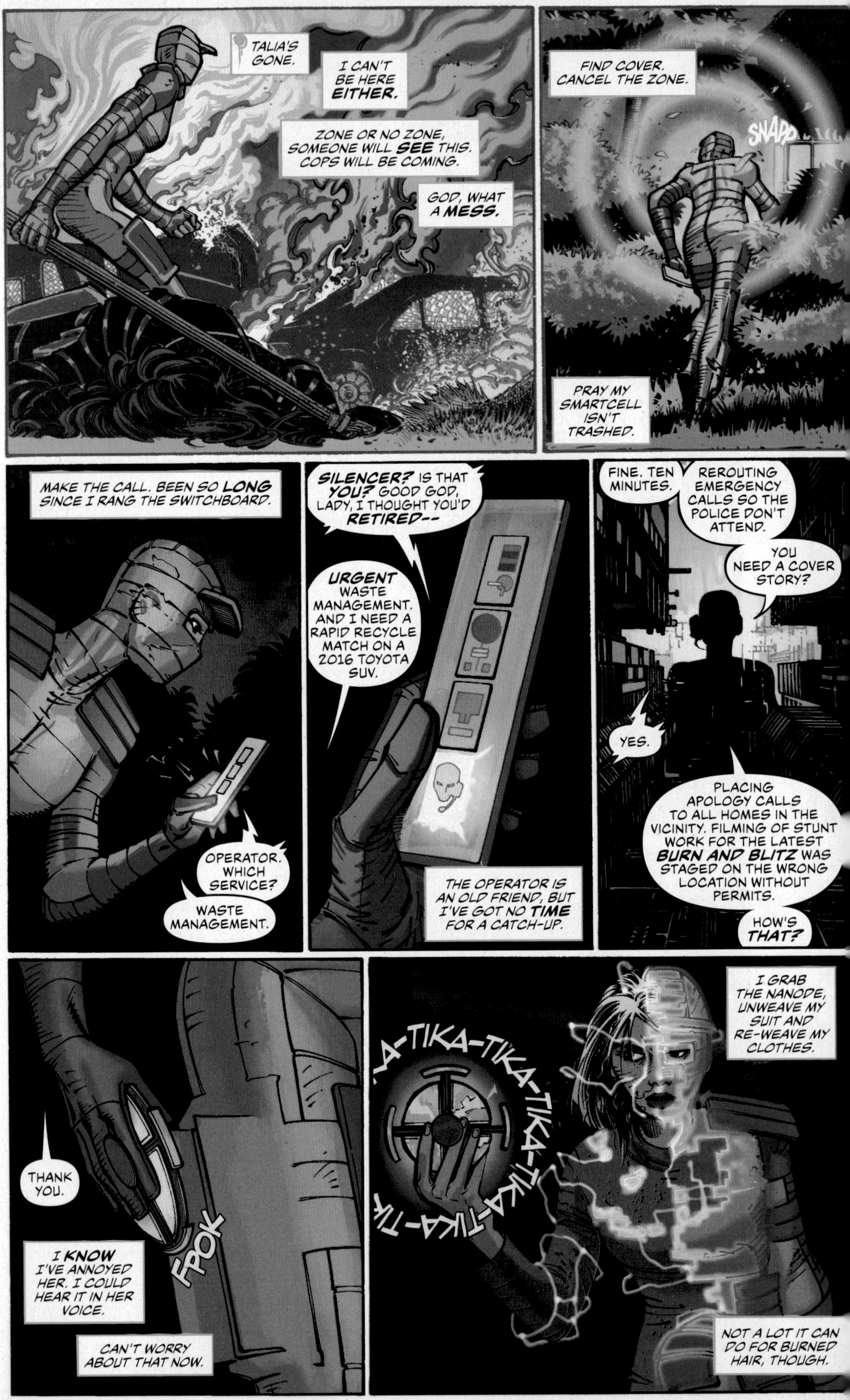
TALIA'S GONE.
I CAN'T BE HERE EITHER.
ZONE OR NO ZONE, SOMEONE WILL SEE THIS. COPS WILL BE COMING.
GOD, WHAT A MESS.
FIND COVER. CANCEL THE ZONE.
SNAPP
PRAY MY SMARTCELL ISN'T TRASHED.
MAKE THE CALL. BEEN SO LONG SINCE I RANG THE SWITCHBOARD.
OPERATOR. WHICH SERVICE?
WASTE MANAGEMENT.
SILENCER? IS THAT YOU? GOOD GOD, LADY, I THOUGHT YOU'D RETIRED--
URGENT WASTE MANAGEMENT. AND I NEED A RAPID RECYCLE MATCH ON A 2016 TOYOTA SUV.
THE OPERATOR IS AN OLD FRIEND, BUT I'VE GOT NO TIME FOR A CATCH-UP.
FINE. TEN MINUTES.
REROUTING EMERGENCY CALLS SO THE POLICE DON'T ATTEND.
YOU NEED A COVER STORY?
YES.
PLACING APOLOGY CALLS TO ALL HOMES IN THE VICINITY. FILMING OF STUNT WORK FOR THE LATEST BURN AND BLITZ WAS STAGED ON THE WRONG LOCATION WITHOUT PERMITS.
HOW'S THAT?
THANK YOU.
FPOK
I KNOW I'VE ANNOYED HER. I COULD HEAR IT IN HER VOICE.
CAN'T WORRY ABOUT THAT NOW.
I GRAB THE NANODE, UNWEAVE MY SUIT AND RE-WEAVE MY CLOTHES.
-TIKA-TIKA-TIKA-TIKA-TIKA-TIK
NOT A LOT IT CAN DO FOR BURNED HAIR, THOUGH.

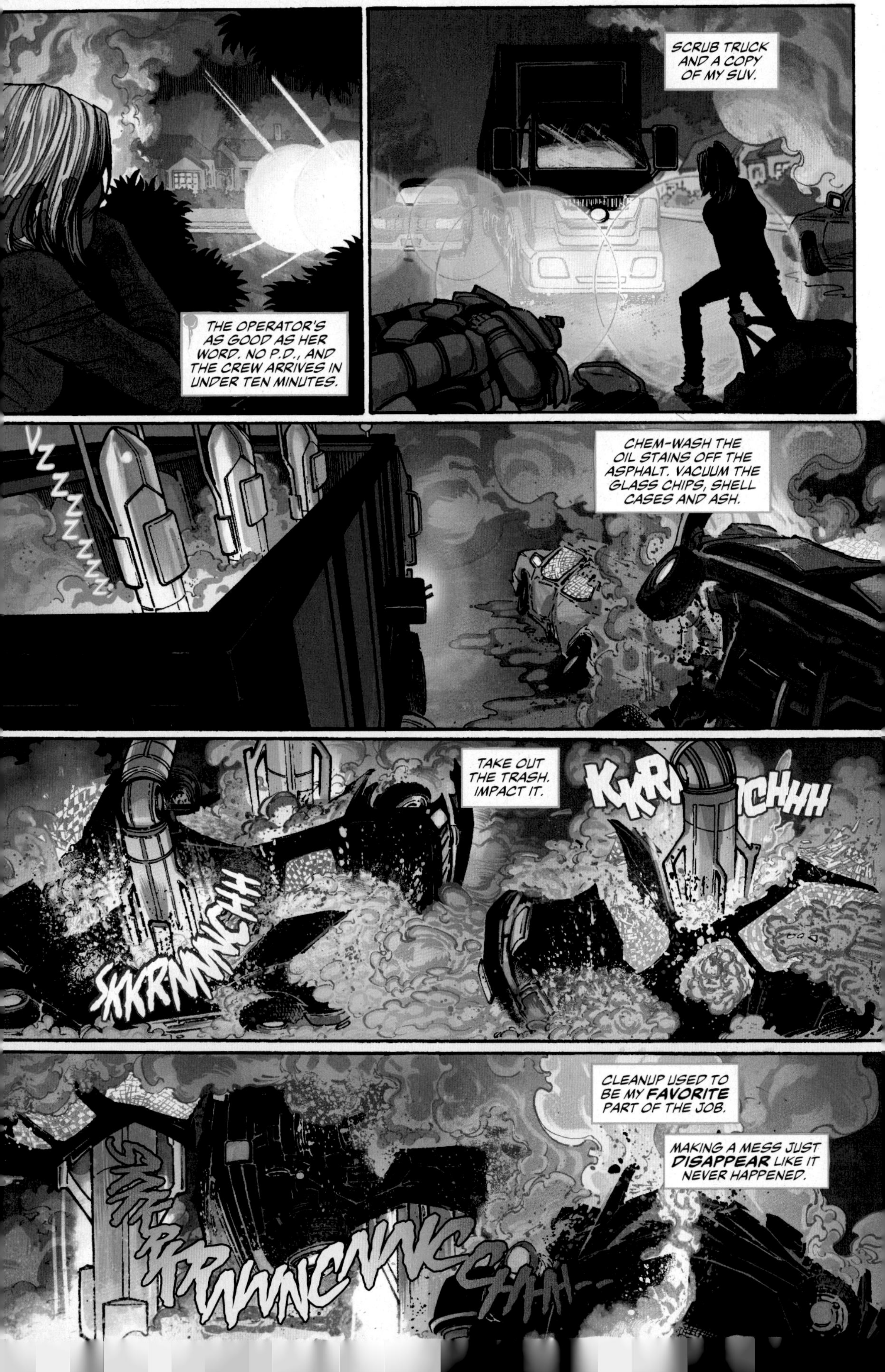
THE OPERATOR'S AS GOOD AS HER WORD. NO P.D., AND THE CREW ARRIVES IN UNDER TEN MINUTES.
SCRUB TRUCK AND A COPY OF MY SUV.
VZZZZZZZ
CHEM-WASH THE OIL STAINS OFF THE ASPHALT. VACUUM THE GLASS CHIPS, SHELL CASES AND ASH.
SKKRNNNCHHH
TAKE OUT THE TRASH. IMPACT IT.
CLEANUP USED TO BE MY **FAVORITE** PART OF THE JOB.
MAKING A MESS JUST **DISAPPEAR** LIKE IT NEVER HAPPENED.

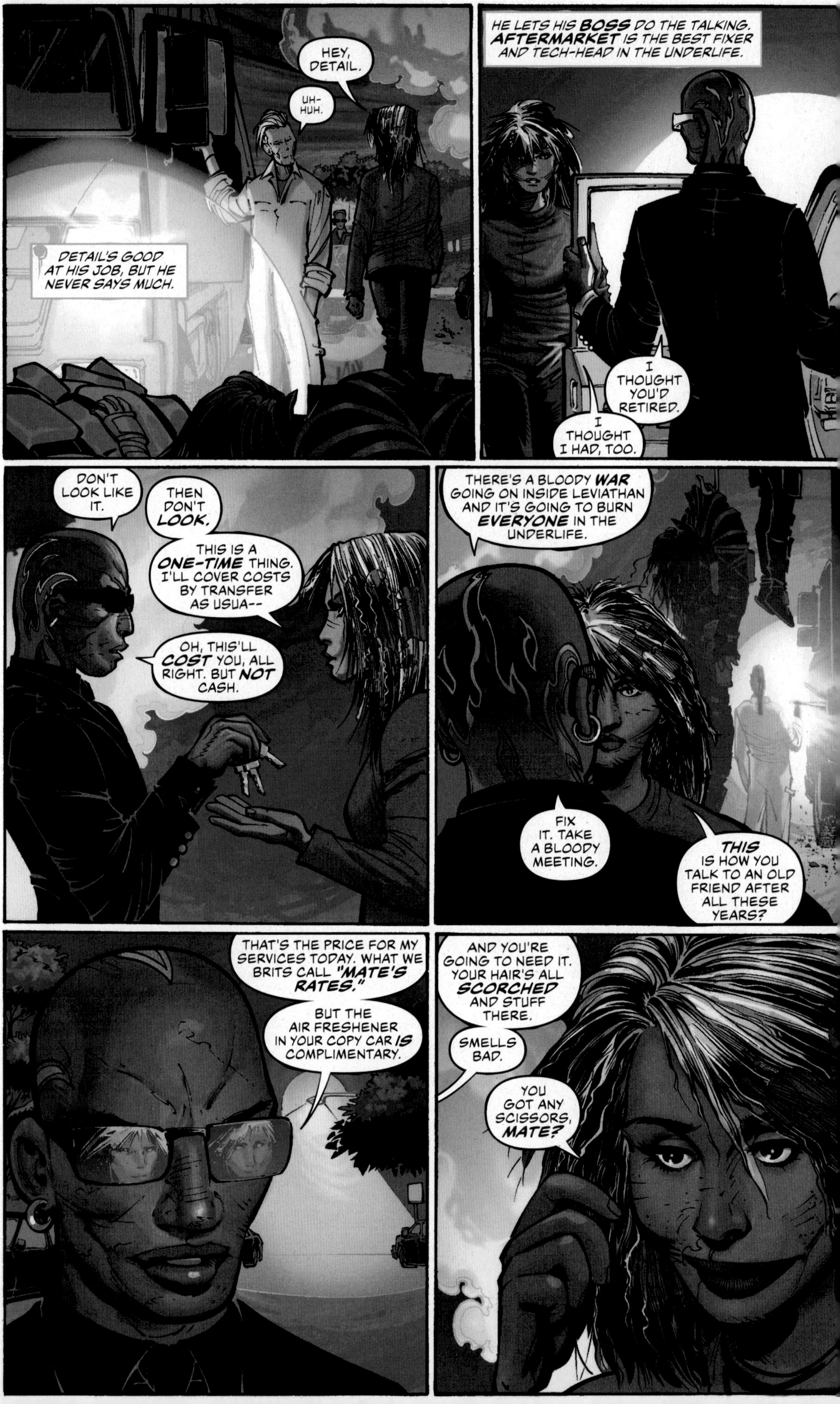
HEY, DETAIL.
UH-HUH.
DETAIL'S GOOD AT HIS JOB, BUT HE NEVER SAYS MUCH.
HE LETS HIS BOSS DO THE TALKING. AFTERMARKET IS THE BEST FIXER AND TECH-HEAD IN THE UNDERLIFE.
I THOUGHT YOU'D RETIRED.
I THOUGHT I HAD, TOO.
DON'T LOOK LIKE IT.
THEN DON'T LOOK.
THIS IS A ONE-TIME THING. I'LL COVER COSTS BY TRANSFER AS USUA--
OH, THIS'LL COST YOU, ALL RIGHT. BUT NOT CASH.
THERE'S A BLOODY WAR GOING ON INSIDE LEVIATHAN AND IT'S GOING TO BURN EVERYONE IN THE UNDERLIFE.
FIX IT. TAKE A BLOODY MEETING.
THIS IS HOW YOU TALK TO AN OLD FRIEND AFTER ALL THESE YEARS?
THAT'S THE PRICE FOR MY SERVICES TODAY. WHAT WE BRITS CALL "MATE'S RATES."
BUT THE AIR FRESHENER IN YOUR COPY CAR IS COMPLIMENTARY.
AND YOU'RE GOING TO NEED IT. YOUR HAIR'S ALL SCORCHED AND STUFF THERE.
SMELLS BAD.
YOU GOT ANY SCISSORS, MATE?

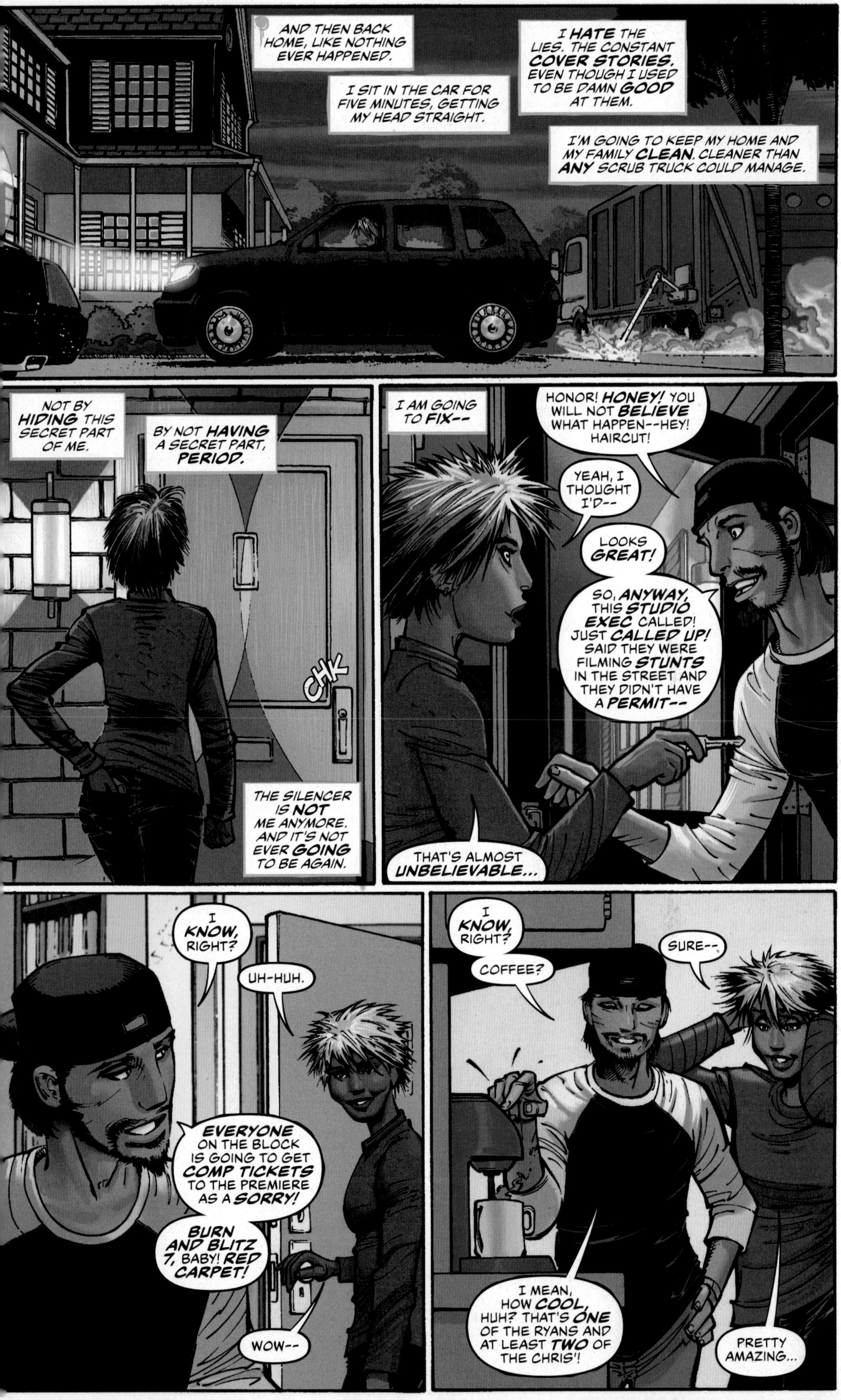
AND THEN BACK HOME, LIKE NOTHING EVER HAPPENED.
I SIT IN THE CAR FOR FIVE MINUTES, GETTING MY HEAD STRAIGHT.
I HATE THE LIES. THE CONSTANT COVER STORIES. EVEN THOUGH I USED TO BE DAMN GOOD AT THEM.
I'M GOING TO KEEP MY HOME AND MY FAMILY CLEAN. CLEANER THAN ANY SCRUB TRUCK COULD MANAGE.
NOT BY HIDING THIS SECRET PART OF ME.
BY NOT HAVING A SECRET PART, PERIOD.
CHK
THE SILENCER IS NOT ME ANYMORE. AND IT'S NOT EVER GOING TO BE AGAIN.
I AM GOING TO FIX--
HONOR! HONEY! YOU WILL NOT BELIEVE WHAT HAPPEN--HEY! HAIRCUT!
YEAH, I THOUGHT I'D--
LOOKS GREAT!
SO, ANYWAY, THIS STUDIO EXEC CALLED! JUST CALLED UP! SAID THEY WERE FILMING STUNTS IN THE STREET AND THEY DIDN'T HAVE A PERMIT--
THAT'S ALMOST UNBELIEVABLE...
I KNOW, RIGHT?
UH-HUH.
EVERYONE ON THE BLOCK IS GOING TO GET COMP TICKETS TO THE PREMIERE AS A SORRY!
BURN AND BLITZ 7, BABY! RED CARPET!
WOW--
I KNOW, RIGHT?
SURE--
COFFEE?
I MEAN, HOW COOL, HUH? THAT'S ONE OF THE RYANS AND AT LEAST TWO OF THE CHRIS'!
PRETTY AMAZING...

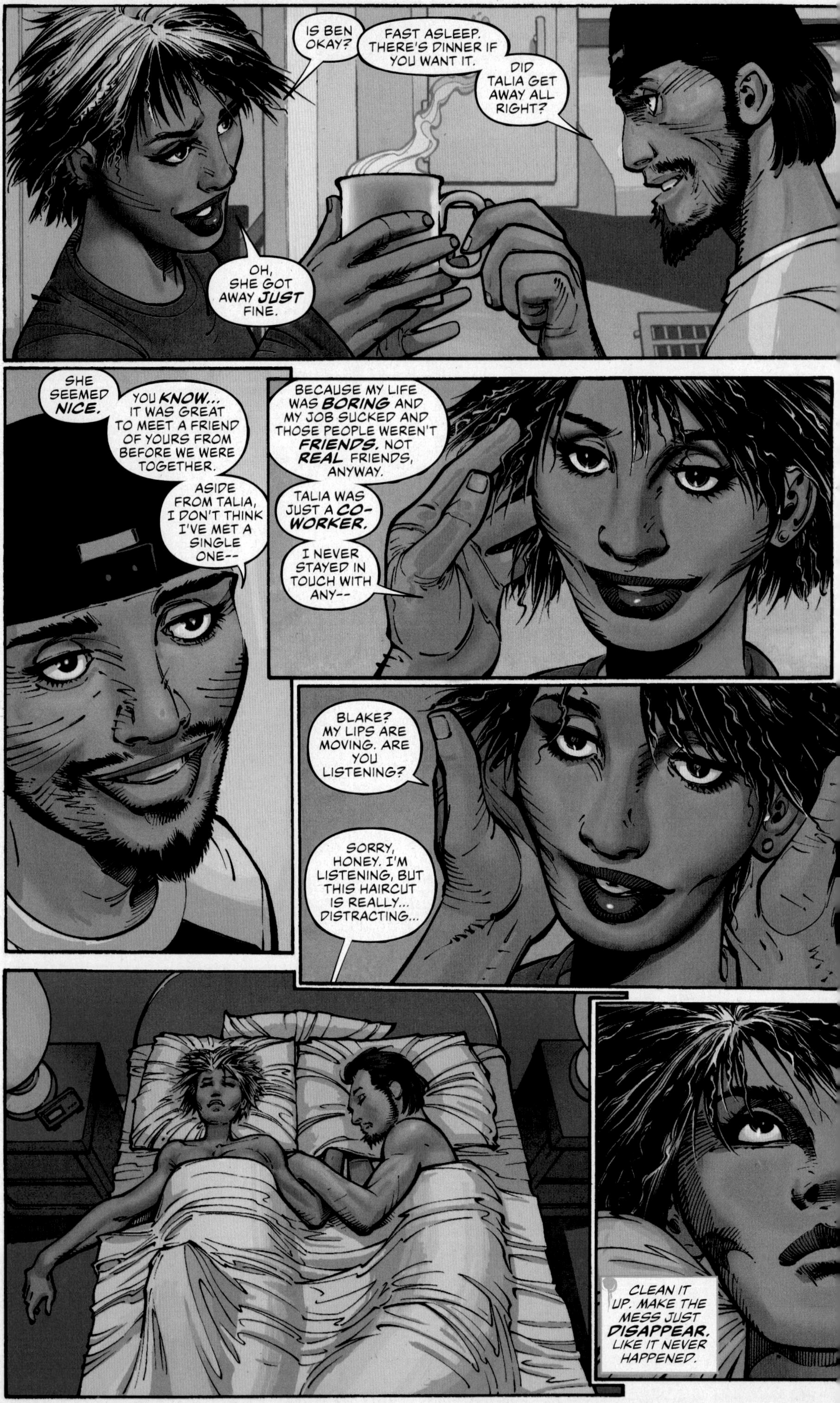
IS BEN OKAY?
FAST ASLEEP. THERE'S DINNER IF YOU WANT IT.
DID TALIA GET AWAY ALL RIGHT?
OH, SHE GOT AWAY JUST FINE.
SHE SEEMED NICE.
YOU KNOW... IT WAS GREAT TO MEET A FRIEND OF YOURS FROM BEFORE WE WERE TOGETHER.
ASIDE FROM TALIA, I DON'T THINK I'VE MET A SINGLE ONE--
BECAUSE MY LIFE WAS BORING AND MY JOB SUCKED AND THOSE PEOPLE WEREN'T FRIENDS. NOT REAL FRIENDS, ANYWAY.
TALIA WAS JUST A CO-WORKER.
I NEVER STAYED IN TOUCH WITH ANY--
BLAKE? MY LIPS ARE MOVING. ARE YOU LISTENING?
SORRY, HONEY. I'M LISTENING, BUT THIS HAIRCUT IS REALLY... DISTRACTING...
CLEAN IT UP. MAKE THE MESS JUST DISAPPEAR. LIKE IT NEVER HAPPENED.

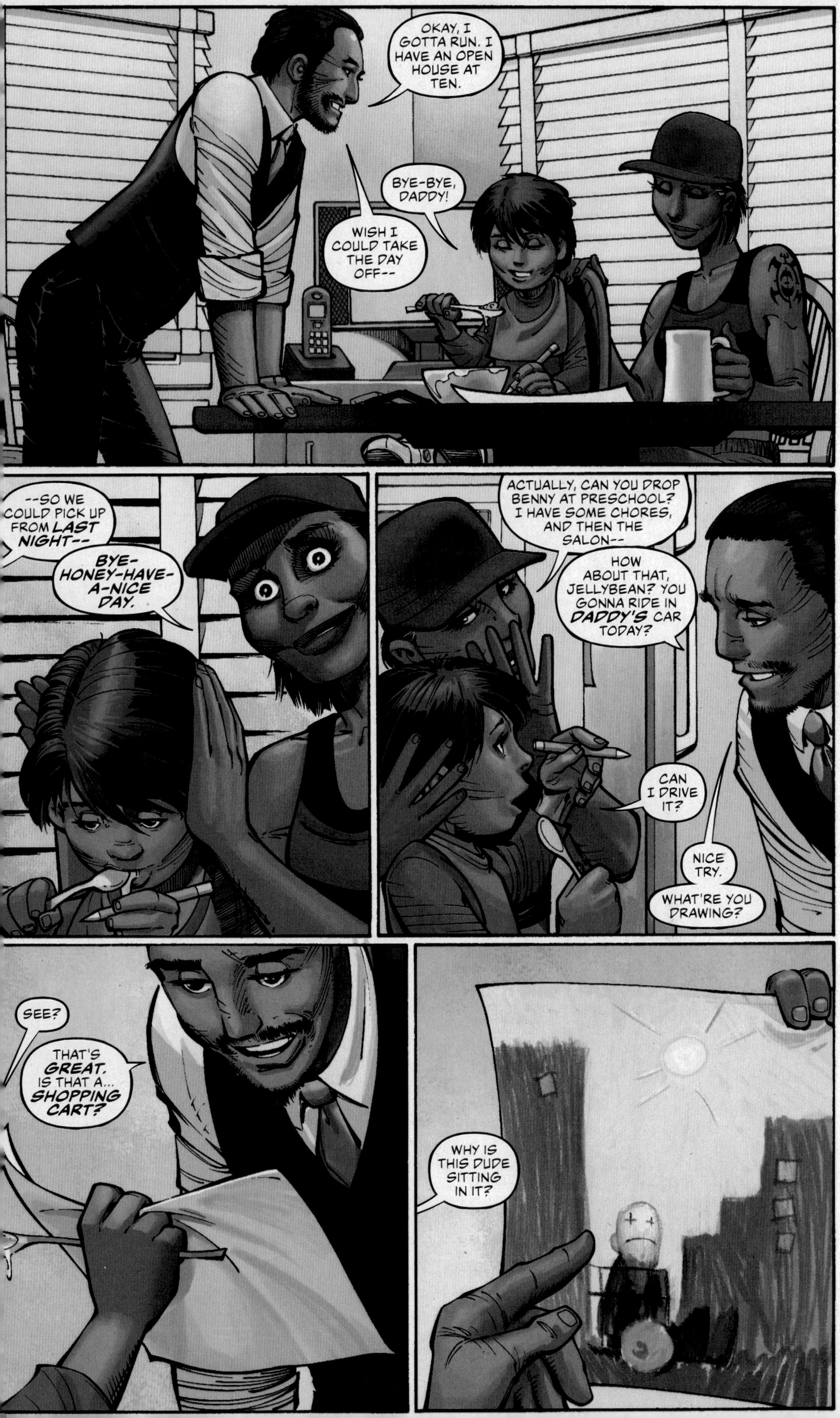
OKAY, I GOTTA RUN. I HAVE AN OPEN HOUSE AT TEN.
WISH I COULD TAKE THE DAY OFF--
BYE-BYE, DADDY!
--SO WE COULD PICK UP FROM LAST NIGHT--
BYE-HONEY-HAVE-A-NICE DAY.
ACTUALLY, CAN YOU DROP BENNY AT PRESCHOOL? I HAVE SOME CHORES, AND THEN THE SALON--
HOW ABOUT THAT, JELLYBEAN? YOU GONNA RIDE IN DADDY'S CAR TODAY?
CAN I DRIVE IT?
NICE TRY.
WHAT'RE YOU DRAWING?
SEE?
THAT'S GREAT. IS THAT A... SHOPPING CART?
WHY IS THIS DUDE SITTING IN IT?

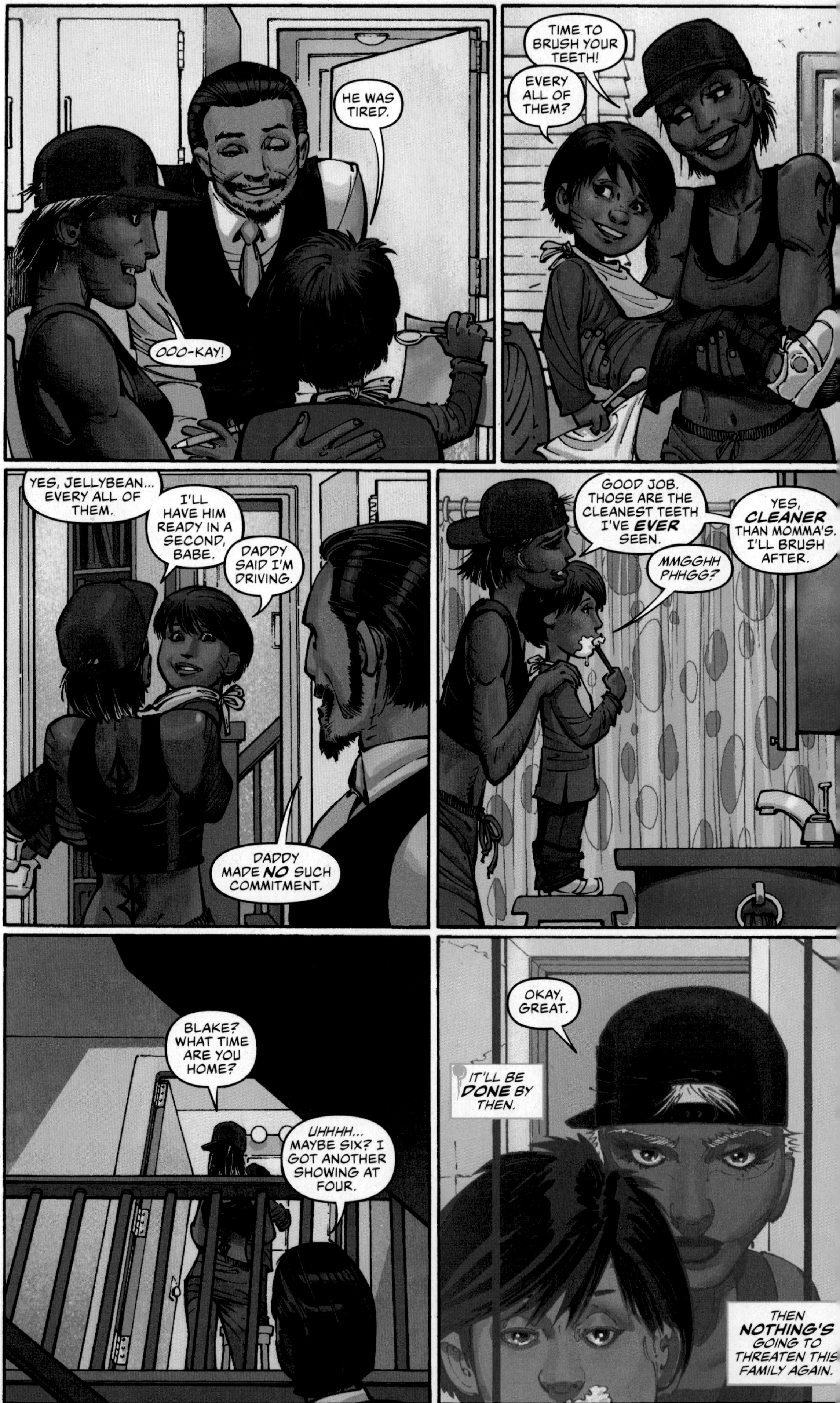
HE WAS TIRED.
OOO-KAY!
TIME TO BRUSH YOUR TEETH!
EVERY ALL OF THEM?
YES, JELLYBEAN... EVERY ALL OF THEM.
I'LL HAVE HIM READY IN A SECOND, BABE.
DADDY SAID I'M DRIVING.
DADDY MADE NO SUCH COMMITMENT.
GOOD JOB. THOSE ARE THE CLEANEST TEETH I'VE EVER SEEN.
MMGGHH PHHGG?
YES, CLEANER THAN MOMMA'S. I'LL BRUSH AFTER.
BLAKE? WHAT TIME ARE YOU HOME?
UHHHH... MAYBE SIX? I GOT ANOTHER SHOWING AT FOUR.
OKAY, GREAT.
IT'LL BE DONE BY THEN.
THEN NOTHING'S GOING TO THREATEN THIS FAMILY AGAIN.

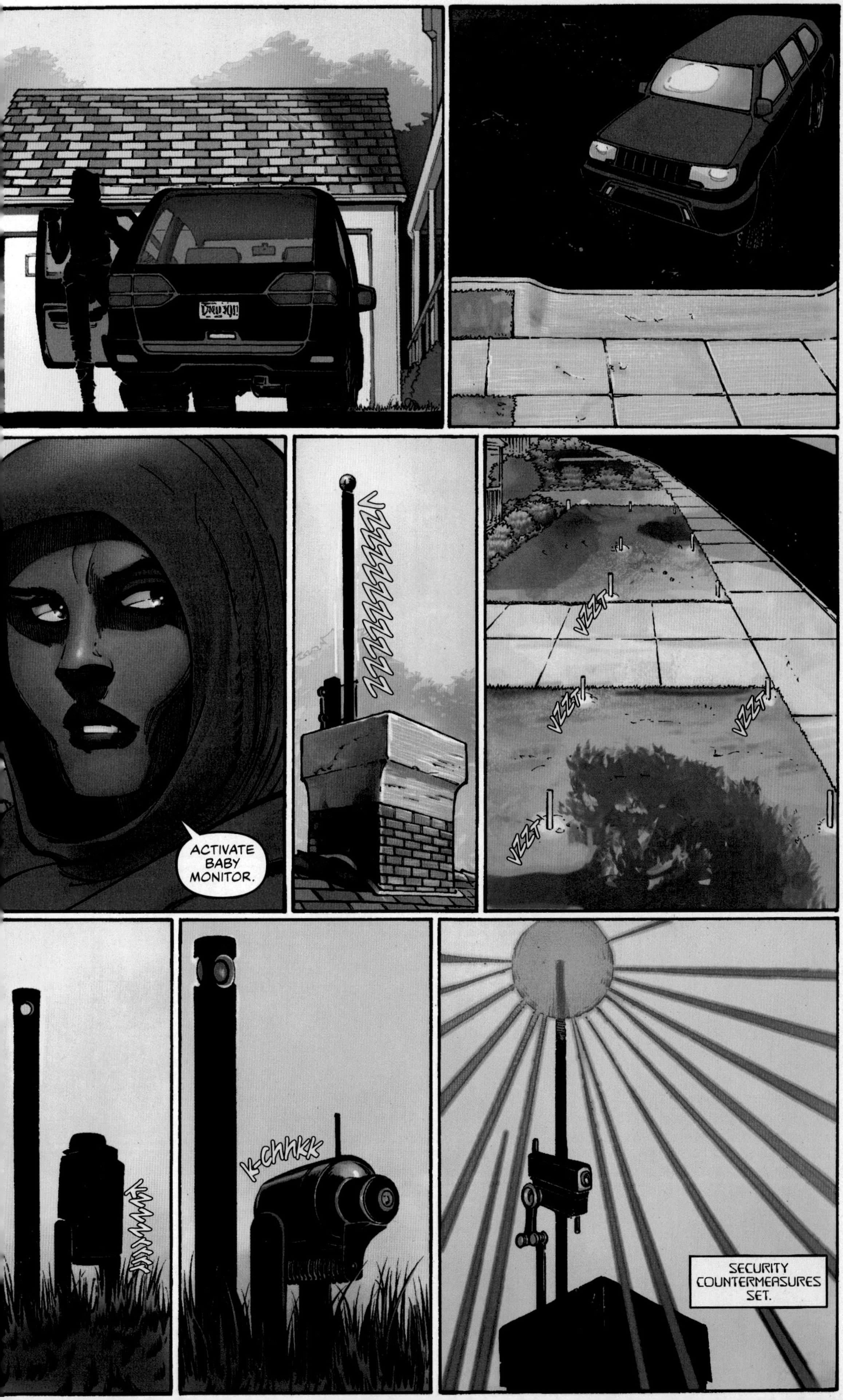
ACTIVATE BABY MONITOR.
VZZZT
VZZZT
VZZZT
VZZZT
K-CHHKK
SECURITY COUNTERMEASURES SET.

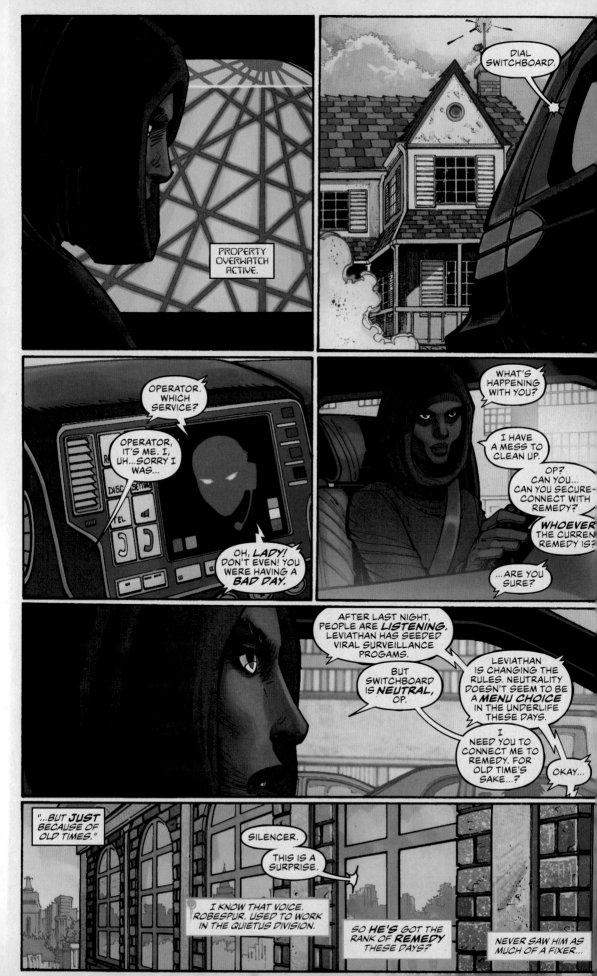

PROPERTY OVERWATCH ACTIVE.

DIAL SWITCHBOARD.

OPERATOR. WHICH SERVICE?

OPERATOR, IT'S ME. I, UH...SORRY I WAS...

OH, *LADY!* DON'T EVEN! YOU WERE HAVING A *BAD DAY.*

WHAT'S HAPPENING WITH YOU?

I HAVE A MESS TO CLEAN UP.

OP? CAN YOU... CAN YOU SECURE-CONNECT WITH REMEDY? *WHOEVER* THE CURRENT REMEDY IS?

...ARE YOU SURE?

AFTER LAST NIGHT, PEOPLE ARE *LISTENING.* LEVIATHAN HAS SEEDED VIRAL SURVEILLANCE PROGAMS.

BUT SWITCHBOARD IS *NEUTRAL,* OP.

LEVIATHAN IS CHANGING THE RULES. NEUTRALITY DOESN'T SEEM TO BE A *MENU CHOICE* IN THE UNDERLIFE THESE DAYS.

I NEED YOU TO CONNECT ME TO REMEDY. FOR OLD TIME'S SAKE...?

OKAY...

"...BUT *JUST* BECAUSE OF OLD TIMES."

SILENCER. THIS IS A SURPRISE.

I KNOW THAT VOICE. ROBESPUR. USED TO WORK IN THE QUIETUS DIVISION.

SO *HE'S* GOT THE RANK OF *REMEDY* THESE DAYS?

NEVER SAW HIM AS MUCH OF A *FIXER...*

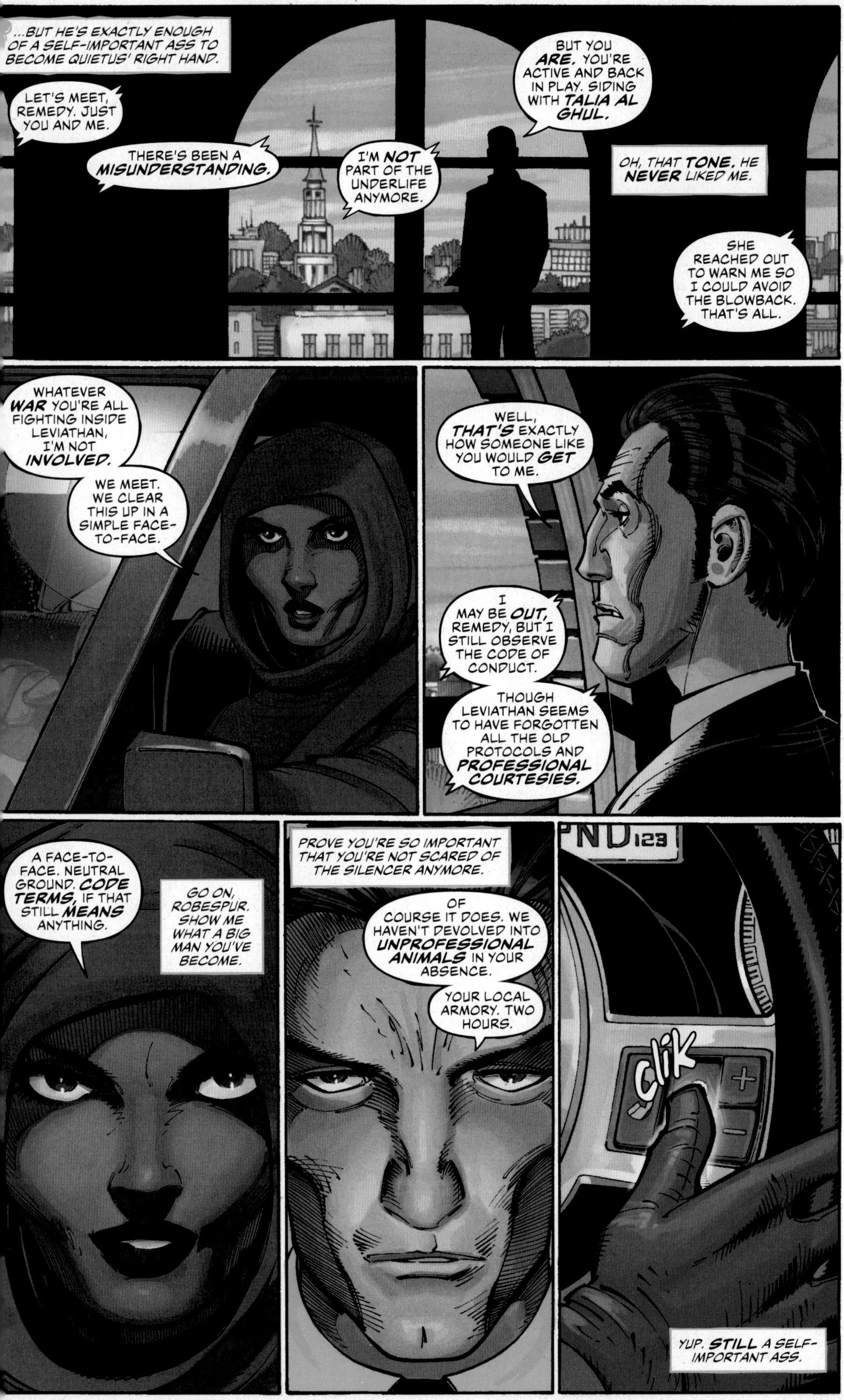
...BUT HE'S EXACTLY ENOUGH OF A SELF-IMPORTANT ASS TO BECOME QUIETUS' RIGHT HAND.
LET'S MEET, REMEDY. JUST YOU AND ME.
THERE'S BEEN A MISUNDERSTANDING.
I'M NOT PART OF THE UNDERLIFE ANYMORE.
BUT YOU ARE. YOU'RE ACTIVE AND BACK IN PLAY. SIDING WITH TALIA AL GHUL.
OH, THAT TONE. HE NEVER LIKED ME.
SHE REACHED OUT TO WARN ME SO I COULD AVOID THE BLOWBACK. THAT'S ALL.
WHATEVER WAR YOU'RE ALL FIGHTING INSIDE LEVIATHAN, I'M NOT INVOLVED.
WE MEET. WE CLEAR THIS UP IN A SIMPLE FACE-TO-FACE.
WELL, THAT'S EXACTLY HOW SOMEONE LIKE YOU WOULD GET TO ME.
I MAY BE OUT, REMEDY, BUT I STILL OBSERVE THE CODE OF CONDUCT.
THOUGH LEVIATHAN SEEMS TO HAVE FORGOTTEN ALL THE OLD PROTOCOLS AND PROFESSIONAL COURTESIES.
A FACE-TO-FACE. NEUTRAL GROUND. CODE TERMS, IF THAT STILL MEANS ANYTHING.
GO ON, ROBESPUR. SHOW ME WHAT A BIG MAN YOU'VE BECOME.
PROVE YOU'RE SO IMPORTANT THAT YOU'RE NOT SCARED OF THE SILENCER ANYMORE.
OF COURSE IT DOES. WE HAVEN'T DEVOLVED INTO UNPROFESSIONAL ANIMALS IN YOUR ABSENCE.
YOUR LOCAL ARMORY. TWO HOURS.
PND 123
CLIK
YUP. STILL A SELF-IMPORTANT ASS.

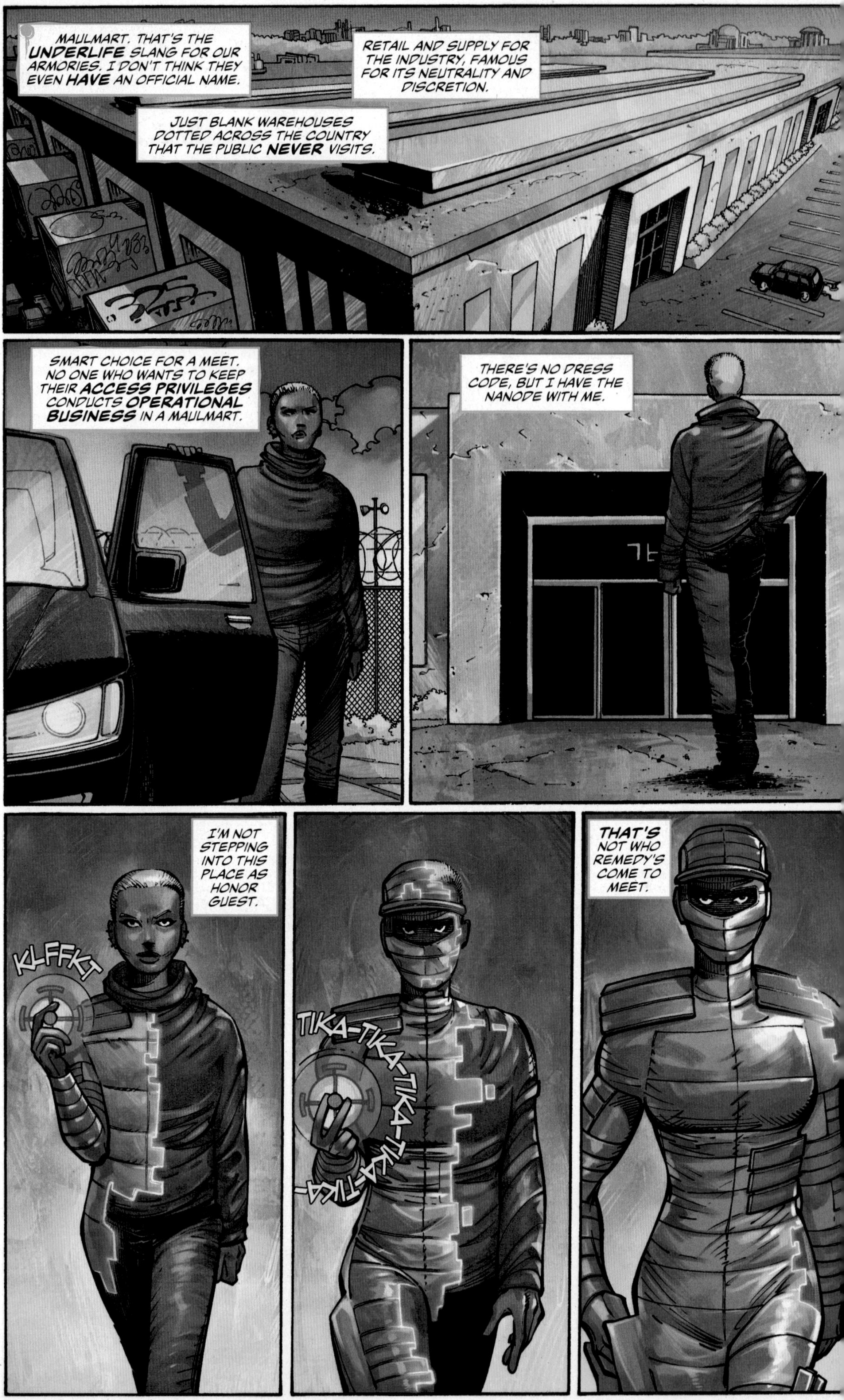
MAULMART. THAT'S THE UNDERLIFE SLANG FOR OUR ARMORIES. I DON'T THINK THEY EVEN HAVE AN OFFICIAL NAME.
RETAIL AND SUPPLY FOR THE INDUSTRY, FAMOUS FOR ITS NEUTRALITY AND DISCRETION.
JUST BLANK WAREHOUSES DOTTED ACROSS THE COUNTRY THAT THE PUBLIC NEVER VISITS.
SMART CHOICE FOR A MEET. NO ONE WHO WANTS TO KEEP THEIR ACCESS PRIVILEGES CONDUCTS OPERATIONAL BUSINESS IN A MAULMART.
THERE'S NO DRESS CODE, BUT I HAVE THE NANODE WITH ME.
I'M NOT STEPPING INTO THIS PLACE AS HONOR GUEST.
KLFFKT
TIKA-TIKA-TIKA-TIKA-TIKA
THAT'S NOT WHO REMEDY'S COME TO MEET.

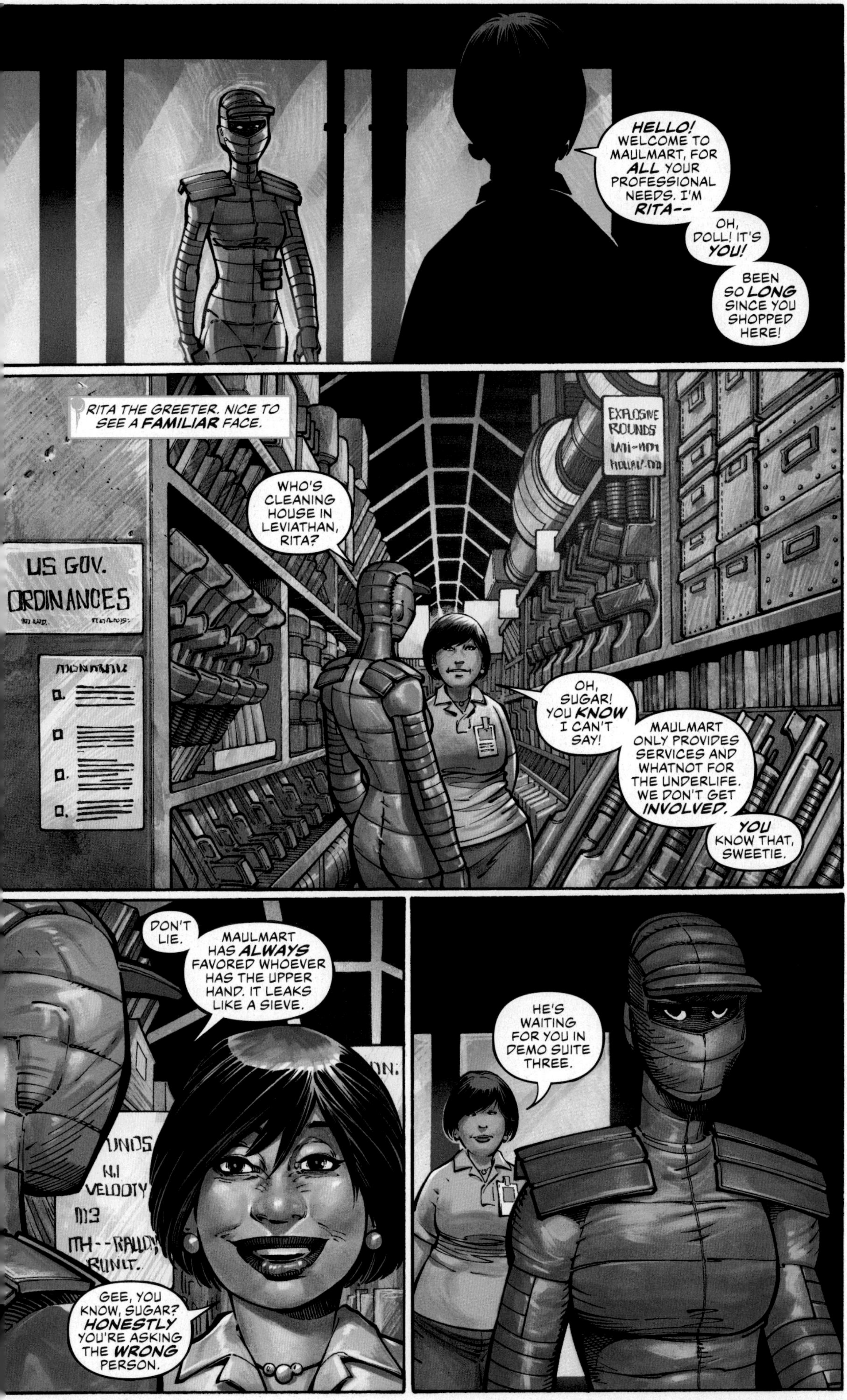
HELLO! WELCOME TO MAULMART, FOR ALL YOUR PROFESSIONAL NEEDS. I'M RITA--
OH, DOLL! IT'S YOU!
BEEN SO LONG SINCE YOU SHOPPED HERE!
RITA THE GREETER. NICE TO SEE A FAMILIAR FACE.
EXPLOSIVE ROUNDS
WHO'S CLEANING HOUSE IN LEVIATHAN, RITA?
US GOV. ORDINANCES
OH, SUGAR! YOU KNOW I CAN'T SAY!
MAULMART ONLY PROVIDES SERVICES AND WHATNOT FOR THE UNDERLIFE. WE DON'T GET INVOLVED.
YOU KNOW THAT, SWEETIE.
DON'T LIE.
MAULMART HAS ALWAYS FAVORED WHOEVER HAS THE UPPER HAND. IT LEAKS LIKE A SIEVE.
GEE, YOU KNOW, SUGAR? HONESTLY YOU'RE ASKING THE WRONG PERSON.
HE'S WAITING FOR YOU IN DEMO SUITE THREE.

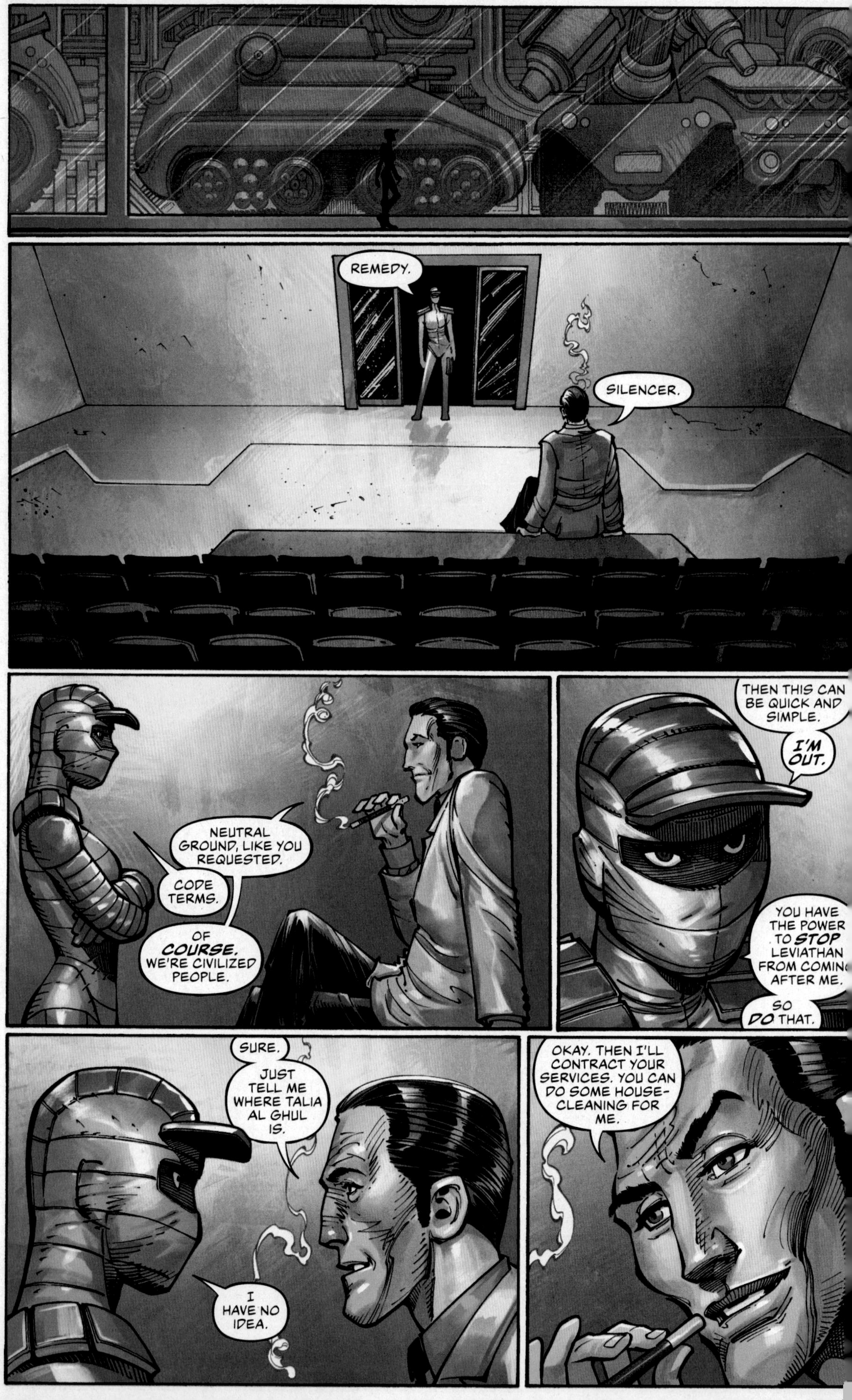
REMEDY.
SILENCER.
NEUTRAL GROUND, LIKE YOU REQUESTED.
CODE TERMS.
OF COURSE. WE'RE CIVILIZED PEOPLE.
THEN THIS CAN BE QUICK AND SIMPLE.
I'M OUT.
YOU HAVE THE POWER TO STOP LEVIATHAN FROM COMIN AFTER ME.
SO DO THAT.
SURE.
JUST TELL ME WHERE TALIA AL GHUL IS.
I HAVE NO IDEA.
OKAY. THEN I'LL CONTRACT YOUR SERVICES. YOU CAN DO SOME HOUSE-CLEANING FOR ME.

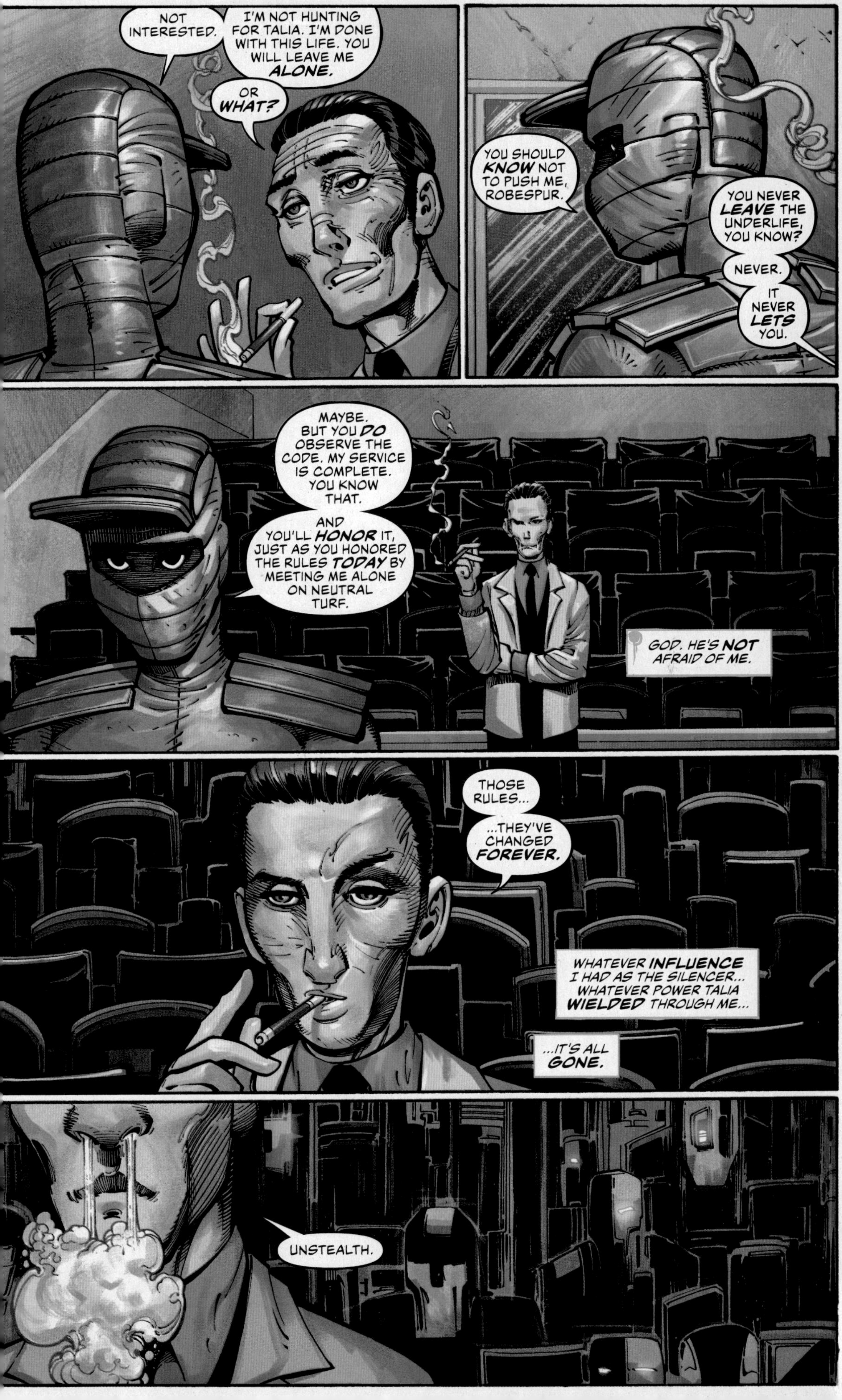
NOT INTERESTED.
I'M NOT HUNTING FOR TALIA. I'M DONE WITH THIS LIFE. YOU WILL LEAVE ME ALONE.
OR WHAT?
YOU SHOULD KNOW NOT TO PUSH ME, ROBESPUR.
YOU NEVER LEAVE THE UNDERLIFE, YOU KNOW?
NEVER.
IT NEVER LETS YOU.
MAYBE. BUT YOU DO OBSERVE THE CODE. MY SERVICE IS COMPLETE. YOU KNOW THAT.
AND YOU'LL HONOR IT, JUST AS YOU HONORED THE RULES TODAY BY MEETING ME ALONE ON NEUTRAL TURF.
GOD. HE'S NOT AFRAID OF ME.
THOSE RULES...
...THEY'VE CHANGED FOREVER.
WHATEVER INFLUENCE I HAD AS THE SILENCER... WHATEVER POWER TALIA WIELDED THROUGH ME...
...IT'S ALL GONE.
UNSTEALTH.

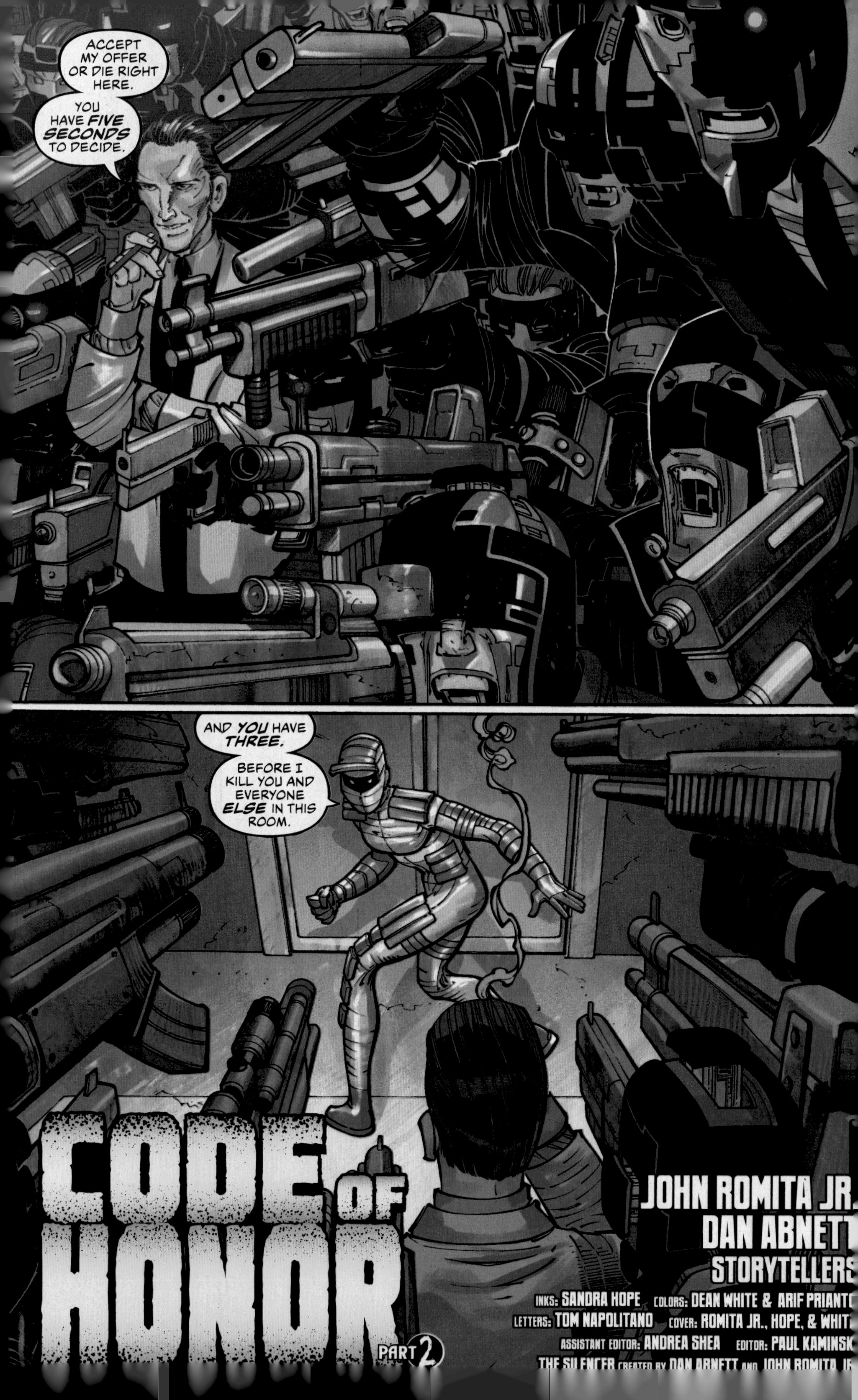
ACCEPT MY OFFER OR DIE RIGHT HERE.
YOU HAVE FIVE SECONDS TO DECIDE.
AND YOU HAVE THREE.
BEFORE I KILL YOU AND EVERYONE ELSE IN THIS ROOM.
CODE OF HONOR
PART 2
JOHN ROMITA JR.
DAN ABNETT
STORYTELLERS
INKS: SANDRA HOPE COLORS: DEAN WHITE & ARIF PRIANTO
LETTERS: TOM NAPOLITANO COVER: ROMITA JR., HOPE, & WHITE
ASSISTANT EDITOR: ANDREA SHEA EDITOR: PAUL KAMINSKI
THE SILENCER CREATED BY DAN ABNETT AND JOHN ROMITA JR.

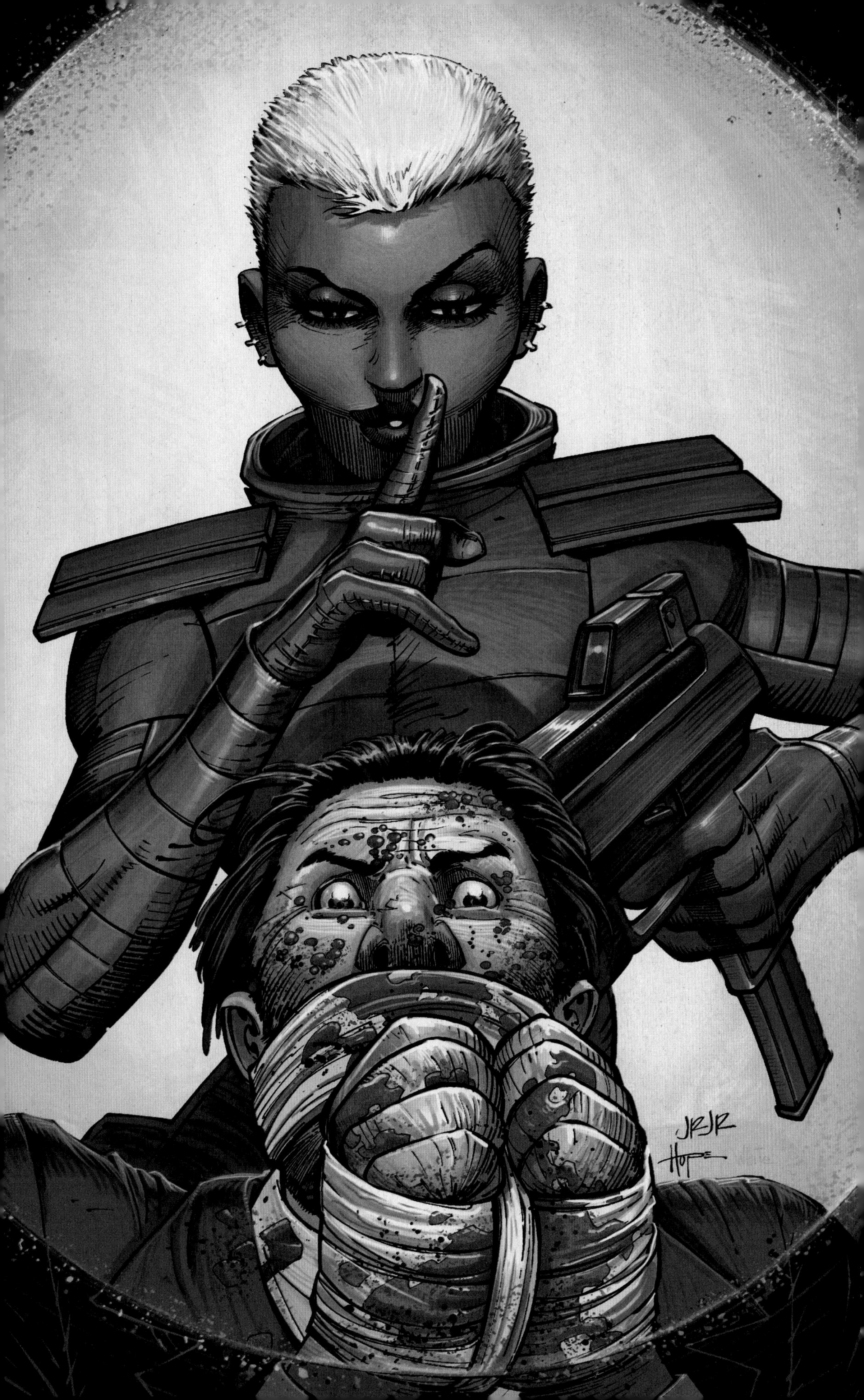
JRJR
HOPE

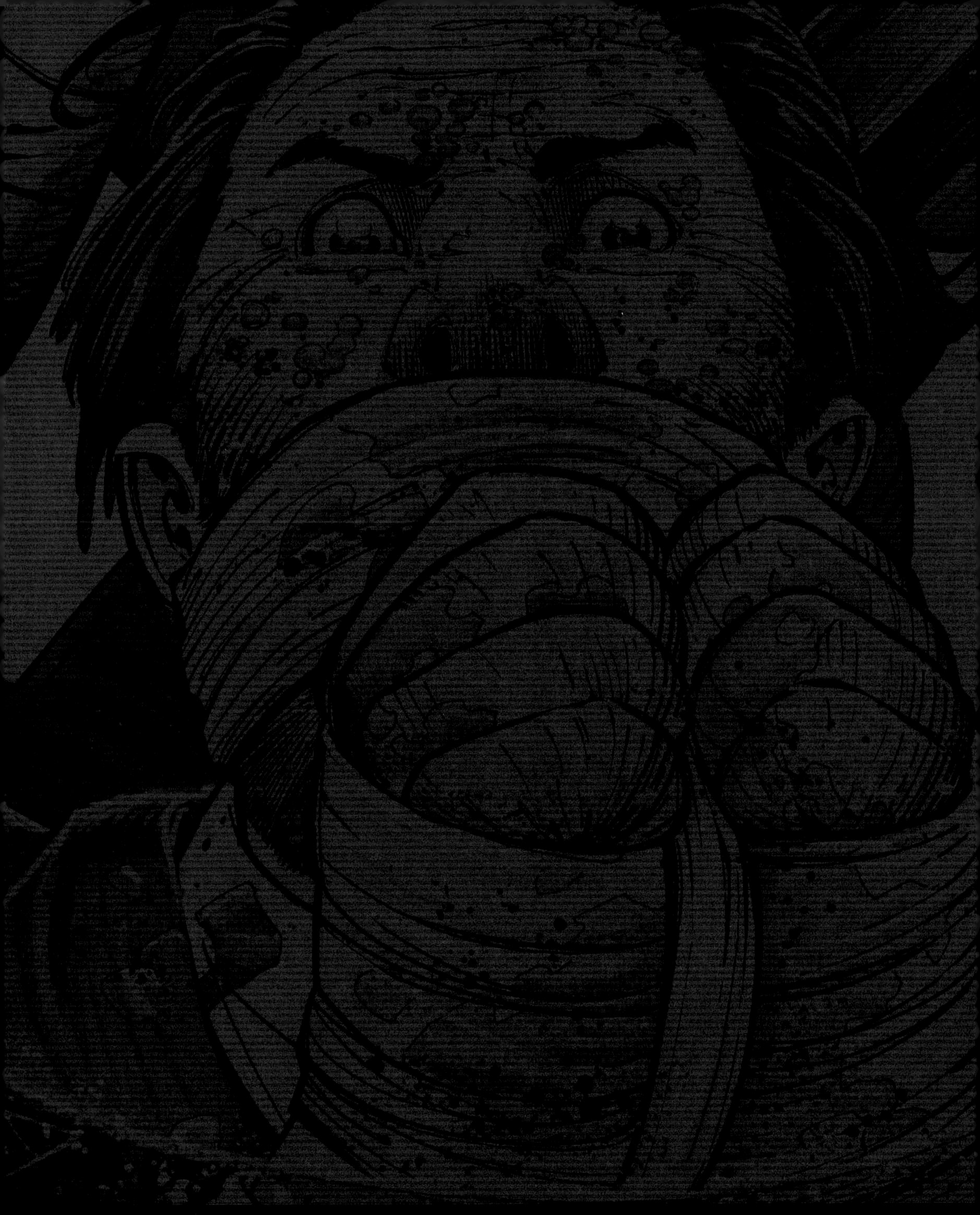

THE SILENCER

#3

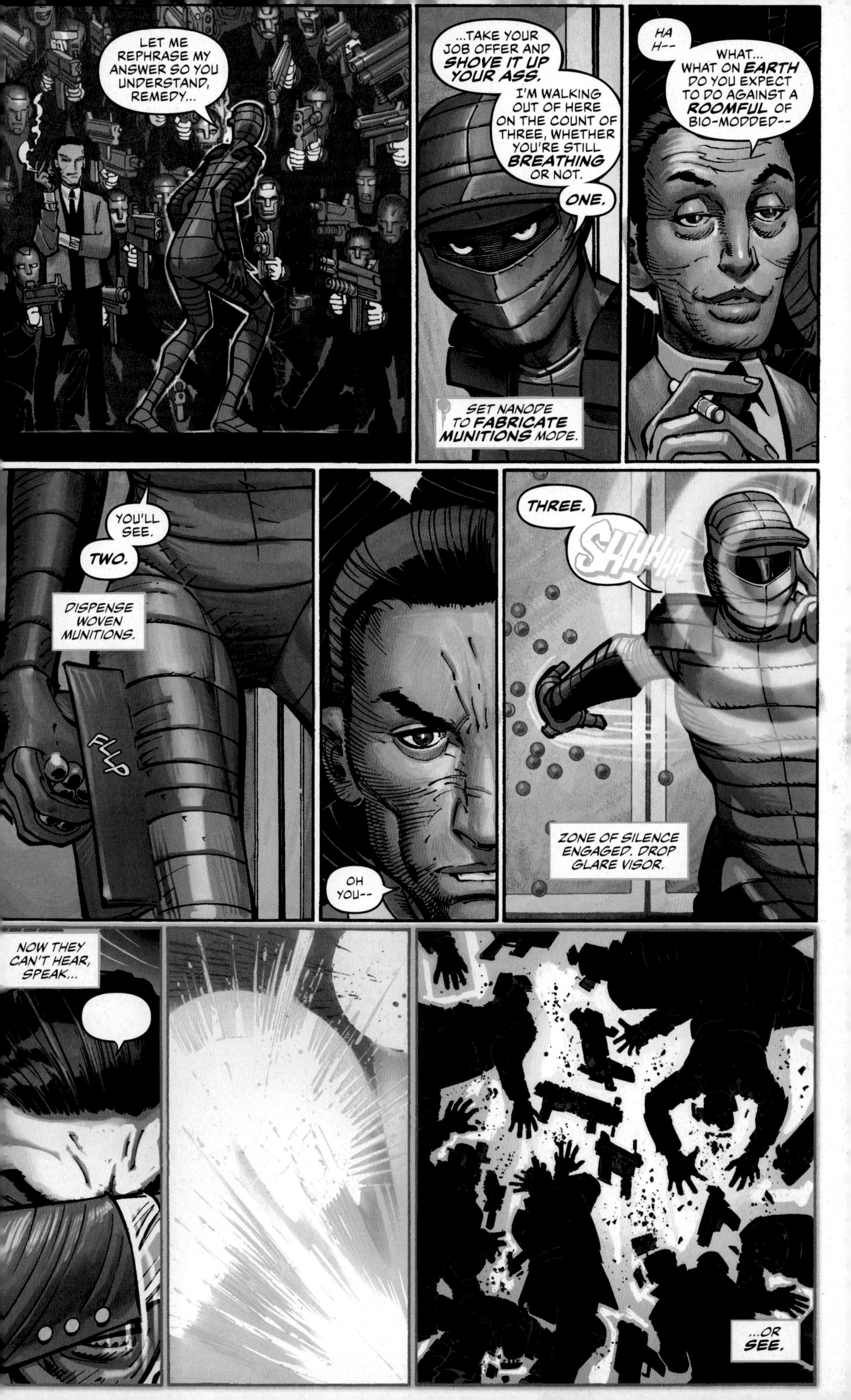
LET ME REPHRASE MY ANSWER SO YOU UNDERSTAND, REMEDY...
...TAKE YOUR JOB OFFER AND SHOVE IT UP YOUR ASS.
I'M WALKING OUT OF HERE ON THE COUNT OF THREE, WHETHER YOU'RE STILL BREATHING OR NOT.
ONE.
SET NANODE TO FABRICATE MUNITIONS MODE.
HA H--
WHAT... WHAT ON EARTH DO YOU EXPECT TO DO AGAINST A ROOMFUL OF BIO-MODDED--
YOU'LL SEE.
TWO.
DISPENSE WOVEN MUNITIONS.
FLIP
OH YOU--
THREE.
SHHHHH
ZONE OF SILENCE ENGAGED. DROP GLARE VISOR.
NOW THEY CAN'T HEAR, SPEAK...
...OR SEE.

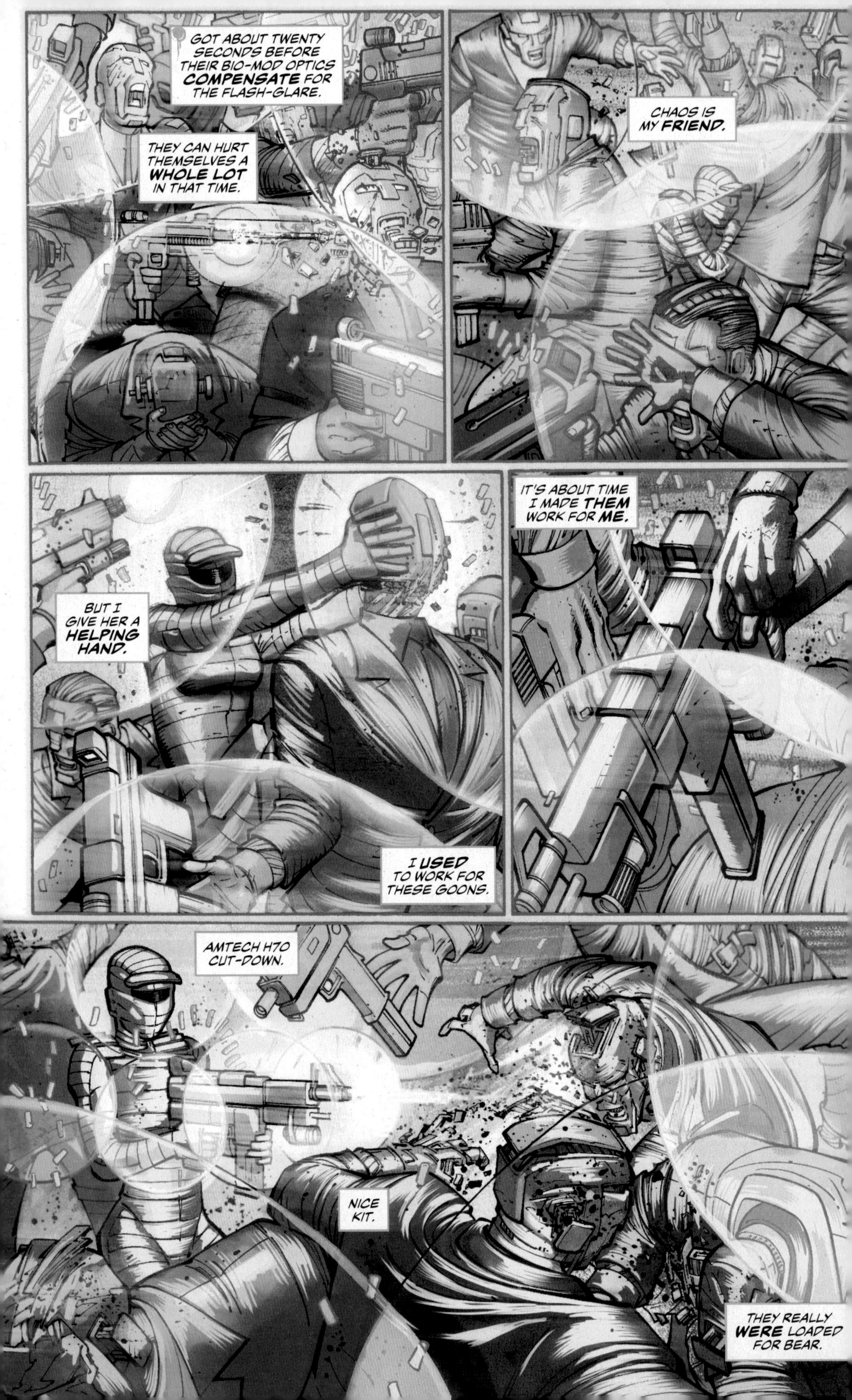
GOT ABOUT TWENTY SECONDS BEFORE THEIR BIO-MOD OPTICS COMPENSATE FOR THE FLASH-GLARE.
THEY CAN HURT THEMSELVES A WHOLE LOT IN THAT TIME.
CHAOS IS MY FRIEND.
BUT I GIVE HER A HELPING HAND.
I USED TO WORK FOR THESE GOONS.
IT'S ABOUT TIME I MADE THEM WORK FOR ME.
AMTECH H70 CUT-DOWN.
NICE KIT.
THEY REALLY WERE LOADED FOR BEAR.

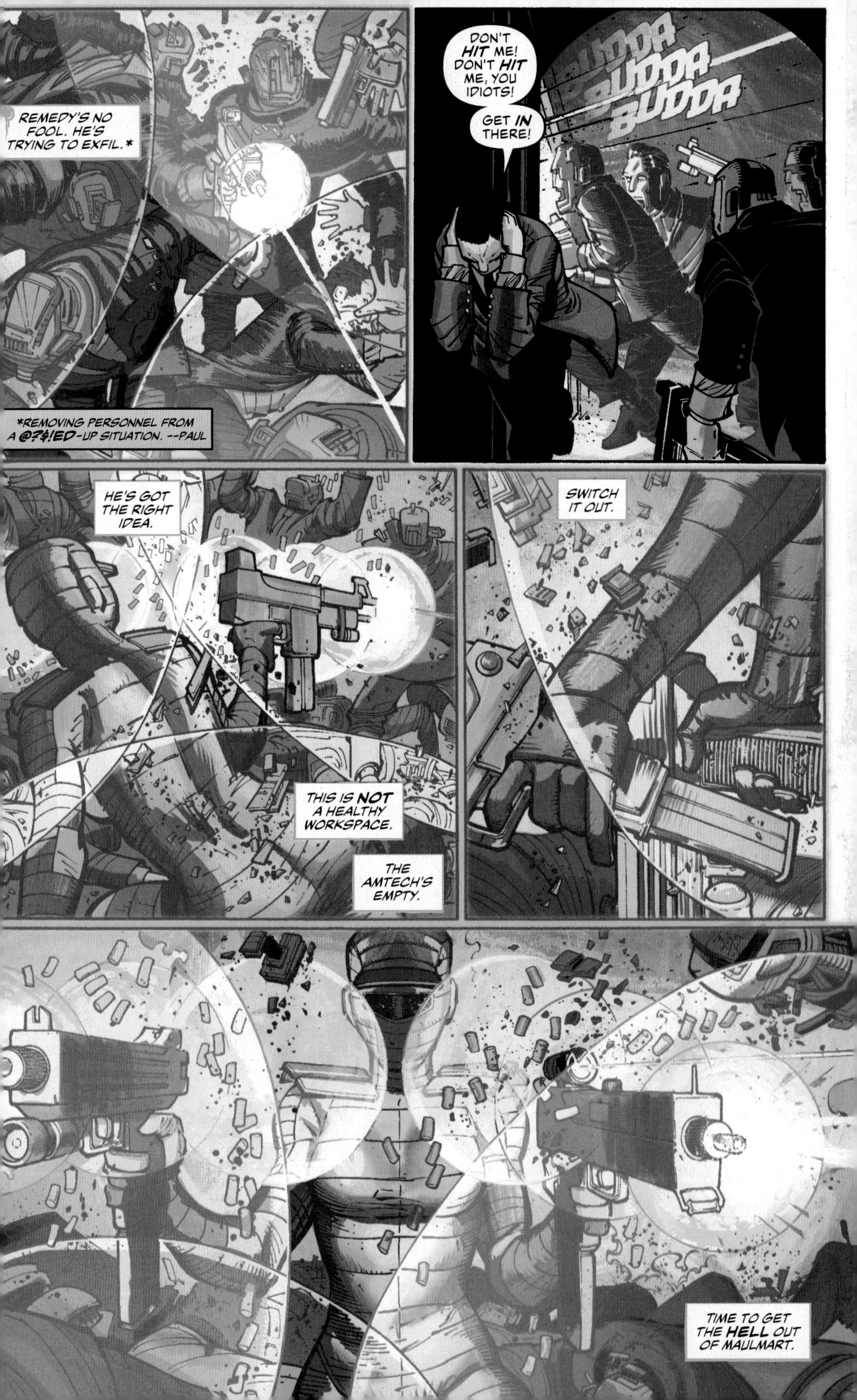
REMEDY'S NO FOOL. HE'S TRYING TO EXFIL.*
*REMOVING PERSONNEL FROM A @?$!ED-UP SITUATION. --PAUL
DON'T HIT ME! DON'T HIT ME, YOU IDIOTS!
GET IN THERE!
BUDDA BUDDA BUDDA
HE'S GOT THE RIGHT IDEA.
THIS IS NOT A HEALTHY WORKSPACE.
THE AMTECH'S EMPTY.
SWITCH IT OUT.
TIME TO GET THE HELL OUT OF MAULMART.

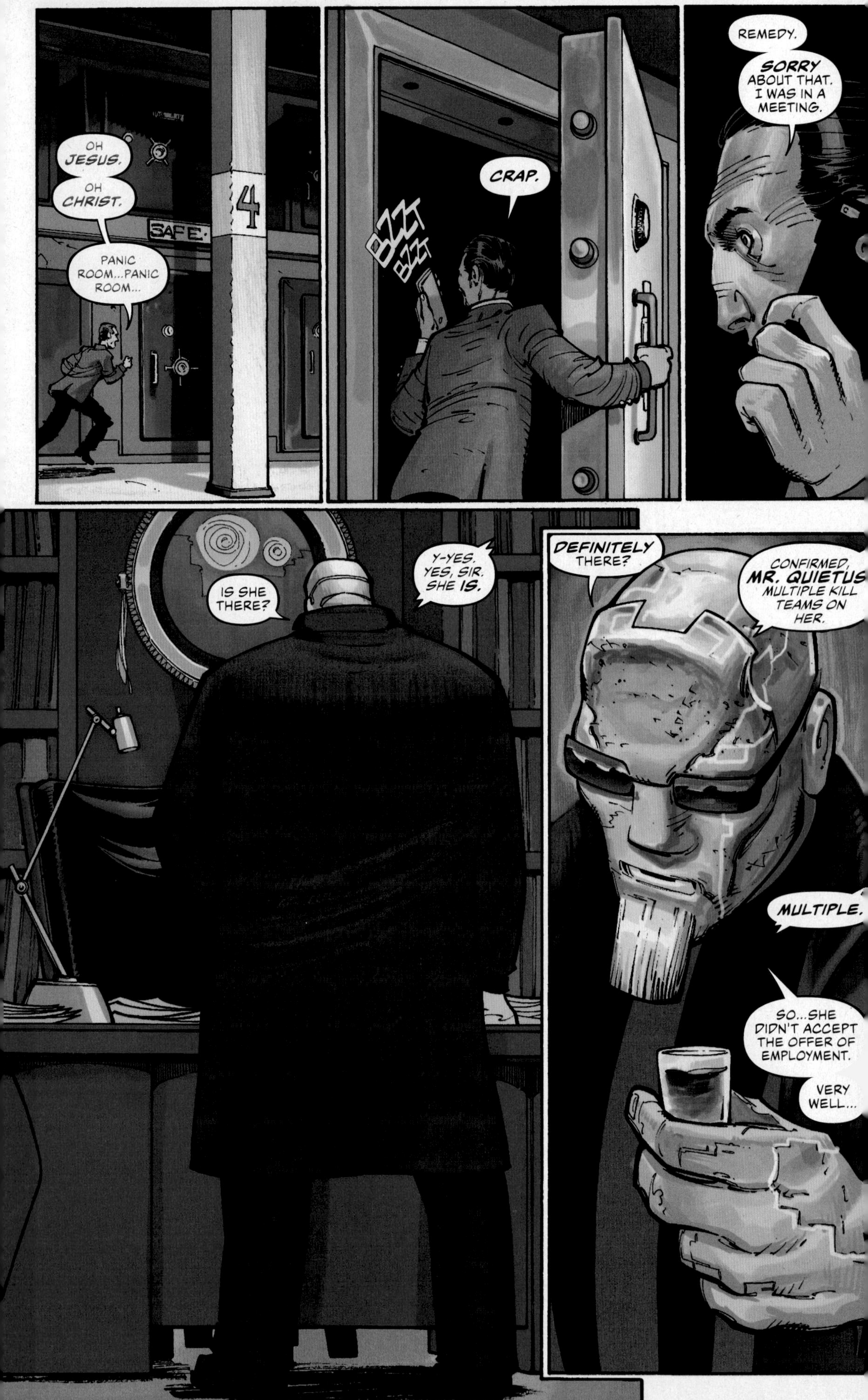

OH JESUS.
OH CHRIST.
PANIC ROOM...PANIC ROOM...
SAFE.
4
CRAP.
BZZT BZZT
REMEDY.
SORRY ABOUT THAT. I WAS IN A MEETING.
IS SHE THERE?
Y-YES. YES, SIR. SHE IS.
DEFINITELY THERE?
CONFIRMED, MR. QUIETUS. MULTIPLE KILL TEAMS ON HER.
MULTIPLE.
SO...SHE DIDN'T ACCEPT THE OFFER OF EMPLOYMENT.
VERY WELL...

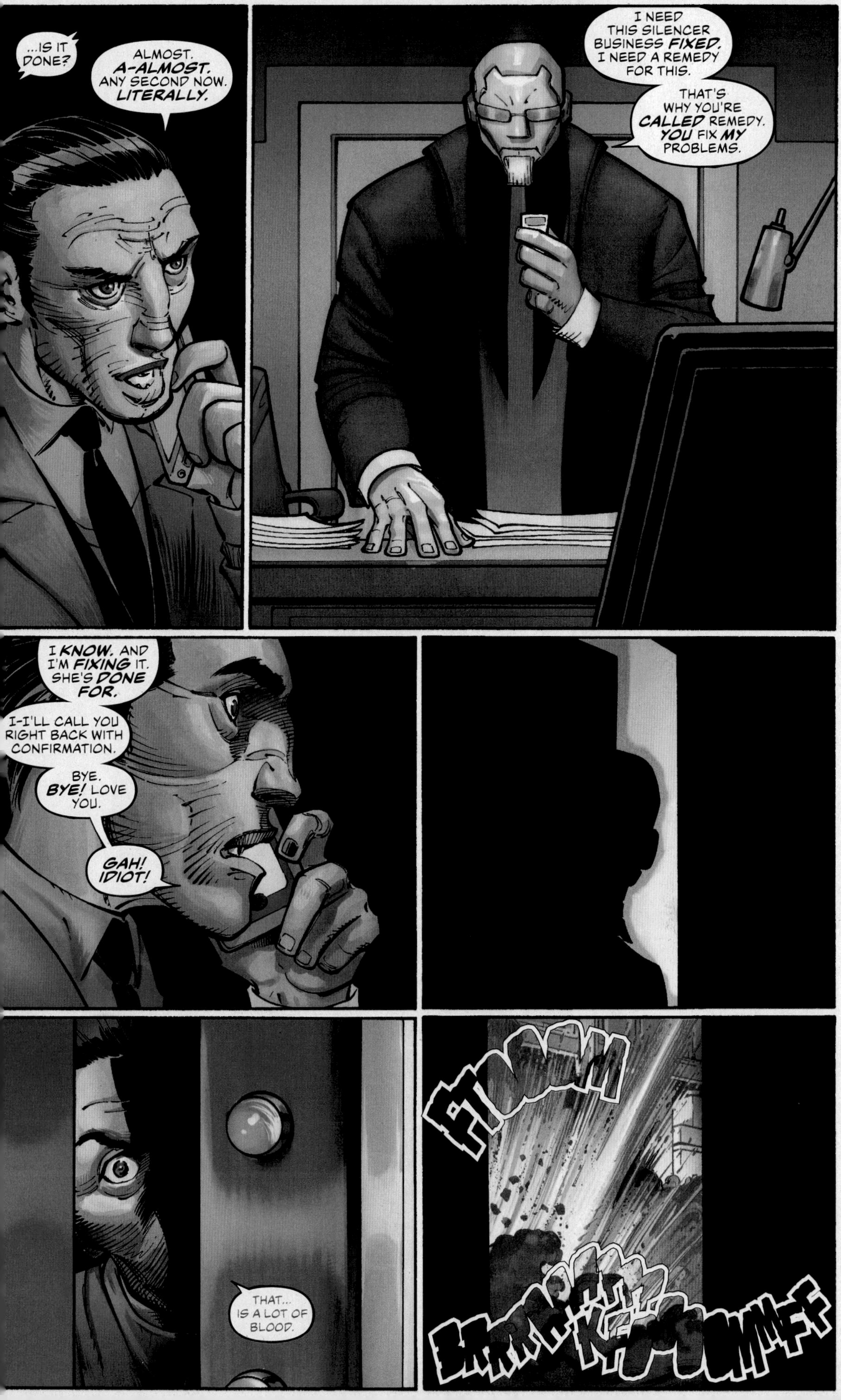
...IS IT DONE?
ALMOST. A-ALMOST. ANY SECOND NOW. LITERALLY.
I NEED THIS SILENCER BUSINESS FIXED. I NEED A REMEDY FOR THIS.
THAT'S WHY YOU'RE CALLED REMEDY. YOU FIX MY PROBLEMS.
I KNOW. AND I'M FIXING IT. SHE'S DONE FOR.
I-I'LL CALL YOU RIGHT BACK WITH CONFIRMATION.
BYE. BYE! LOVE YOU.
GAH! IDIOT!
THAT... IS A LOT OF BLOOD.

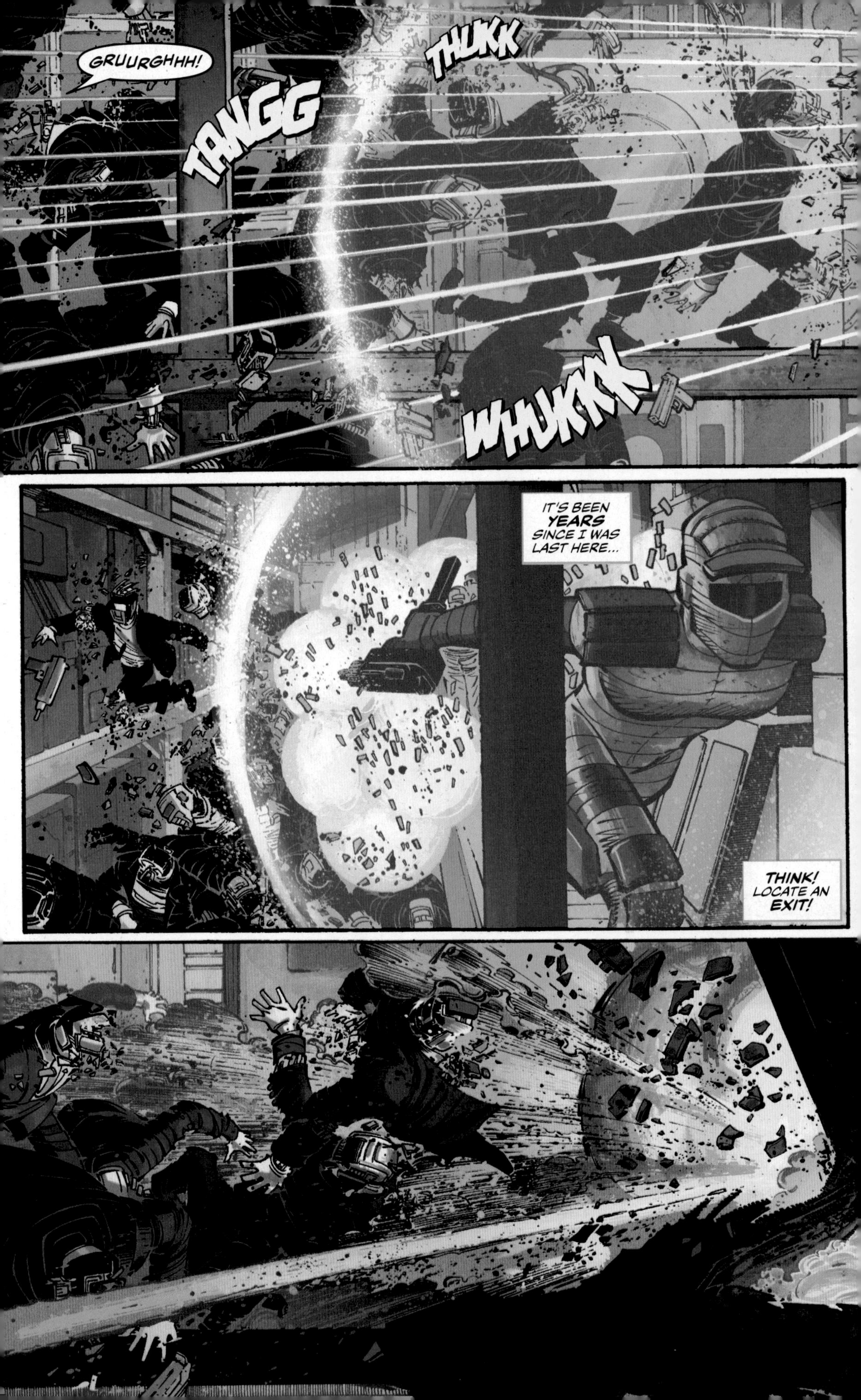
GRUURGHHH!
TANGG
THUKK
WHUKKK
IT'S BEEN YEARS SINCE I WAS LAST HERE...
THINK! LOCATE AN EXIT!

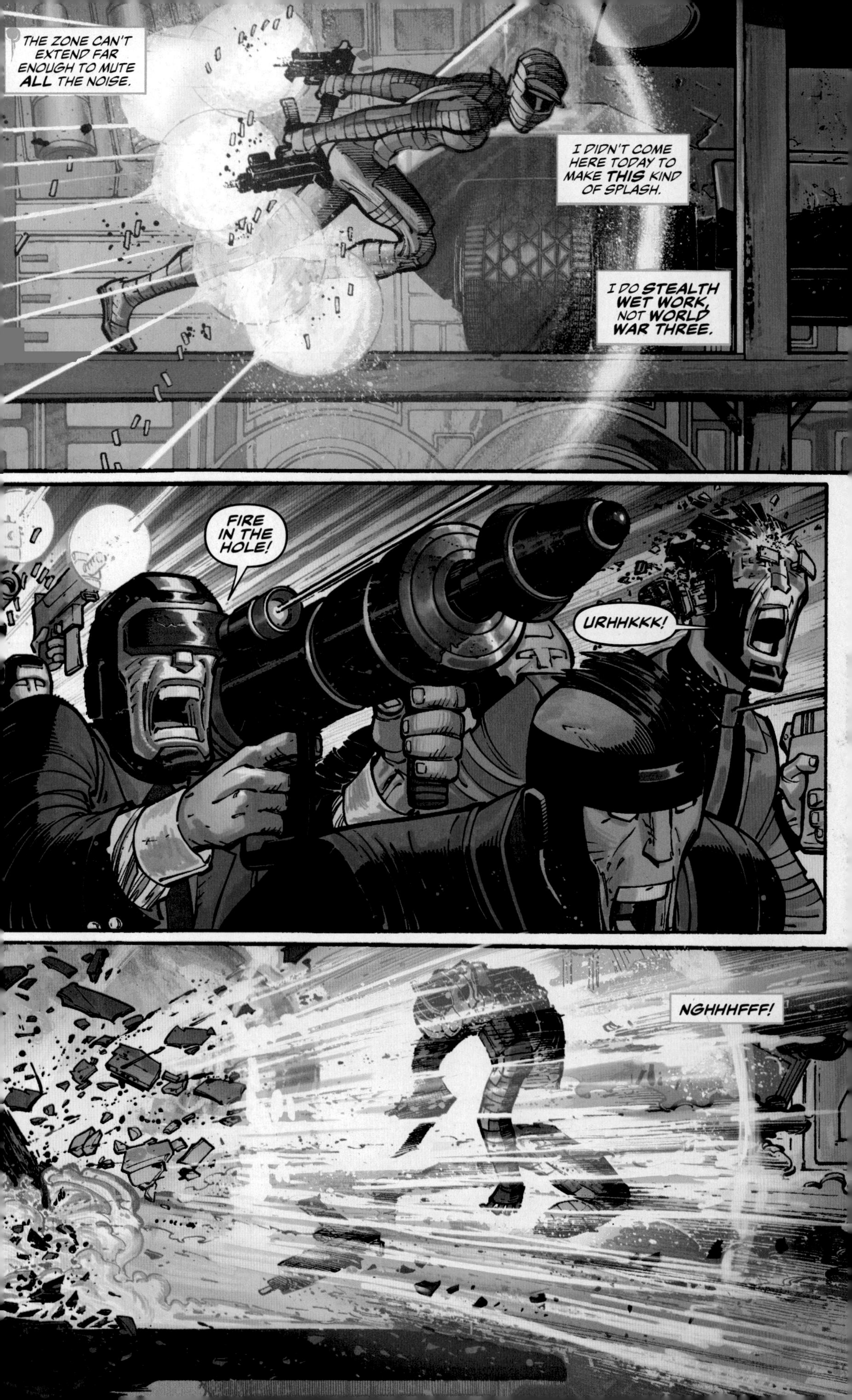
THE ZONE CAN'T EXTEND FAR ENOUGH TO MUTE ALL THE NOISE.
I DIDN'T COME HERE TODAY TO MAKE THIS KIND OF SPLASH.
I DO STEALTH WET WORK, NOT WORLD WAR THREE.
FIRE IN THE HOLE!
URHHKKK!
NGHHHFFF!

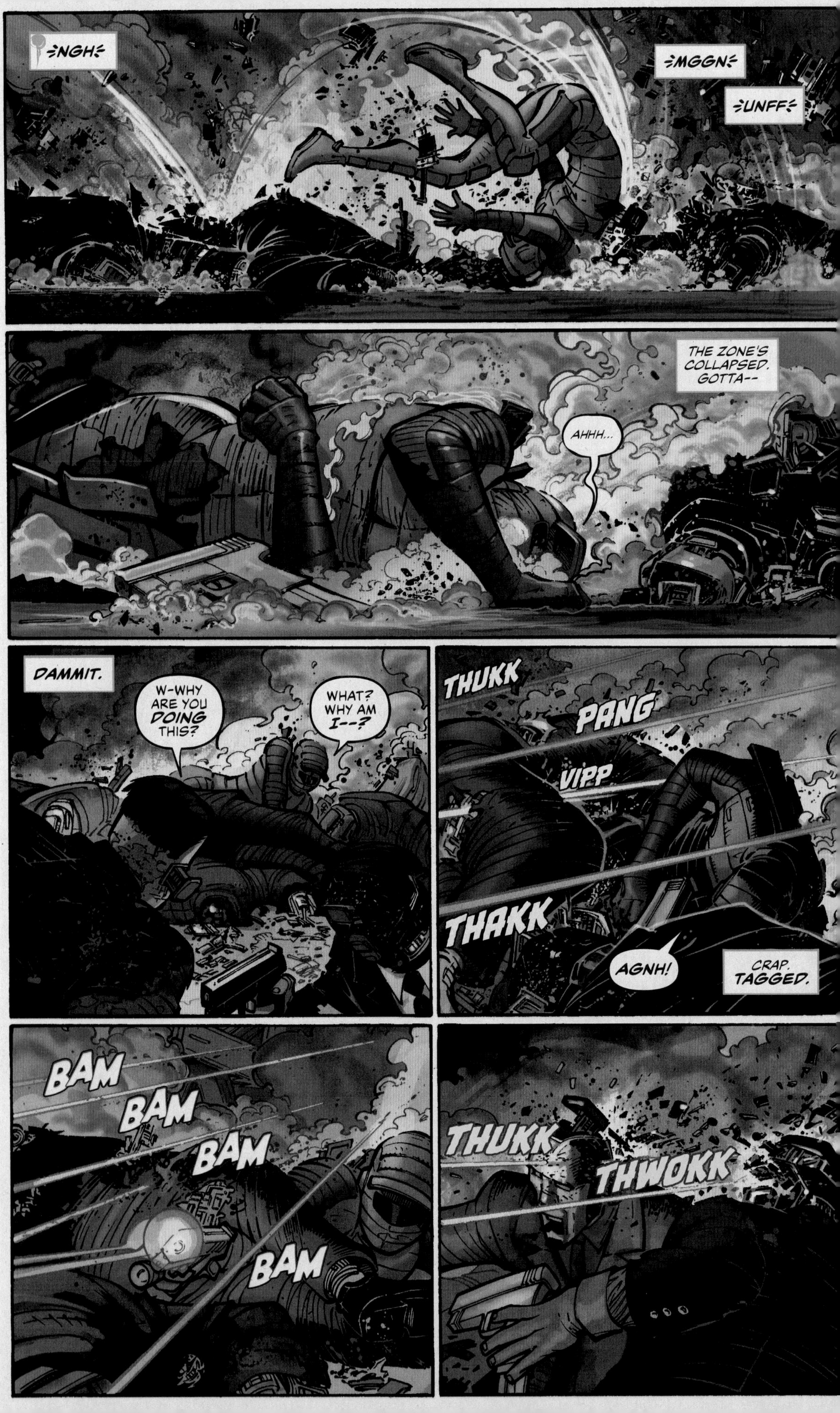
=NGH=
=MGGN=
=UNFF=
THE ZONE'S COLLAPSED. GOTTA--
AHHH...
DAMMIT.
W-WHY ARE YOU DOING THIS?
WHAT? WHY AM I--?
THUKK
PANG
VIPP
THAKK
AGNH!
CRAP. TAGGED.
BAM
BAM
BAM
BAM
THUKK
THWOKK

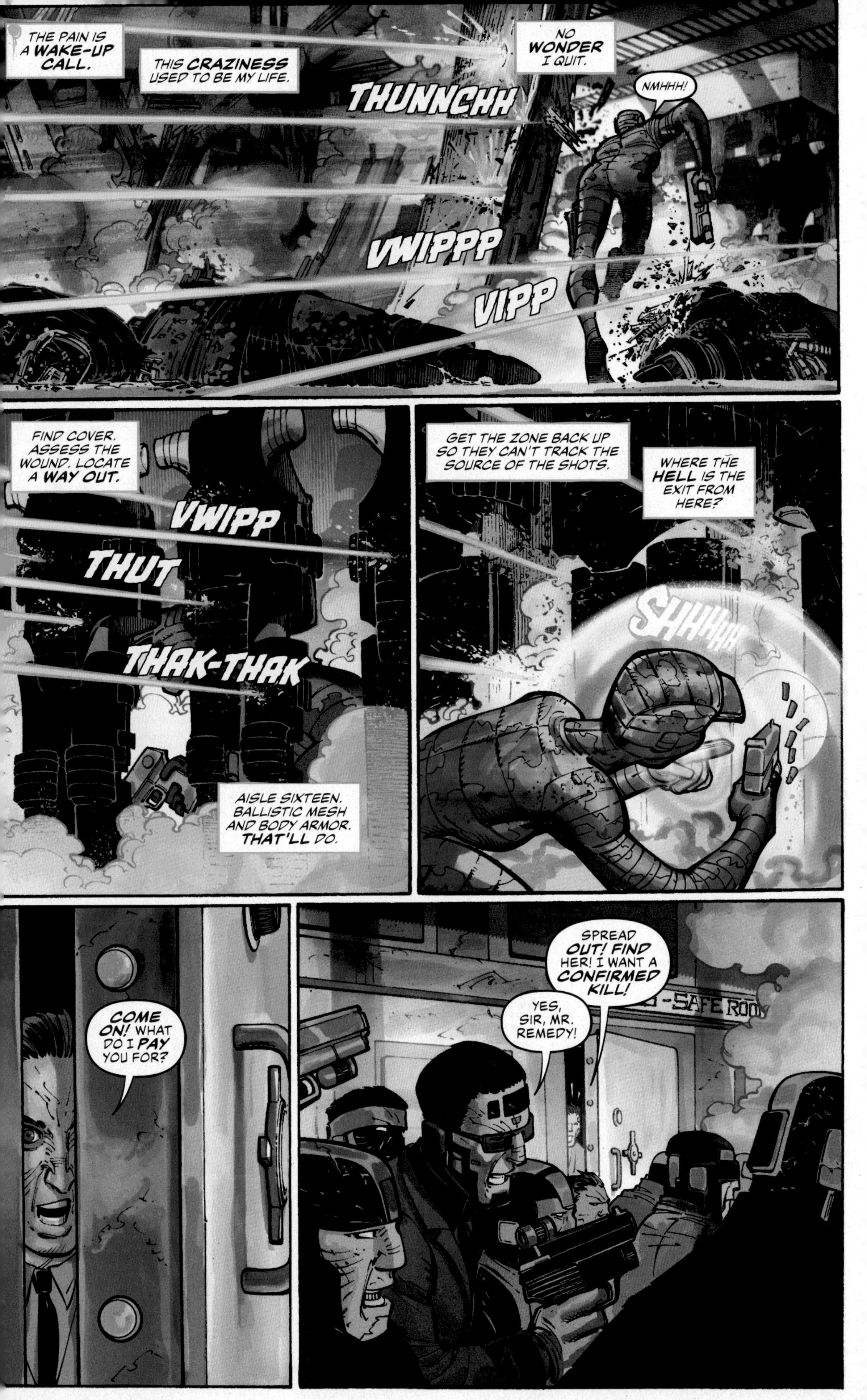
THE PAIN IS A WAKE-UP CALL.
THIS CRAZINESS USED TO BE MY LIFE.
NO WONDER I QUIT.
THUNNCHH
NMHHH!
VWIPPP
VIPP
FIND COVER. ASSESS THE WOUND. LOCATE A WAY OUT.
VWIPP
THUT
THAK-THAK
AISLE SIXTEEN. BALLISTIC MESH AND BODY ARMOR. THAT'LL DO.
GET THE ZONE BACK UP SO THEY CAN'T TRACK THE SOURCE OF THE SHOTS.
WHERE THE HELL IS THE EXIT FROM HERE?
SHHHHH
COME ON! WHAT DO I PAY YOU FOR?
SPREAD OUT! FIND HER! I WANT A CONFIRMED KILL!
YES, SIR, MR. REMEDY!
-SAFE ROO

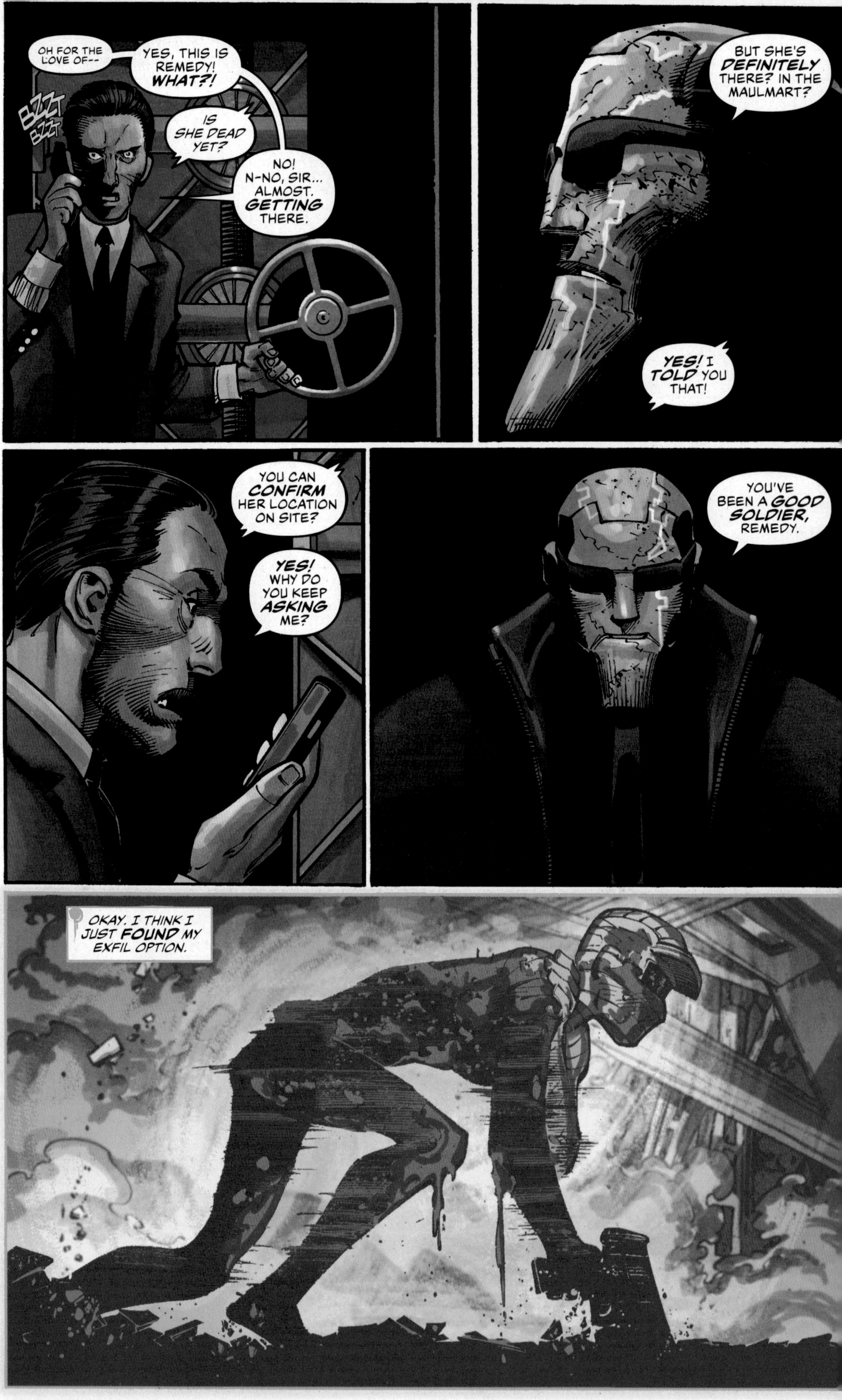
OH FOR THE LOVE OF--
YES, THIS IS REMEDY! WHAT?!
BZZT BZZT
IS SHE DEAD YET?
NO! N-NO, SIR... ALMOST. GETTING THERE.
BUT SHE'S DEFINITELY THERE? IN THE MAULMART?
YES! I TOLD YOU THAT!
YOU CAN CONFIRM HER LOCATION ON SITE?
YES! WHY DO YOU KEEP ASKING ME?
YOU'VE BEEN A GOOD SOLDIER, REMEDY.
OKAY. I THINK I JUST FOUND MY EXFIL OPTION.

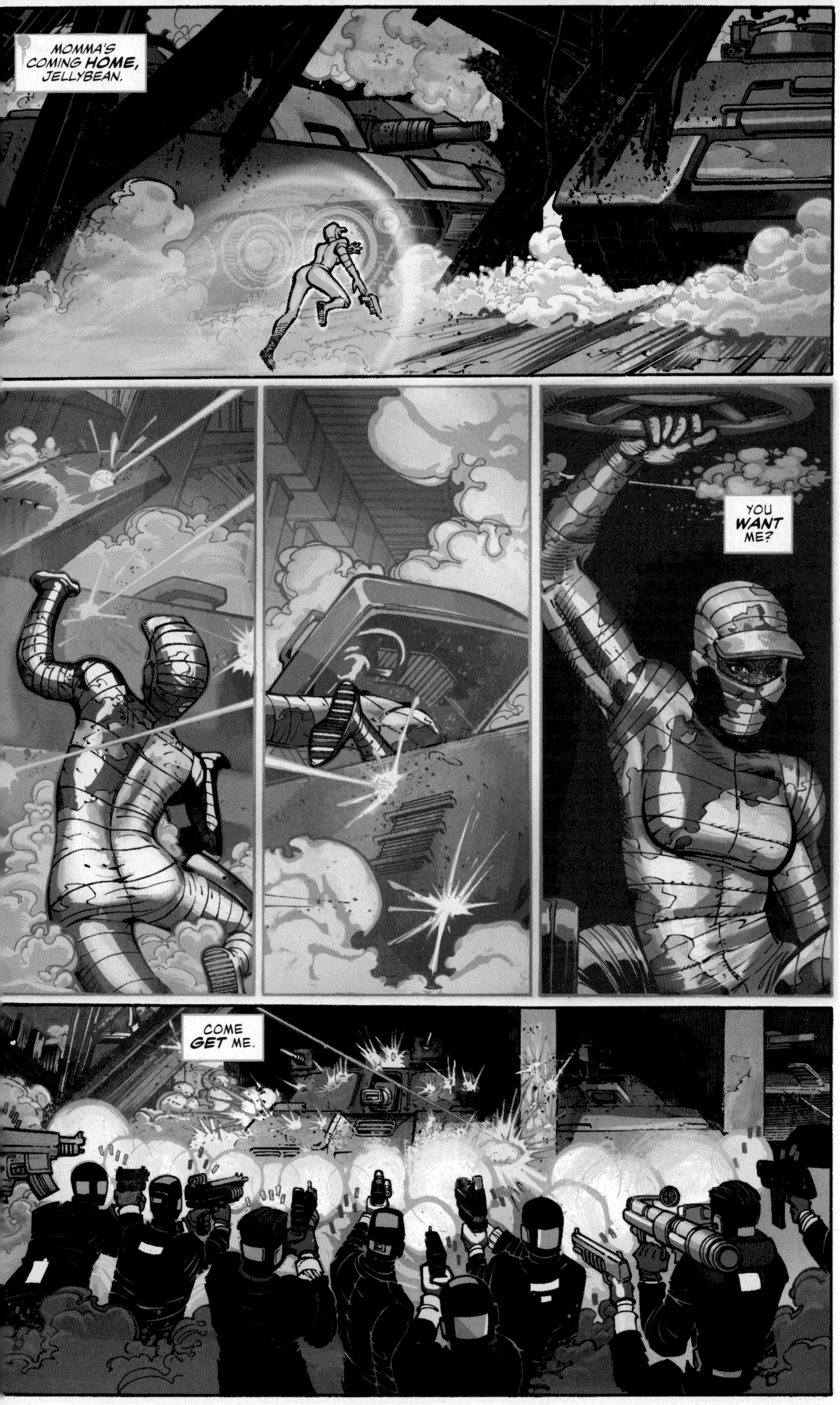
MOMMA'S COMING HOME, JELLYBEAN.
YOU WANT ME?
COME GET ME.

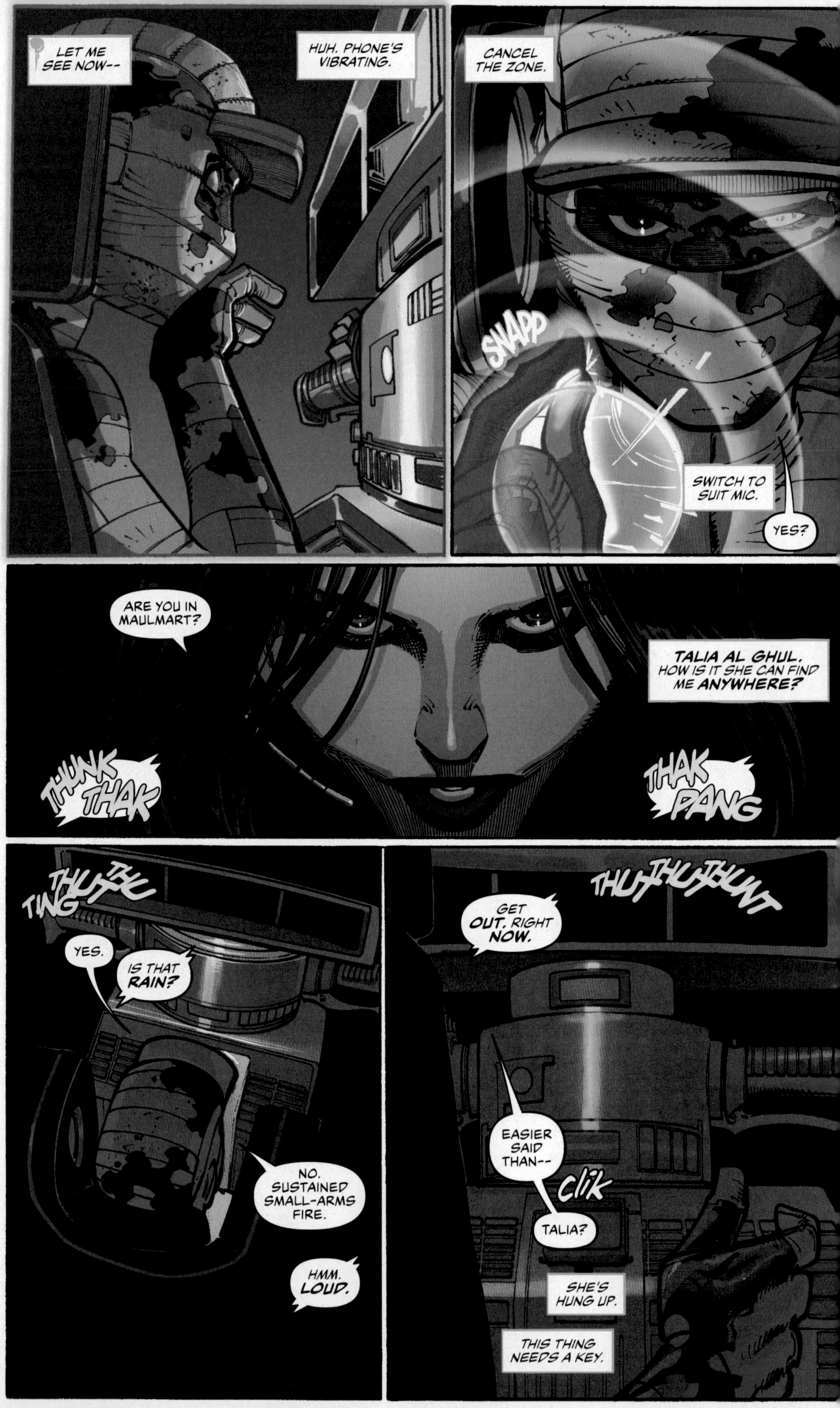
LET ME SEE NOW--
HUH. PHONE'S VIBRATING.
CANCEL THE ZONE.
SNAPP
SWITCH TO SUIT MIC.
YES?
ARE YOU IN MAULMART?
TALIA AL GHUL. HOW IS IT SHE CAN FIND ME ANYWHERE?
THUNK THAK
THAK PANG
THUT THU TING
YES.
IS THAT RAIN?
NO. SUSTAINED SMALL-ARMS FIRE.
HMM. LOUD.
THUTTHUTTHUNT
GET OUT. RIGHT NOW.
EASIER SAID THAN--
CLIK
TALIA?
SHE'S HUNG UP.
THIS THING NEEDS A KEY.

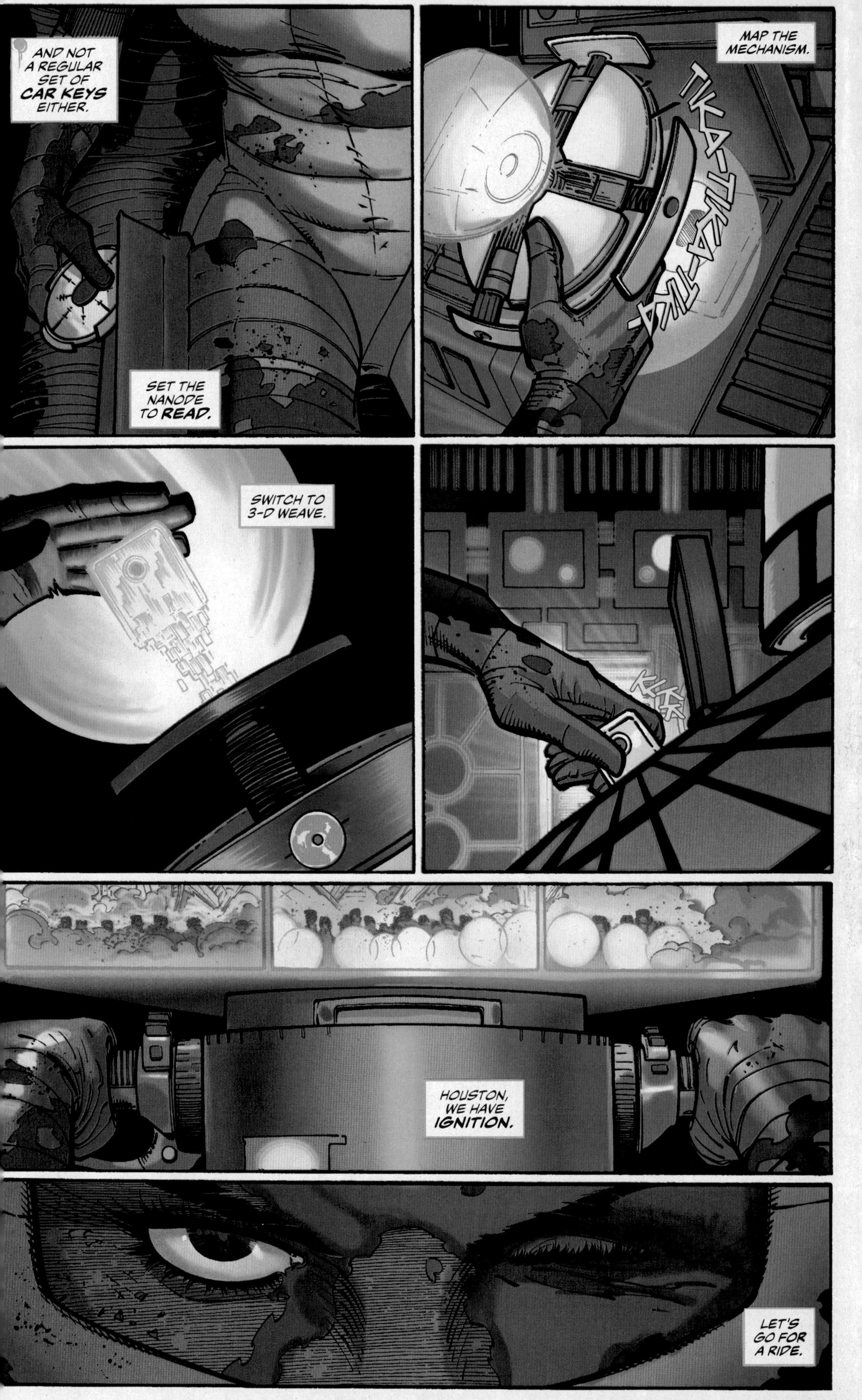
AND NOT A REGULAR SET OF CAR KEYS EITHER.
SET THE NANODE TO READ.
MAP THE MECHANISM.
TIKA-TIKA-TIKA-TIKA
SWITCH TO 3-D WEAVE.
KLIK
HOUSTON, WE HAVE IGNITION.
LET'S GO FOR A RIDE.

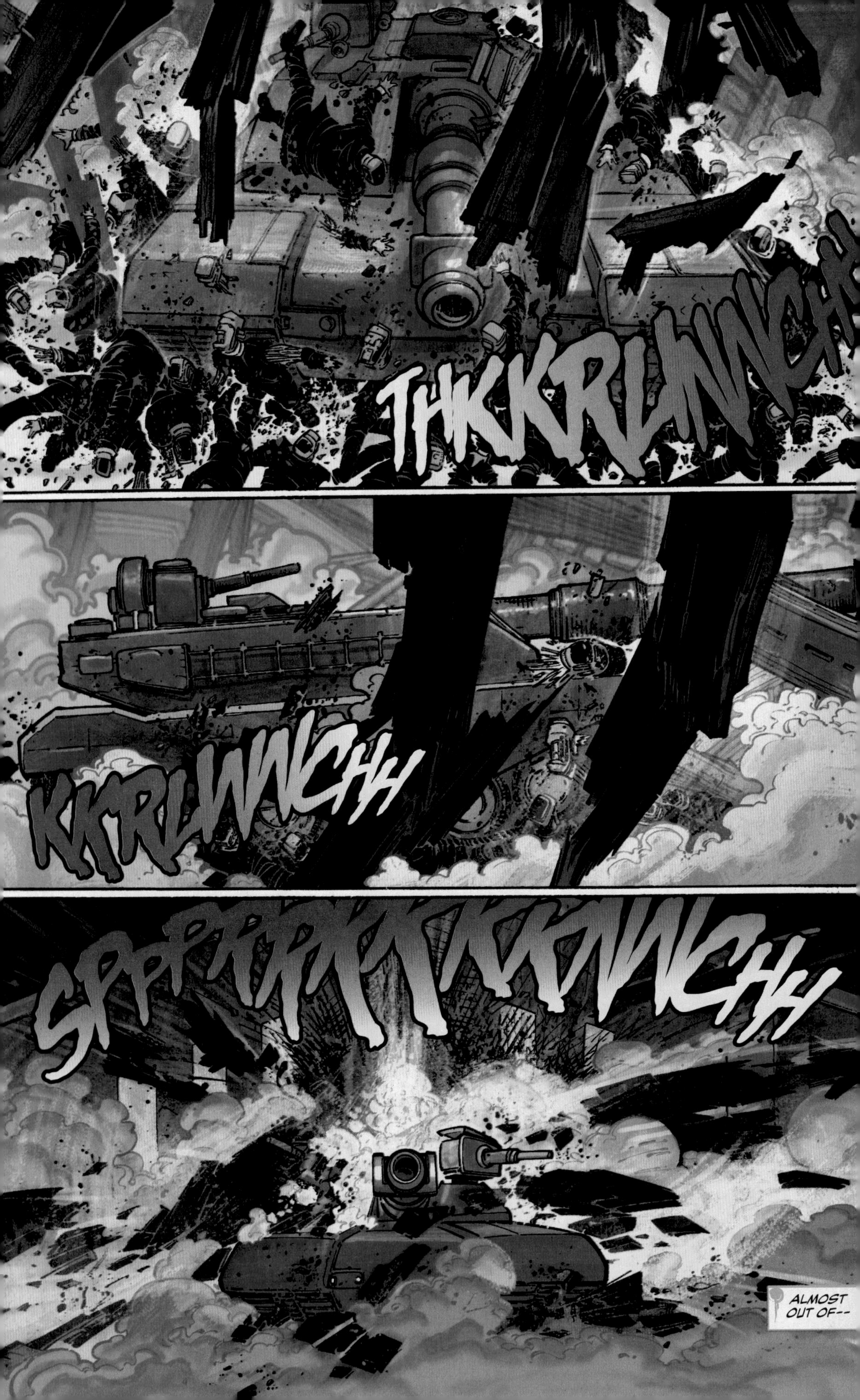
THKKRUNNCH
KKRUNNCHH
SPPRRRRKKRONNCHH
ALMOST OUT OF--

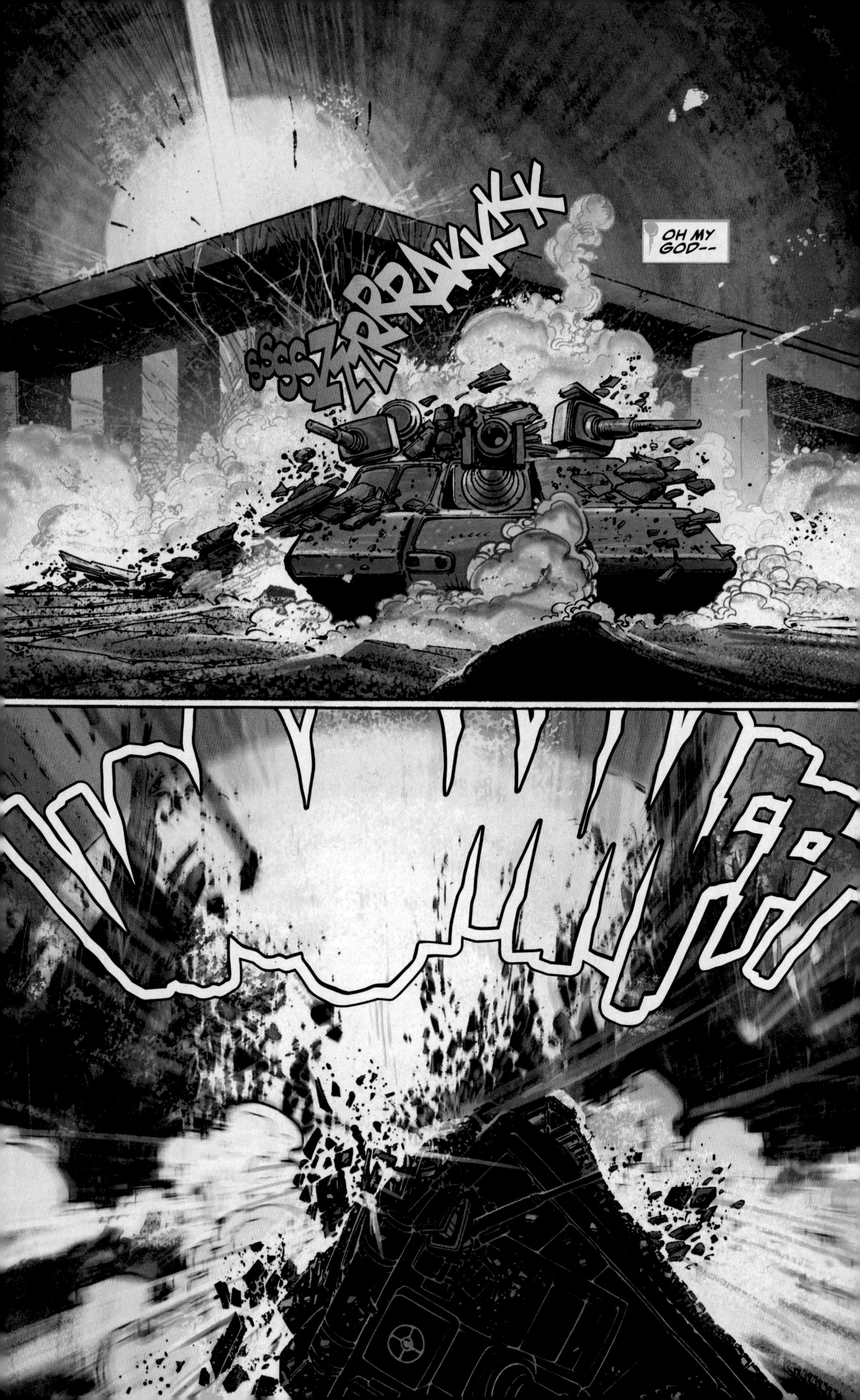
SSSSZZRRAKKK
OH MY GOD--

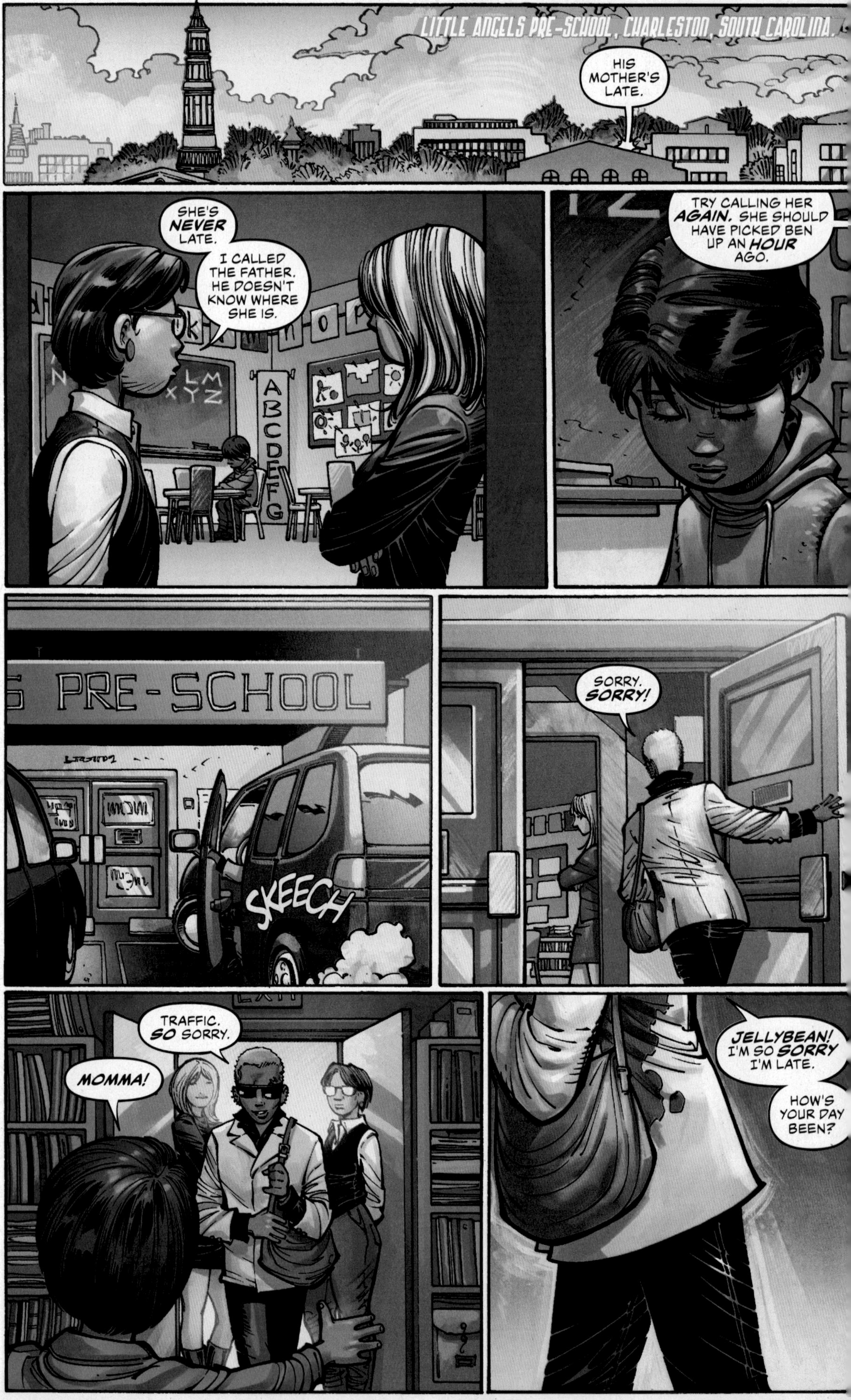
LITTLE ANGELS PRE-SCHOOL, CHARLESTON, SOUTH CAROLINA.
HIS MOTHER'S LATE.
SHE'S NEVER LATE.
I CALLED THE FATHER. HE DOESN'T KNOW WHERE SHE IS.
TRY CALLING HER AGAIN. SHE SHOULD HAVE PICKED BEN UP AN HOUR AGO.
PRE-SCHOOL
SKEECH
SORRY. SORRY!
TRAFFIC. SO SORRY.
MOMMA!
JELLYBEAN! I'M SO SORRY I'M LATE.
HOW'S YOUR DAY BEEN?

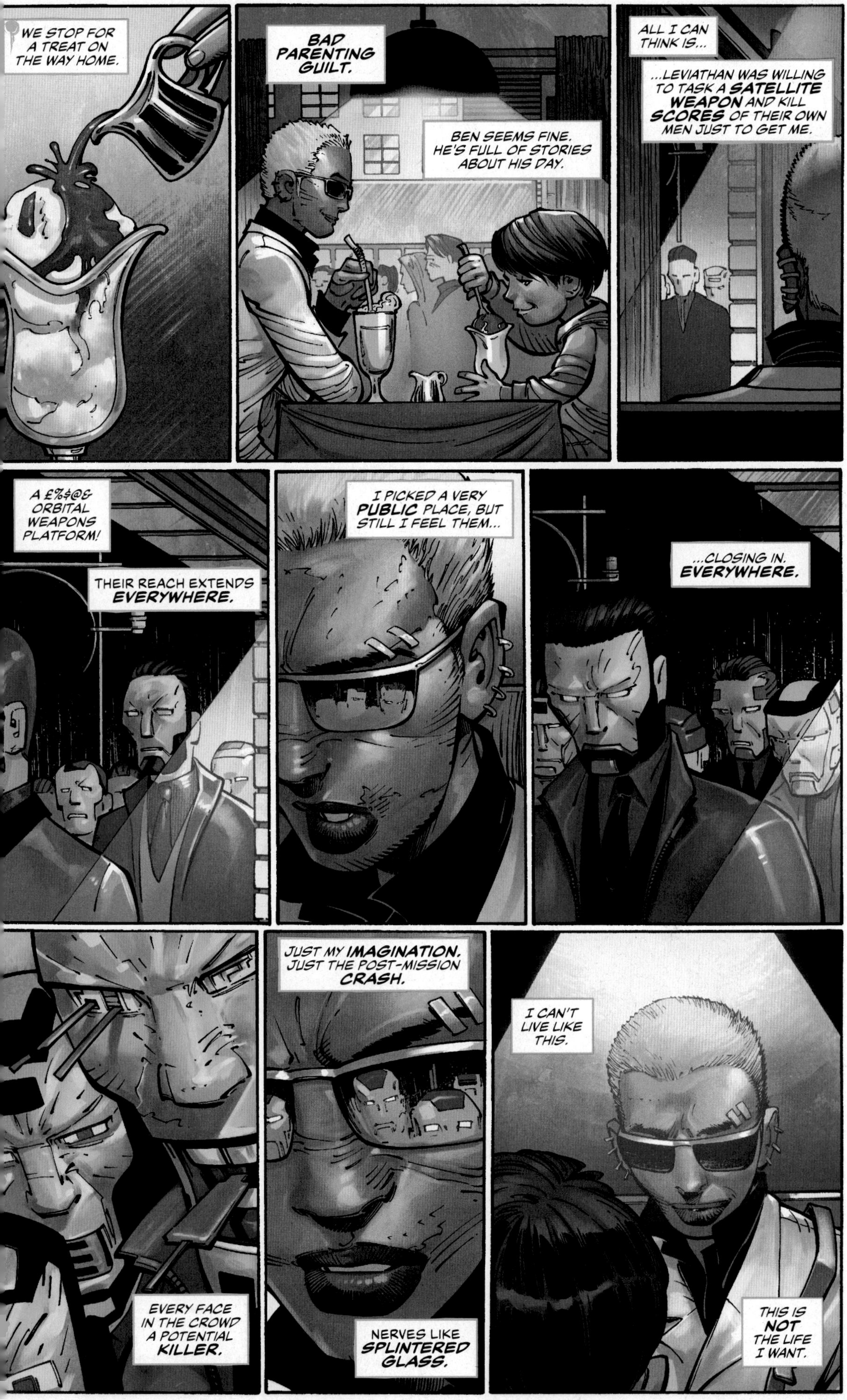

WE STOP FOR A TREAT ON THE WAY HOME.
BAD PARENTING GUILT.
BEN SEEMS FINE. HE'S FULL OF STORIES ABOUT HIS DAY.
ALL I CAN THINK IS...
...LEVIATHAN WAS WILLING TO TASK A SATELLITE WEAPON AND KILL SCORES OF THEIR OWN MEN JUST TO GET ME.
A £%$@& ORBITAL WEAPONS PLATFORM!
THEIR REACH EXTENDS EVERYWHERE.
I PICKED A VERY PUBLIC PLACE, BUT STILL I FEEL THEM...
...CLOSING IN. EVERYWHERE.
EVERY FACE IN THE CROWD A POTENTIAL KILLER.
JUST MY IMAGINATION. JUST THE POST-MISSION CRASH.
NERVES LIKE SPLINTERED GLASS.
I CAN'T LIVE LIKE THIS.
THIS IS NOT THE LIFE I WANT.

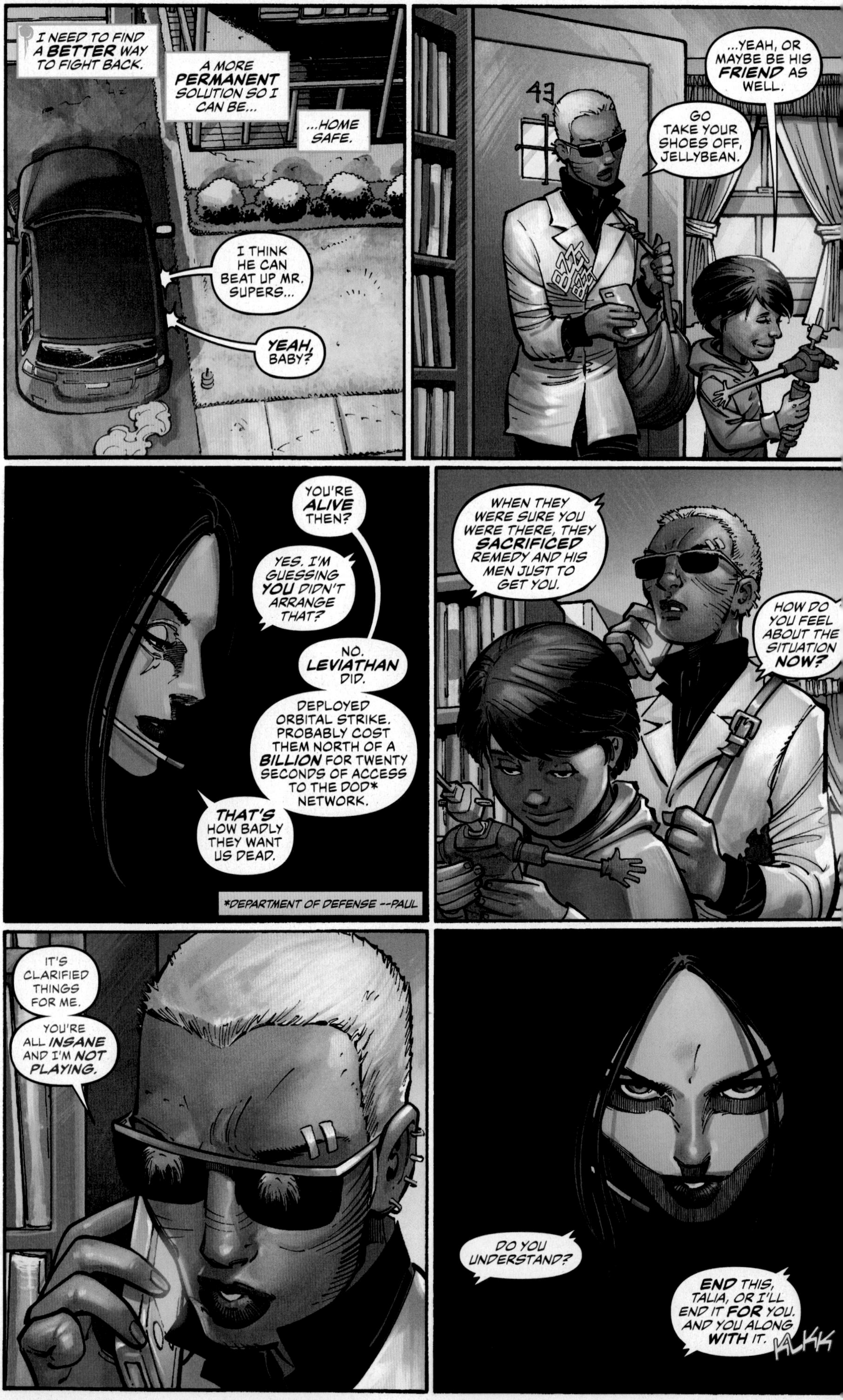
I NEED TO FIND A BETTER WAY TO FIGHT BACK.
A MORE PERMANENT SOLUTION SO I CAN BE...
...HOME SAFE.
I THINK HE CAN BEAT UP MR. SUPERS...
YEAH, BABY?
GO TAKE YOUR SHOES OFF, JELLYBEAN.
...YEAH, OR MAYBE BE HIS FRIEND AS WELL.
YOU'RE ALIVE THEN?
YES. I'M GUESSING YOU DIDN'T ARRANGE THAT?
NO. LEVIATHAN DID.
DEPLOYED ORBITAL STRIKE. PROBABLY COST THEM NORTH OF A BILLION FOR TWENTY SECONDS OF ACCESS TO THE DOD* NETWORK.
THAT'S HOW BADLY THEY WANT US DEAD.
*DEPARTMENT OF DEFENSE --PAUL
WHEN THEY WERE SURE YOU WERE THERE, THEY SACRIFICED REMEDY AND HIS MEN JUST TO GET YOU.
HOW DO YOU FEEL ABOUT THE SITUATION NOW?
IT'S CLARIFIED THINGS FOR ME.
YOU'RE ALL INSANE AND I'M NOT PLAYING.
DO YOU UNDERSTAND?
END THIS, TALIA, OR I'LL END IT FOR YOU. AND YOU ALONG WITH IT.
KLIKK

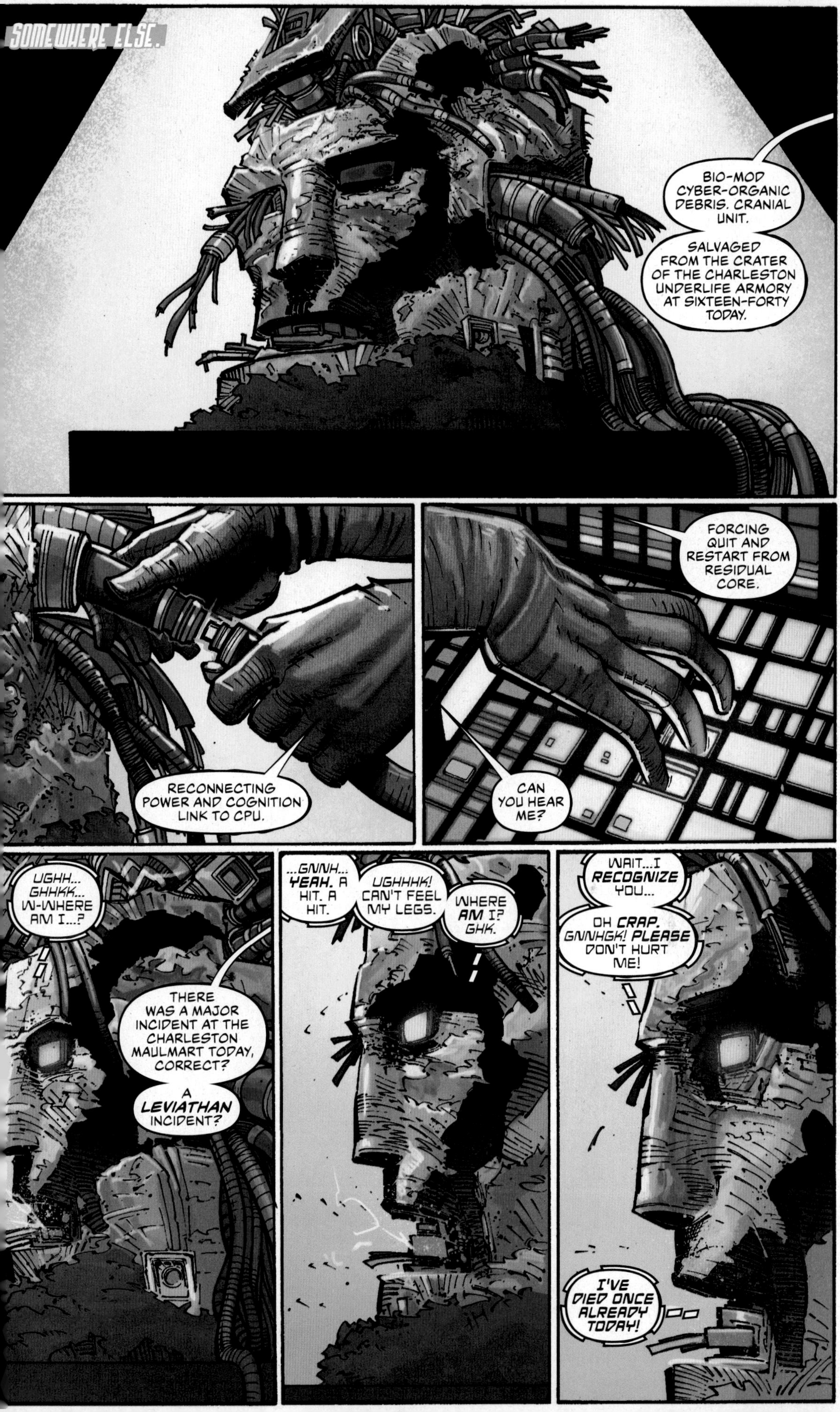
SOMEWHERE ELSE.
BIO-MOD CYBER-ORGANIC DEBRIS. CRANIAL UNIT.
SALVAGED FROM THE CRATER OF THE CHARLESTON UNDERLIFE ARMORY AT SIXTEEN-FORTY TODAY.
RECONNECTING POWER AND COGNITION LINK TO CPU.
FORCING QUIT AND RESTART FROM RESIDUAL CORE.
CAN YOU HEAR ME?
UGHH... GHHKK... W-WHERE AM I...?
THERE WAS A MAJOR INCIDENT AT THE CHARLESTON MAULMART TODAY, CORRECT?
A LEVIATHAN INCIDENT?
...GNNH... YEAH. A HIT. A HIT.
UGHHHK! CAN'T FEEL MY LEGS.
WHERE AM I? GHK.
WAIT...I RECOGNIZE YOU...
OH CRAP. GNNHGK! PLEASE DON'T HURT ME!
I'VE DIED ONCE ALREADY TODAY!

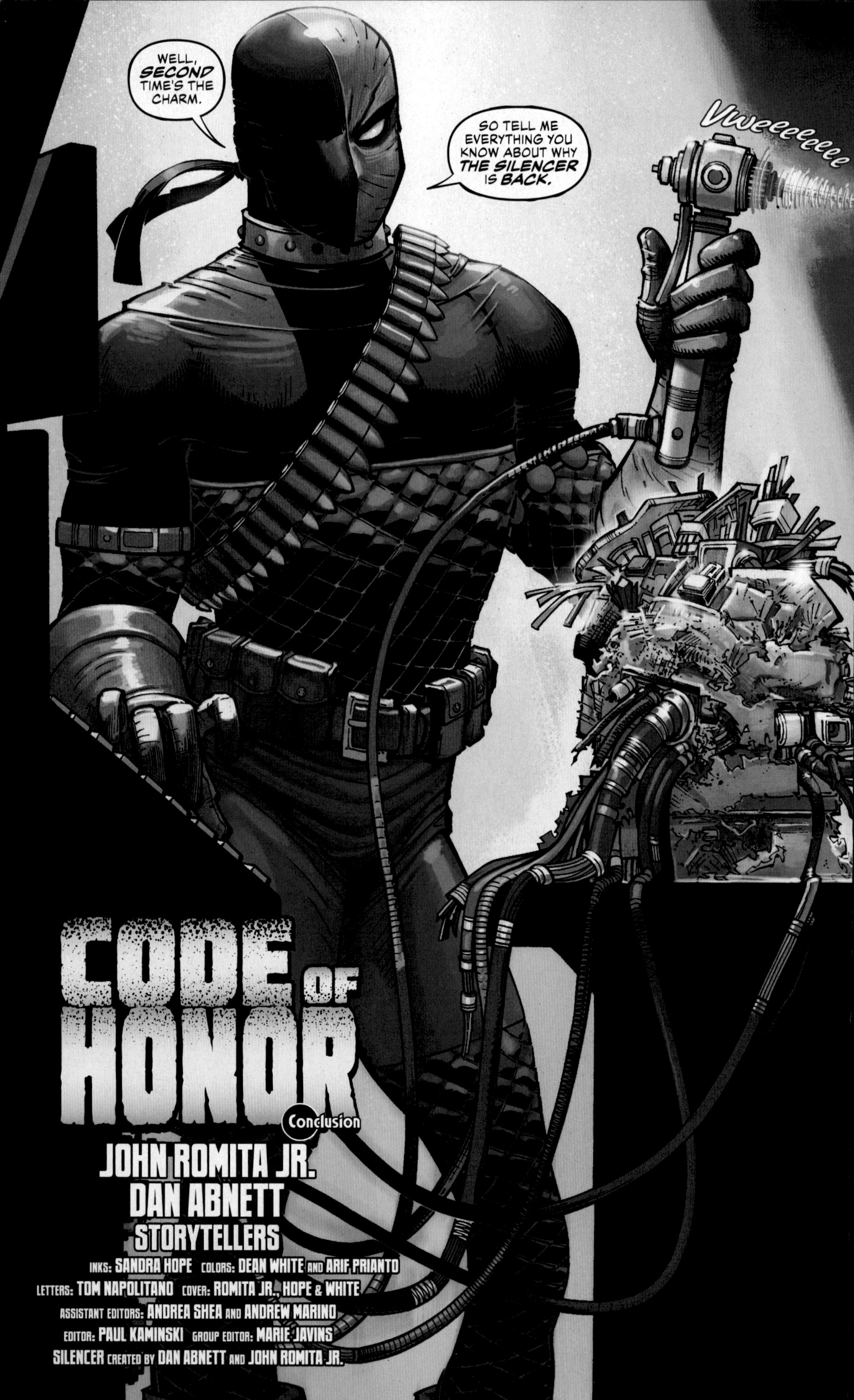
WELL, SECOND TIME'S THE CHARM.
SO TELL ME EVERYTHING YOU KNOW ABOUT WHY THE SILENCER IS BACK.
Vweeeeeeee
CODE OF HONOR
Conclusion
JOHN ROMITA JR.
DAN ABNETT
STORYTELLERS
INKS: SANDRA HOPE COLORS: DEAN WHITE AND ARIF PRIANTO
LETTERS: TOM NAPOLITANO COVER: ROMITA JR., HOPE & WHITE
ASSISTANT EDITORS: ANDREA SHEA AND ANDREW MARINO
EDITOR: PAUL KAMINSKI GROUP EDITOR: MARIE JAVINS
SILENCER CREATED BY DAN ABNETT AND JOHN ROMITA JR.

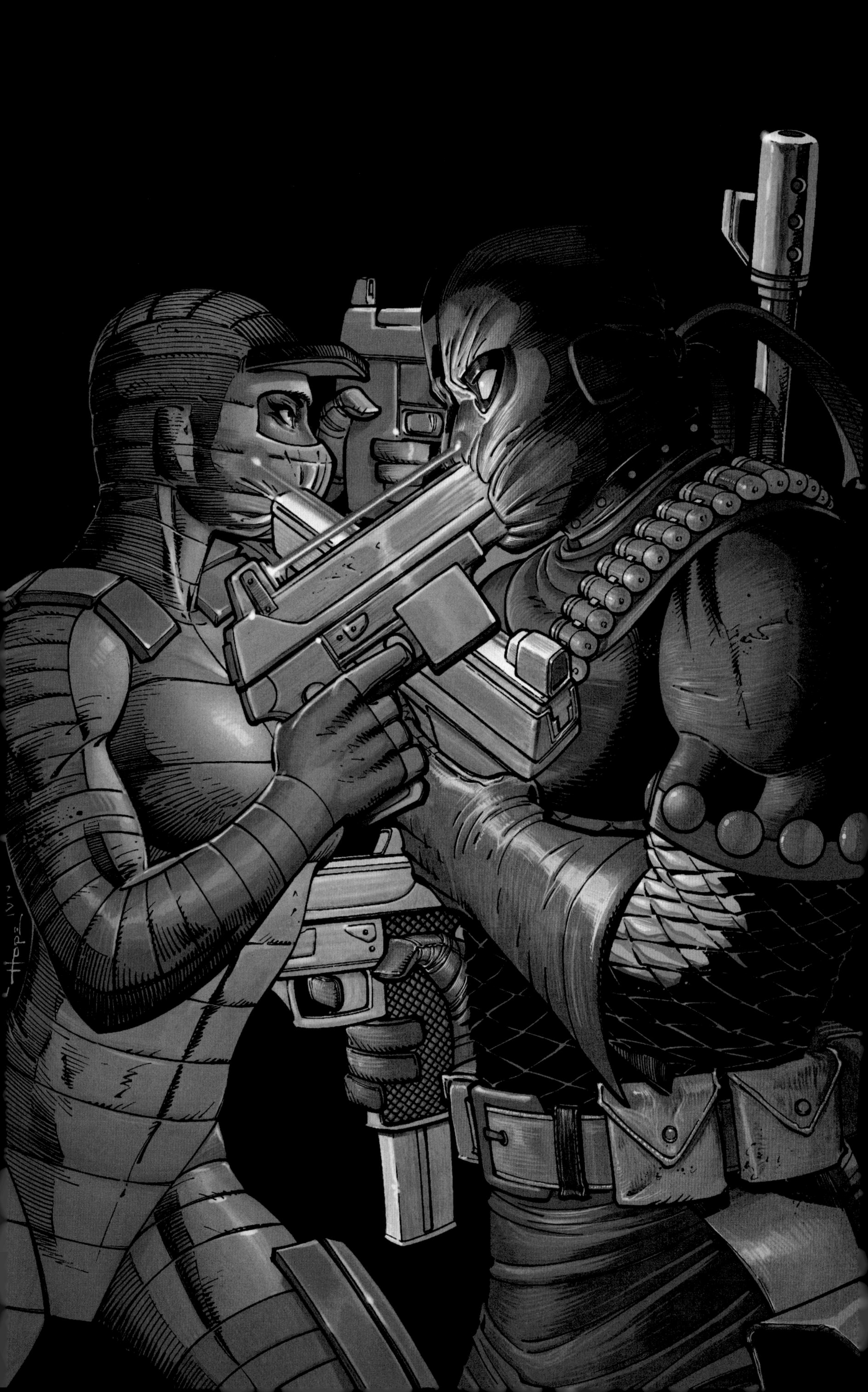

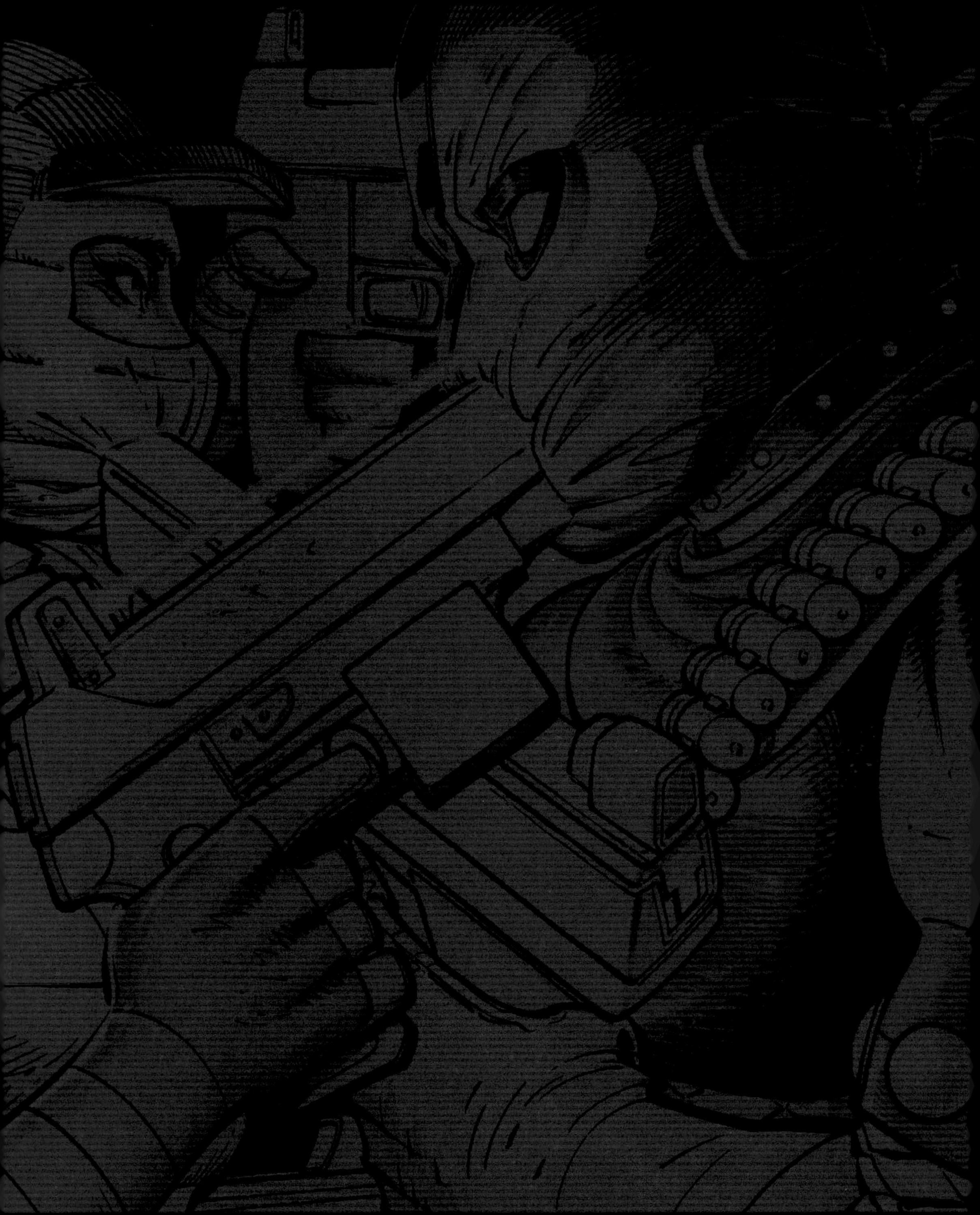

THE SILENCER

#4

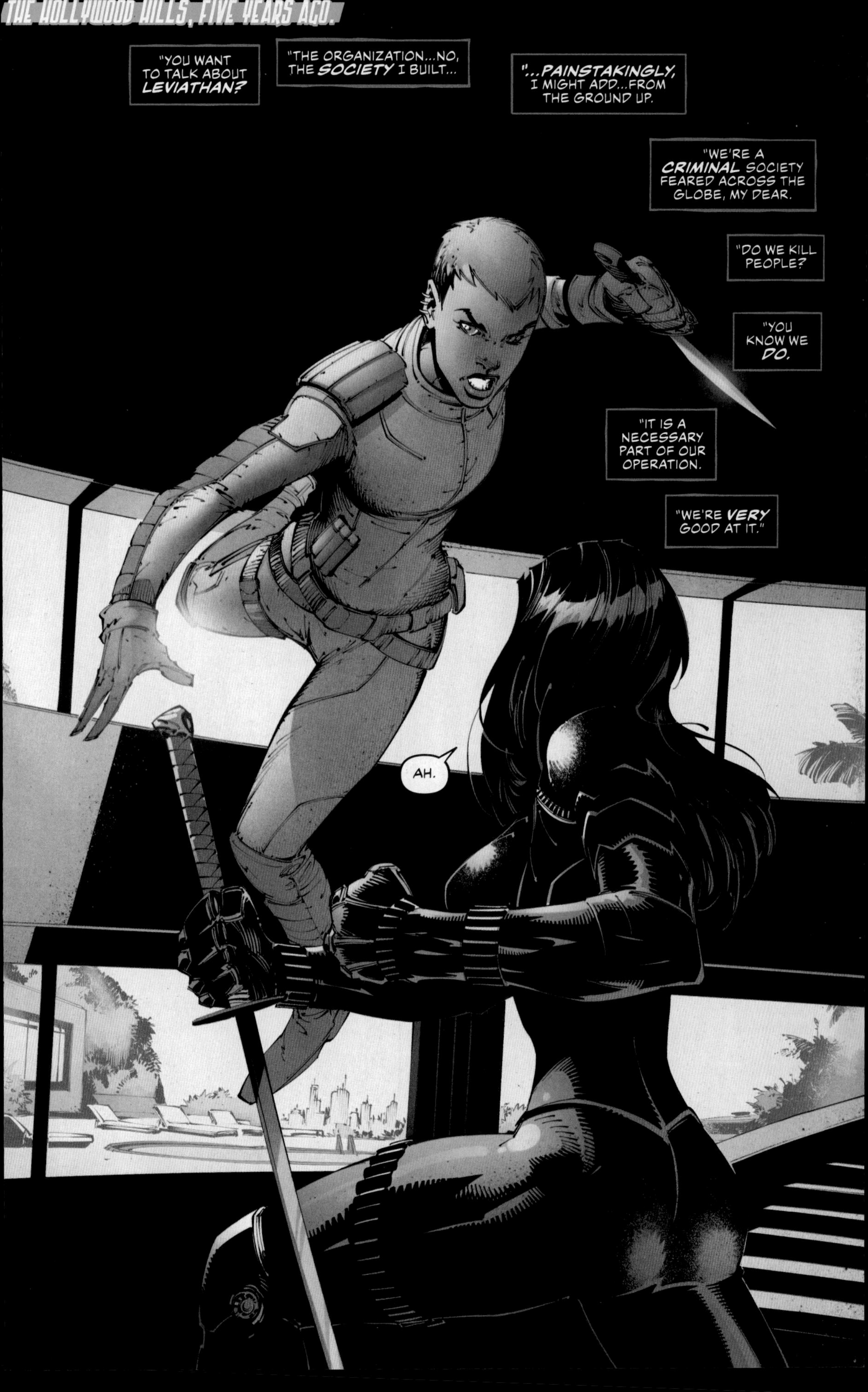
THE HOLLYWOOD HILLS, FIVE YEARS AGO.
"YOU WANT TO TALK ABOUT LEVIATHAN?
"THE ORGANIZATION...NO, THE SOCIETY I BUILT...
"...PAINSTAKINGLY, I MIGHT ADD...FROM THE GROUND UP.
"WE'RE A CRIMINAL SOCIETY FEARED ACROSS THE GLOBE, MY DEAR.
"DO WE KILL PEOPLE?
"YOU KNOW WE DO.
"IT IS A NECESSARY PART OF OUR OPERATION.
"WE'RE VERY GOOD AT IT."
AH.

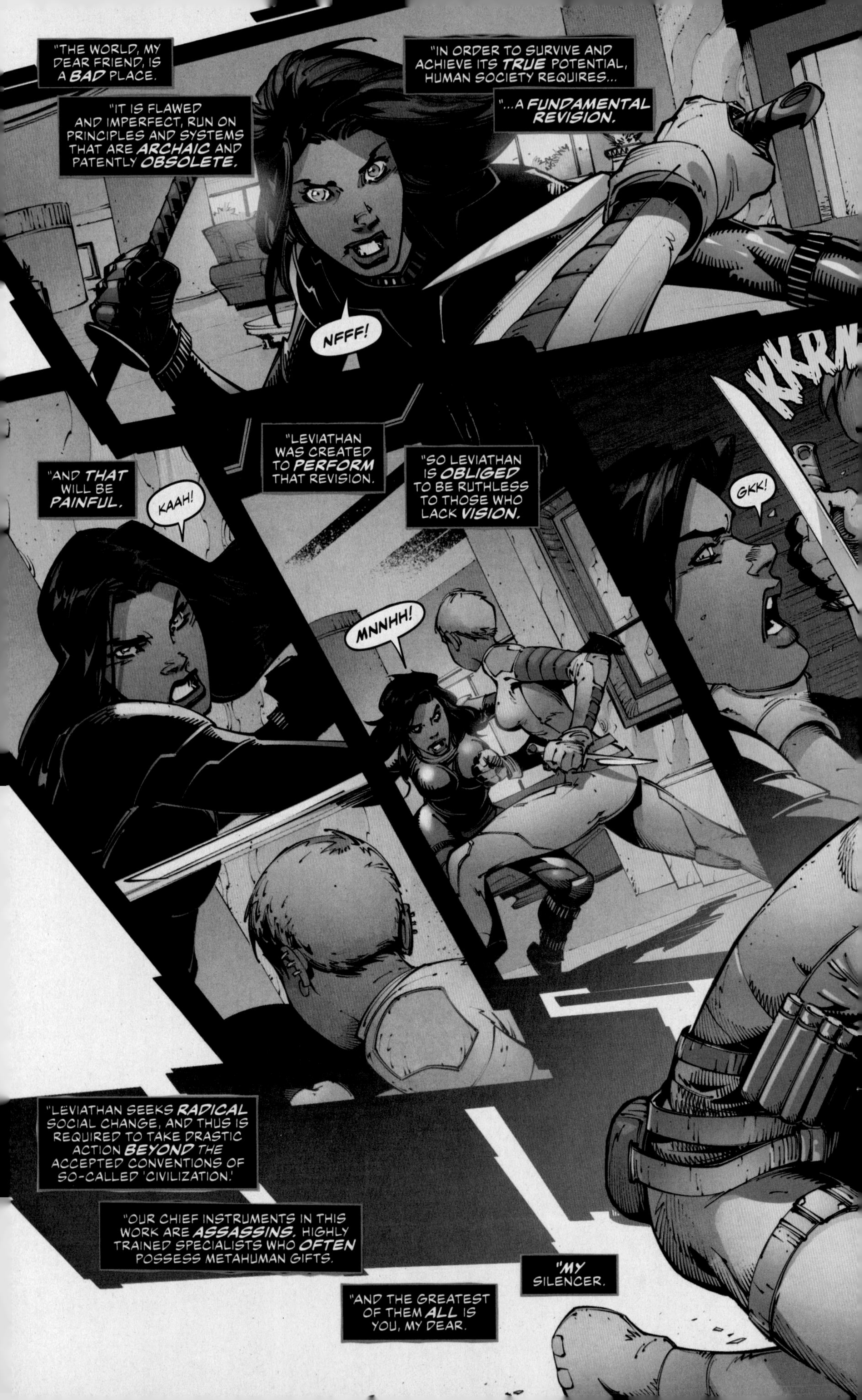
"THE WORLD, MY DEAR FRIEND, IS A BAD PLACE.
"IT IS FLAWED AND IMPERFECT, RUN ON PRINCIPLES AND SYSTEMS THAT ARE ARCHAIC AND PATENTLY OBSOLETE.
"IN ORDER TO SURVIVE AND ACHIEVE ITS TRUE POTENTIAL, HUMAN SOCIETY REQUIRES...
"...A FUNDAMENTAL REVISION.
NFFF!
"AND THAT WILL BE PAINFUL.
KAAH!
"LEVIATHAN WAS CREATED TO PERFORM THAT REVISION.
"SO LEVIATHAN IS OBLIGED TO BE RUTHLESS TO THOSE WHO LACK VISION.
MNNHH!
GKK!
"LEVIATHAN SEEKS RADICAL SOCIAL CHANGE, AND THUS IS REQUIRED TO TAKE DRASTIC ACTION BEYOND THE ACCEPTED CONVENTIONS OF SO-CALLED 'CIVILIZATION.'
"OUR CHIEF INSTRUMENTS IN THIS WORK ARE ASSASSINS, HIGHLY TRAINED SPECIALISTS WHO OFTEN POSSESS METAHUMAN GIFTS.
"AND THE GREATEST OF THEM ALL IS YOU, MY DEAR.
"MY SILENCER.

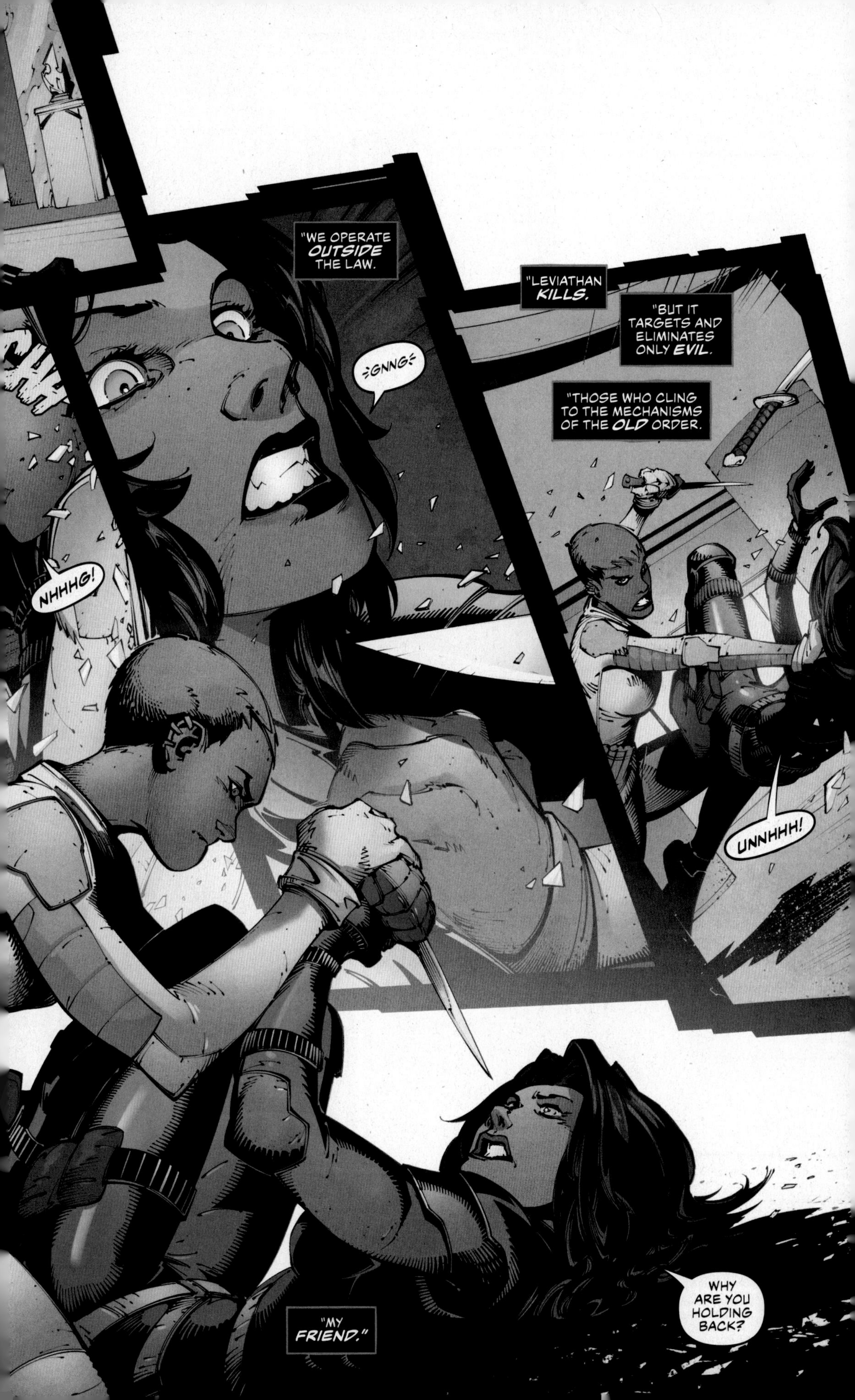
"WE OPERATE OUTSIDE THE LAW.
GNNG
NHHHG!
"LEVIATHAN KILLS.
"BUT IT TARGETS AND ELIMINATES ONLY EVIL.
"THOSE WHO CLING TO THE MECHANISMS OF THE OLD ORDER.
UNNHHH!
"MY FRIEND."
WHY ARE YOU HOLDING BACK?

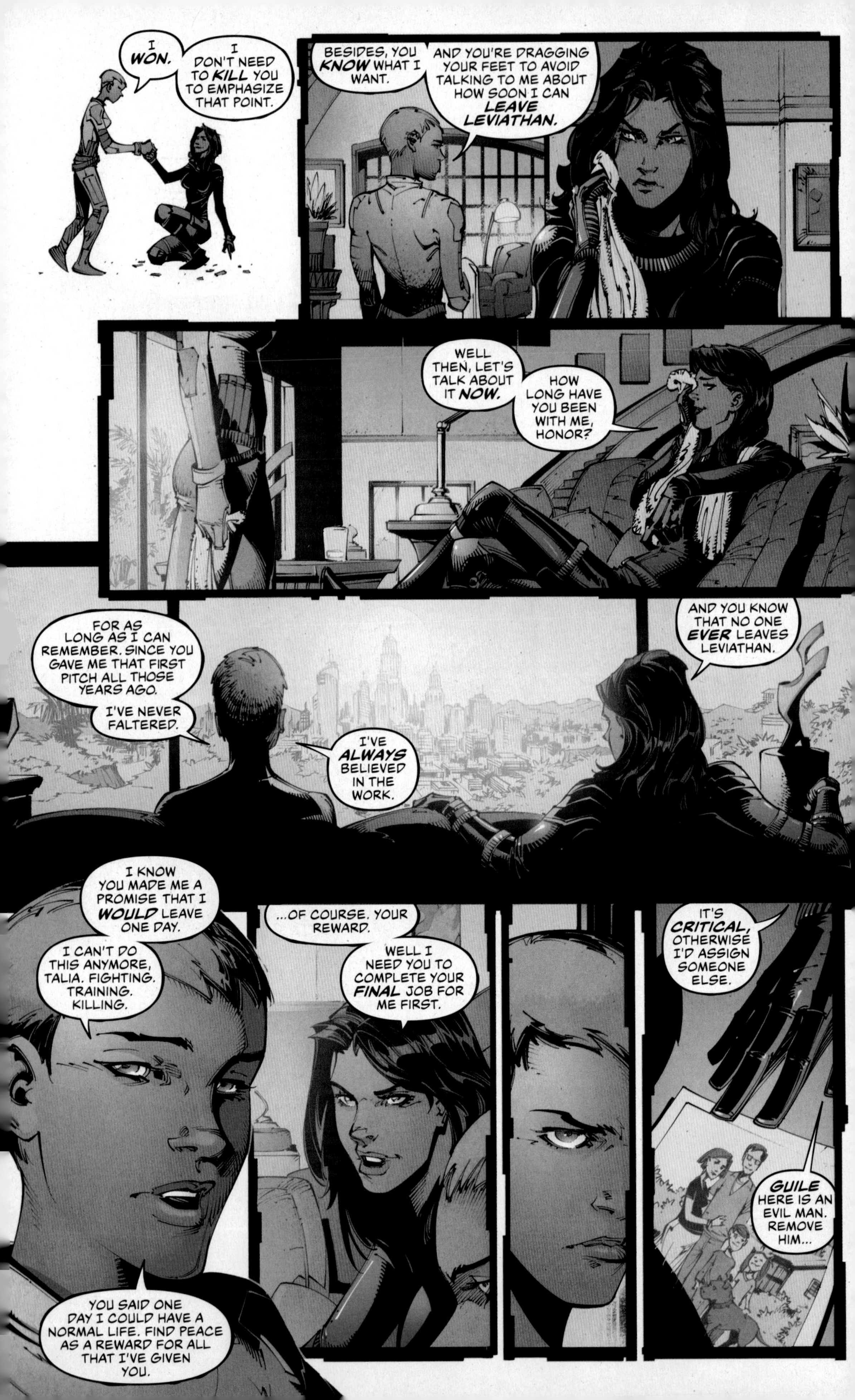
I WON.
I DON'T NEED TO KILL YOU TO EMPHASIZE THAT POINT.
BESIDES, YOU KNOW WHAT I WANT.
AND YOU'RE DRAGGING YOUR FEET TO AVOID TALKING TO ME ABOUT HOW SOON I CAN LEAVE LEVIATHAN.
WELL THEN, LET'S TALK ABOUT IT NOW.
HOW LONG HAVE YOU BEEN WITH ME, HONOR?
FOR AS LONG AS I CAN REMEMBER. SINCE YOU GAVE ME THAT FIRST PITCH ALL THOSE YEARS AGO.
I'VE NEVER FALTERED.
I'VE ALWAYS BELIEVED IN THE WORK.
AND YOU KNOW THAT NO ONE EVER LEAVES LEVIATHAN.
I KNOW YOU MADE ME A PROMISE THAT I WOULD LEAVE ONE DAY.
I CAN'T DO THIS ANYMORE, TALIA. FIGHTING. TRAINING. KILLING.
YOU SAID ONE DAY I COULD HAVE A NORMAL LIFE. FIND PEACE AS A REWARD FOR ALL THAT I'VE GIVEN YOU.
...OF COURSE. YOUR REWARD.
WELL I NEED YOU TO COMPLETE YOUR FINAL JOB FOR ME FIRST.
IT'S CRITICAL, OTHERWISE I'D ASSIGN SOMEONE ELSE.
GUILE HERE IS AN EVIL MAN. REMOVE HIM...

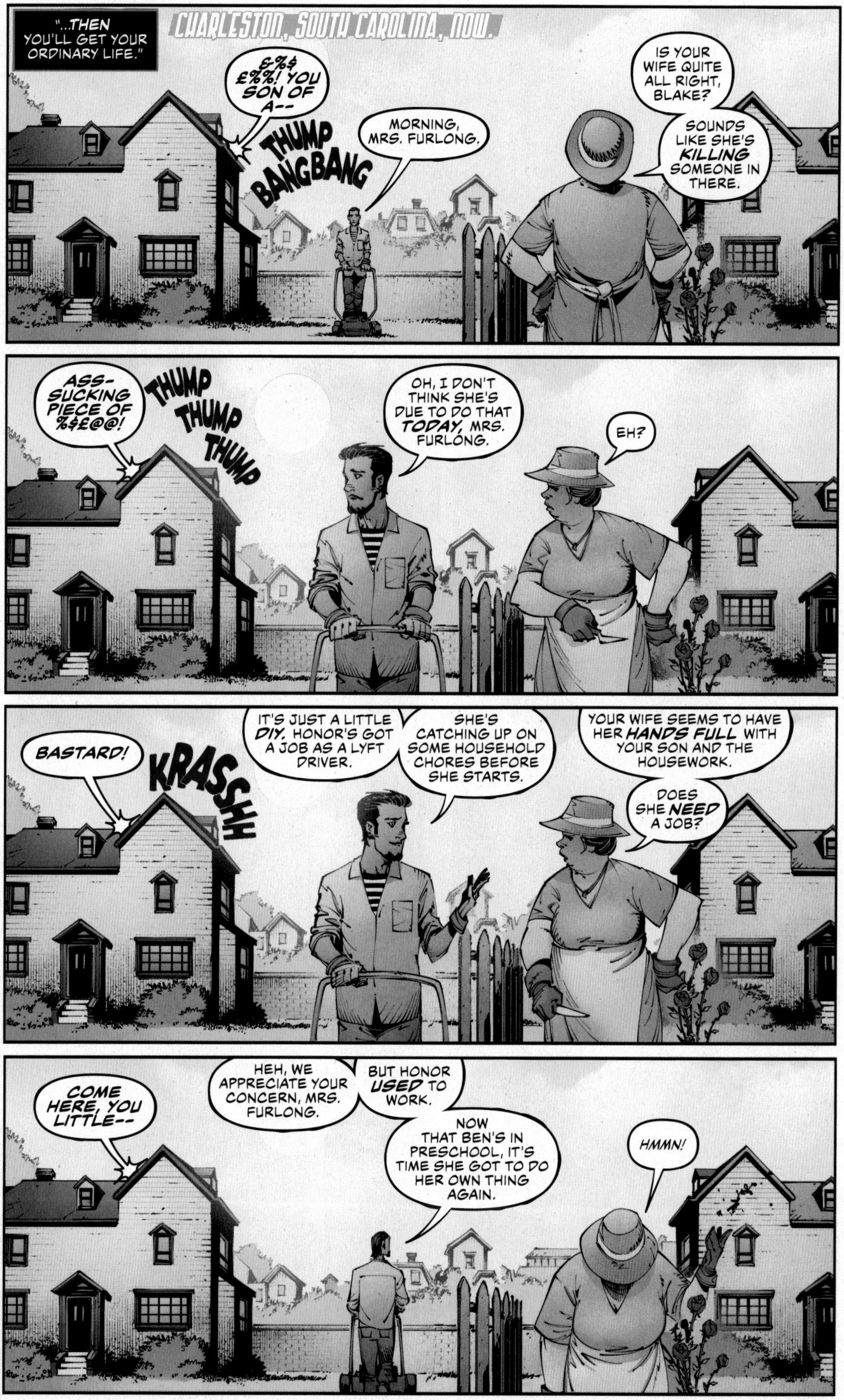
"...THEN YOU'LL GET YOUR ORDINARY LIFE."
CHARLESTON, SOUTH CAROLINA, NOW.
&%$ £%%! YOU SON OF A--
THUMP BANGBANG
MORNING, MRS. FURLONG.
IS YOUR WIFE QUITE ALL RIGHT, BLAKE?
SOUNDS LIKE SHE'S KILLING SOMEONE IN THERE.
ASS-SUCKING PIECE OF %$£@@!
THUMP THUMP THUMP
OH, I DON'T THINK SHE'S DUE TO DO THAT TODAY, MRS. FURLONG.
EH?
BASTARD!
KRASSHH
IT'S JUST A LITTLE DIY. HONOR'S GOT A JOB AS A LYFT DRIVER.
SHE'S CATCHING UP ON SOME HOUSEHOLD CHORES BEFORE SHE STARTS.
YOUR WIFE SEEMS TO HAVE HER HANDS FULL WITH YOUR SON AND THE HOUSEWORK.
DOES SHE NEED A JOB?
COME HERE, YOU LITTLE--
HEH, WE APPRECIATE YOUR CONCERN, MRS. FURLONG.
BUT HONOR USED TO WORK.
NOW THAT BEN'S IN PRESCHOOL, IT'S TIME SHE GOT TO DO HER OWN THING AGAIN.
HMMN!

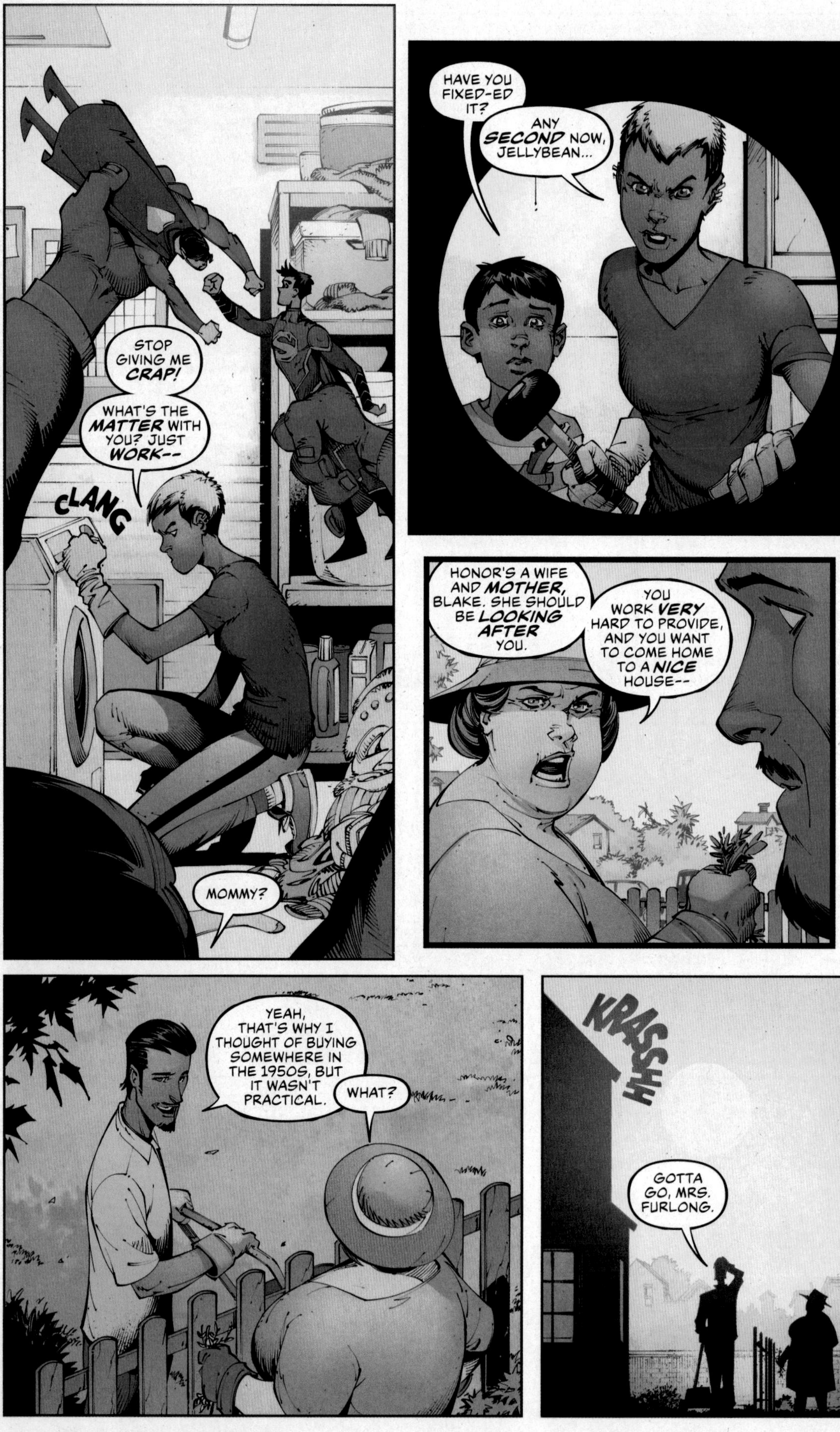
STOP GIVING ME CRAP!
WHAT'S THE MATTER WITH YOU? JUST WORK--
CLANG
MOMMY?
HAVE YOU FIXED-ED IT?
ANY SECOND NOW, JELLYBEAN...
HONOR'S A WIFE AND MOTHER, BLAKE. SHE SHOULD BE LOOKING AFTER YOU.
YOU WORK VERY HARD TO PROVIDE, AND YOU WANT TO COME HOME TO A NICE HOUSE--
YEAH, THAT'S WHY I THOUGHT OF BUYING SOMEWHERE IN THE 1950S, BUT IT WASN'T PRACTICAL.
WHAT?
KRASSHH
GOTTA GO, MRS. FURLONG.

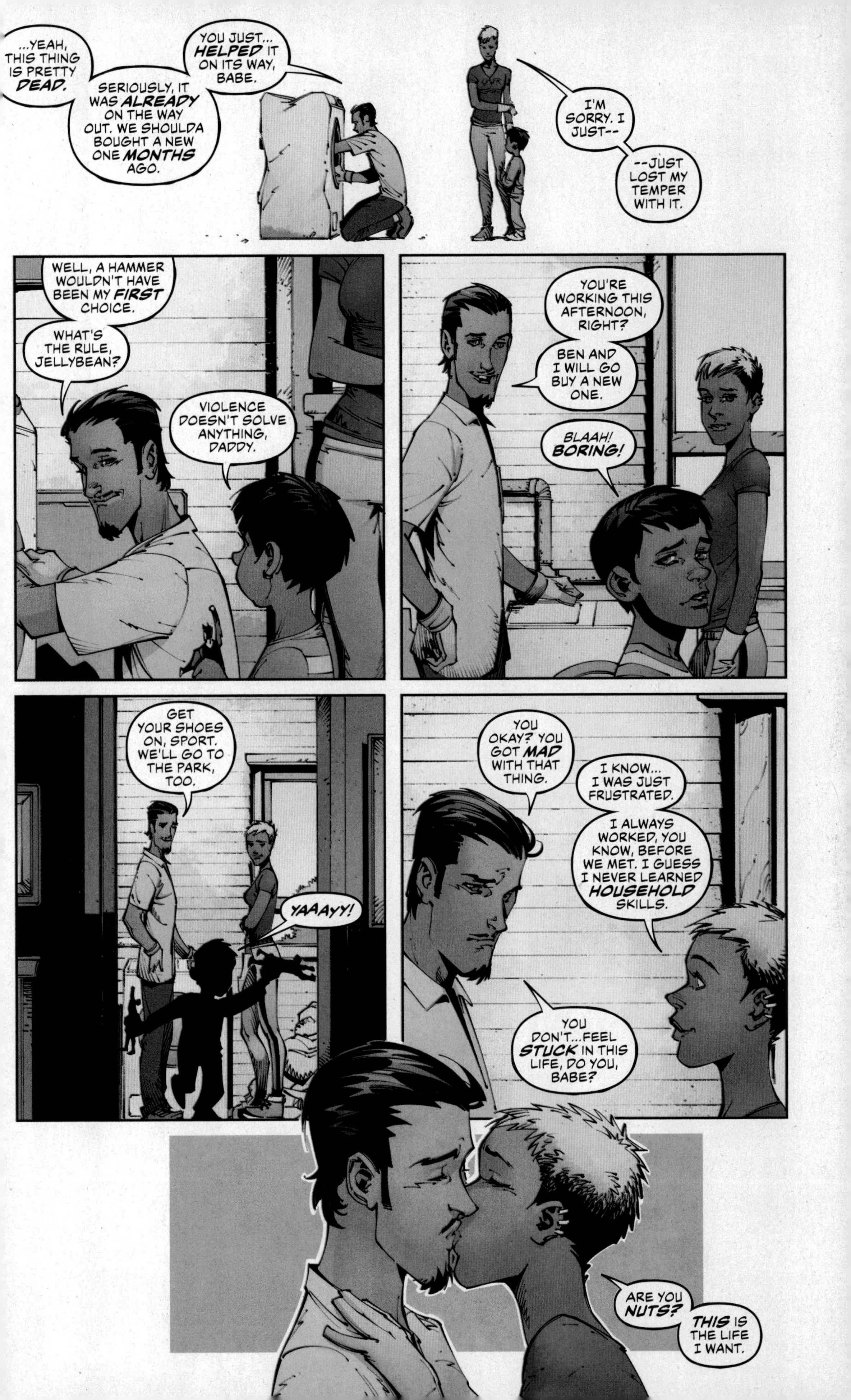

...YEAH, THIS THING IS PRETTY DEAD.
SERIOUSLY, IT WAS ALREADY ON THE WAY OUT. WE SHOULDA BOUGHT A NEW ONE MONTHS AGO.
YOU JUST... HELPED IT ON ITS WAY, BABE.
I'M SORRY. I JUST--
--JUST LOST MY TEMPER WITH IT.
WELL, A HAMMER WOULDN'T HAVE BEEN MY FIRST CHOICE.
WHAT'S THE RULE, JELLYBEAN?
VIOLENCE DOESN'T SOLVE ANYTHING, DADDY.
YOU'RE WORKING THIS AFTERNOON, RIGHT?
BEN AND I WILL GO BUY A NEW ONE.
BLAAH! BORING!
GET YOUR SHOES ON, SPORT. WE'LL GO TO THE PARK, TOO.
YAAAAYY!
YOU OKAY? YOU GOT MAD WITH THAT THING.
I KNOW... I WAS JUST FRUSTRATED.
I ALWAYS WORKED, YOU KNOW, BEFORE WE MET. I GUESS I NEVER LEARNED HOUSEHOLD SKILLS.
YOU DON'T...FEEL STUCK IN THIS LIFE, DO YOU, BABE?
ARE YOU NUTS?
THIS IS THE LIFE I WANT.

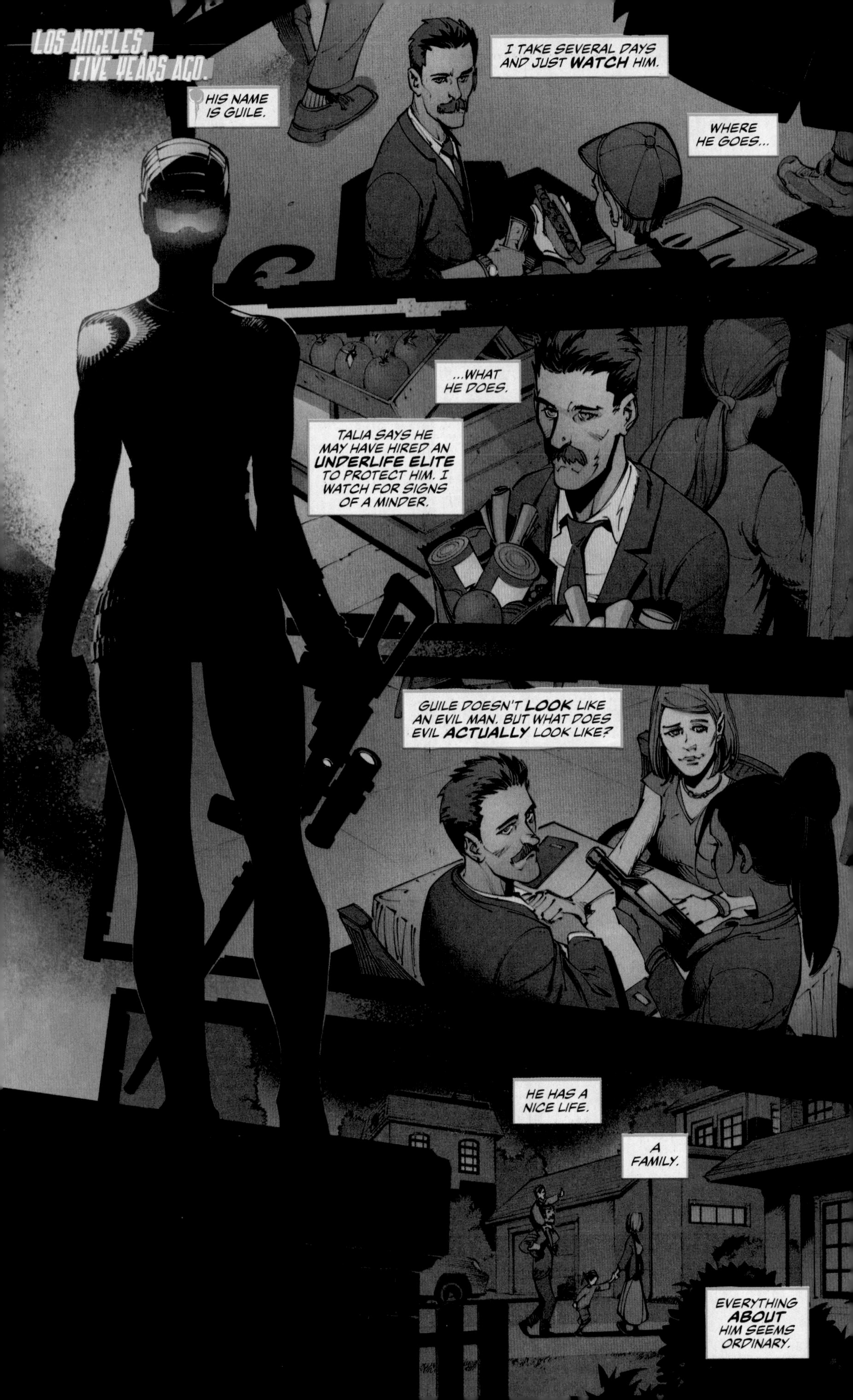
LOS ANGELES, FIVE YEARS AGO.
HIS NAME IS GUILE.
I TAKE SEVERAL DAYS AND JUST WATCH HIM.
WHERE HE GOES...
...WHAT HE DOES.
TALIA SAYS HE MAY HAVE HIRED AN UNDERLIFE ELITE TO PROTECT HIM. I WATCH FOR SIGNS OF A MINDER.
GUILE DOESN'T LOOK LIKE AN EVIL MAN. BUT WHAT DOES EVIL ACTUALLY LOOK LIKE?
HE HAS A NICE LIFE.
A FAMILY.
EVERYTHING ABOUT HIM SEEMS ORDINARY.

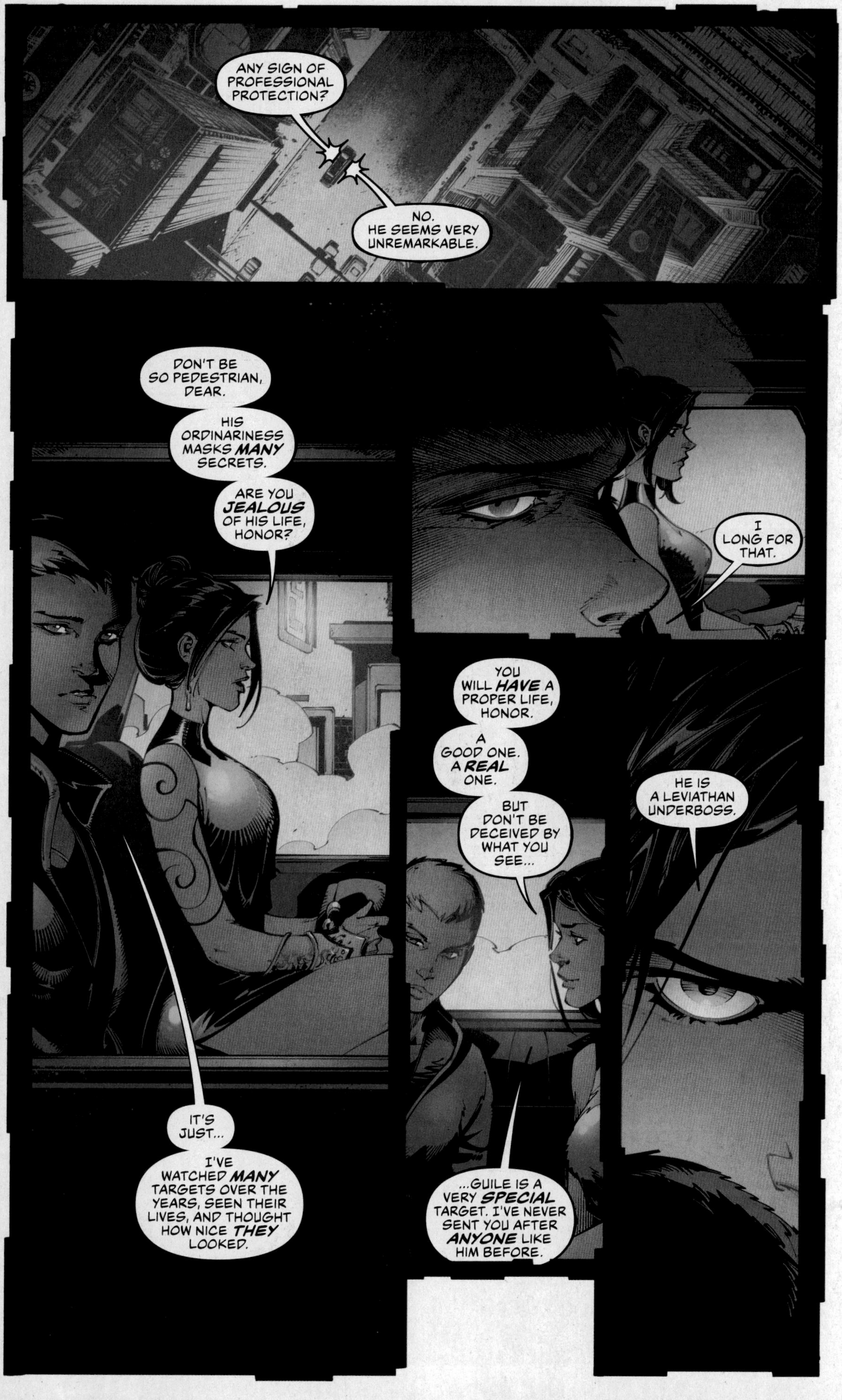
ANY SIGN OF PROFESSIONAL PROTECTION?
NO. HE SEEMS VERY UNREMARKABLE.
DON'T BE SO PEDESTRIAN, DEAR.
HIS ORDINARINESS MASKS MANY SECRETS.
ARE YOU JEALOUS OF HIS LIFE, HONOR?
IT'S JUST...
I'VE WATCHED MANY TARGETS OVER THE YEARS, SEEN THEIR LIVES, AND THOUGHT HOW NICE THEY LOOKED.
I LONG FOR THAT.
YOU WILL HAVE A PROPER LIFE, HONOR.
A GOOD ONE. A REAL ONE.
BUT DON'T BE DECEIVED BY WHAT YOU SEE...
...GUILE IS A VERY SPECIAL TARGET. I'VE NEVER SENT YOU AFTER ANYONE LIKE HIM BEFORE.
HE IS A LEVIATHAN UNDERBOSS.

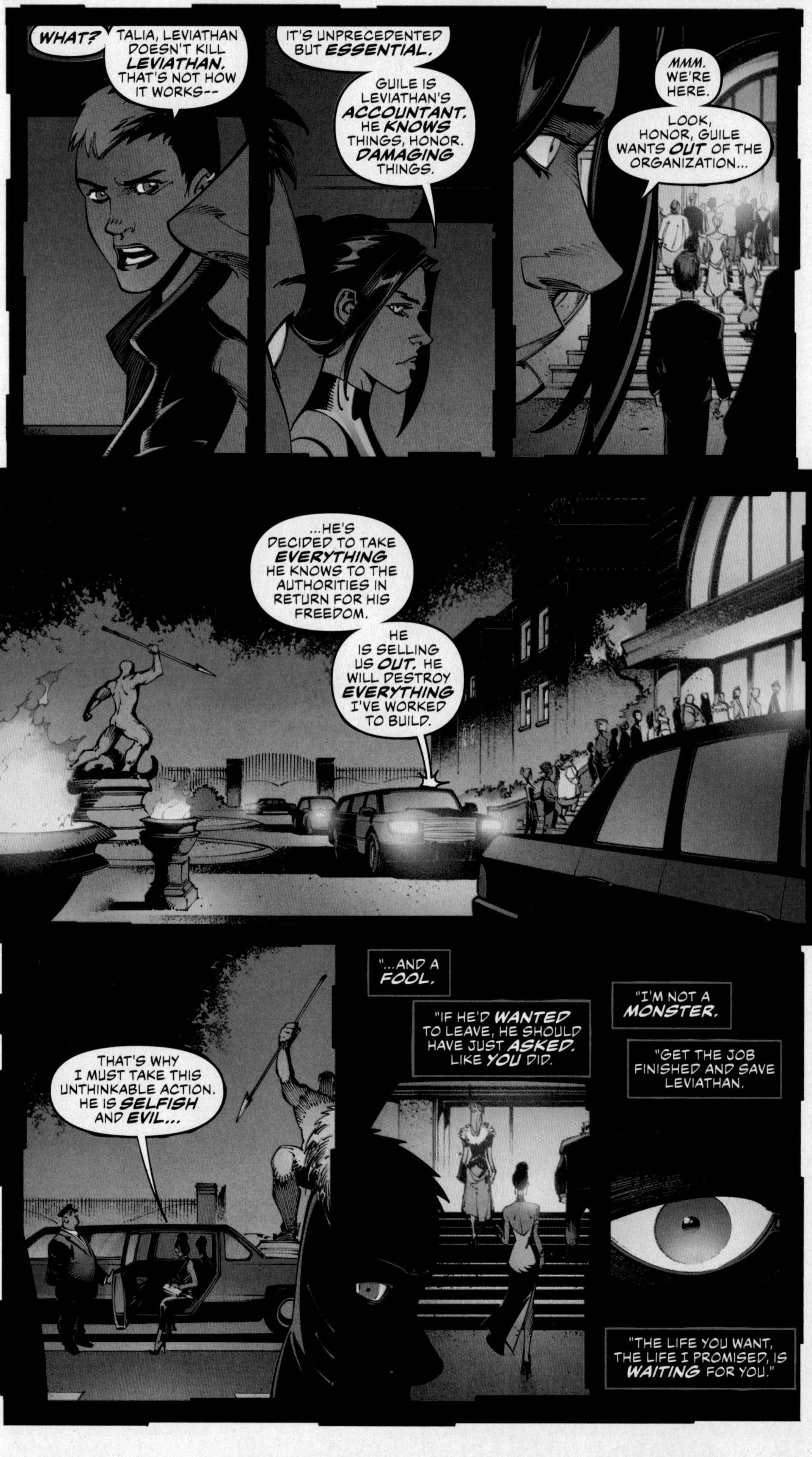
WHAT?
TALIA, LEVIATHAN DOESN'T KILL LEVIATHAN. THAT'S NOT HOW IT WORKS--
IT'S UNPRECEDENTED BUT ESSENTIAL.
GUILE IS LEVIATHAN'S ACCOUNTANT. HE KNOWS THINGS, HONOR. DAMAGING THINGS.
MMM. WE'RE HERE.
LOOK, HONOR, GUILE WANTS OUT OF THE ORGANIZATION...
...HE'S DECIDED TO TAKE EVERYTHING HE KNOWS TO THE AUTHORITIES IN RETURN FOR HIS FREEDOM.
HE IS SELLING US OUT. HE WILL DESTROY EVERYTHING I'VE WORKED TO BUILD.
THAT'S WHY I MUST TAKE THIS UNTHINKABLE ACTION. HE IS SELFISH AND EVIL...
"...AND A FOOL.
"IF HE'D WANTED TO LEAVE, HE SHOULD HAVE JUST ASKED. LIKE YOU DID.
"I'M NOT A MONSTER.
"GET THE JOB FINISHED AND SAVE LEVIATHAN.
"THE LIFE YOU WANT, THE LIFE I PROMISED, IS WAITING FOR YOU."

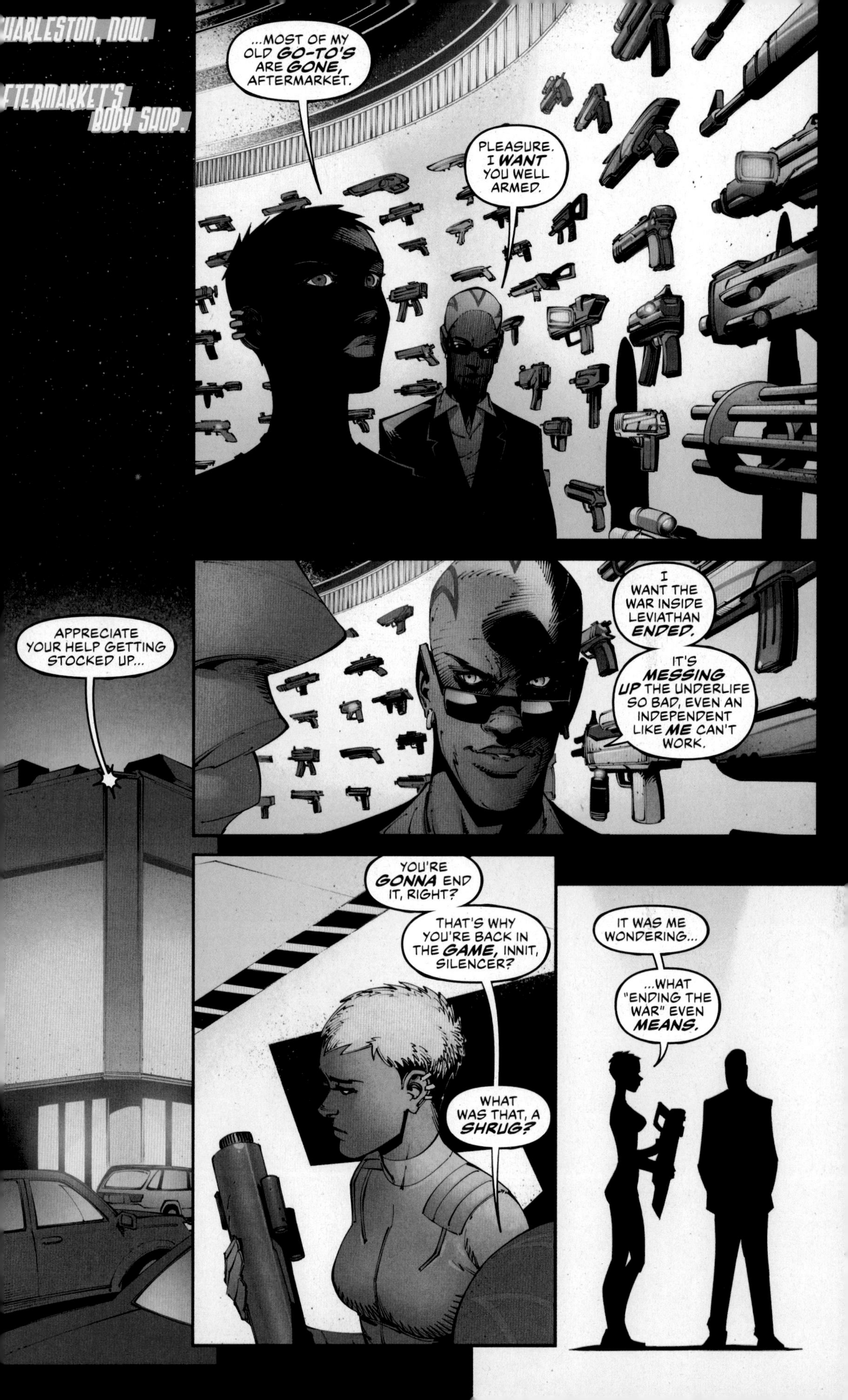
CHARLESTON, NOW.
AFTERMARKET'S BODY SHOP.
...MOST OF MY OLD GO-TO'S ARE GONE, AFTERMARKET.
PLEASURE. I WANT YOU WELL ARMED.
APPRECIATE YOUR HELP GETTING STOCKED UP...
I WANT THE WAR INSIDE LEVIATHAN ENDED.
IT'S MESSING UP THE UNDERLIFE SO BAD, EVEN AN INDEPENDENT LIKE ME CAN'T WORK.
YOU'RE GONNA END IT, RIGHT?
THAT'S WHY YOU'RE BACK IN THE GAME, INNIT, SILENCER?
WHAT WAS THAT, A SHRUG?
IT WAS ME WONDERING...
...WHAT "ENDING THE WAR" EVEN MEANS.

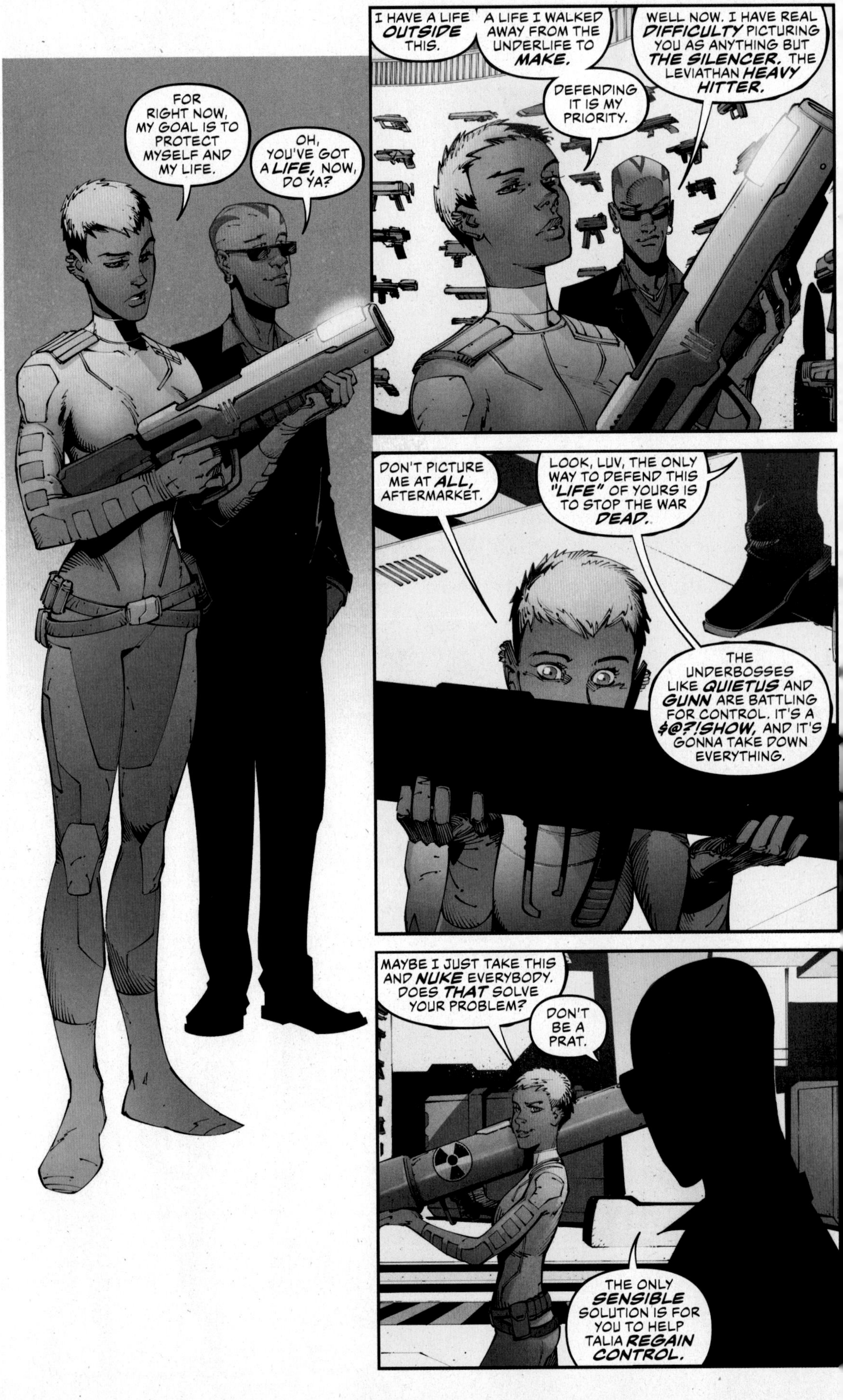
FOR RIGHT NOW, MY GOAL IS TO PROTECT MYSELF AND MY LIFE.
OH, YOU'VE GOT A LIFE, NOW, DO YA?
I HAVE A LIFE OUTSIDE THIS.
A LIFE I WALKED AWAY FROM THE UNDERLIFE TO MAKE.
DEFENDING IT IS MY PRIORITY.
WELL NOW. I HAVE REAL DIFFICULTY PICTURING YOU AS ANYTHING BUT THE SILENCER. THE LEVIATHAN HEAVY HITTER.
DON'T PICTURE ME AT ALL, AFTERMARKET.
LOOK, LUV, THE ONLY WAY TO DEFEND THIS "LIFE" OF YOURS IS TO STOP THE WAR DEAD.
THE UNDERBOSSES LIKE QUIETUS AND GUNN ARE BATTLING FOR CONTROL. IT'S A $@?!SHOW, AND IT'S GONNA TAKE DOWN EVERYTHING.
MAYBE I JUST TAKE THIS AND NUKE EVERYBODY. DOES THAT SOLVE YOUR PROBLEM?
DON'T BE A PRAT.
THE ONLY SENSIBLE SOLUTION IS FOR YOU TO HELP TALIA REGAIN CONTROL.

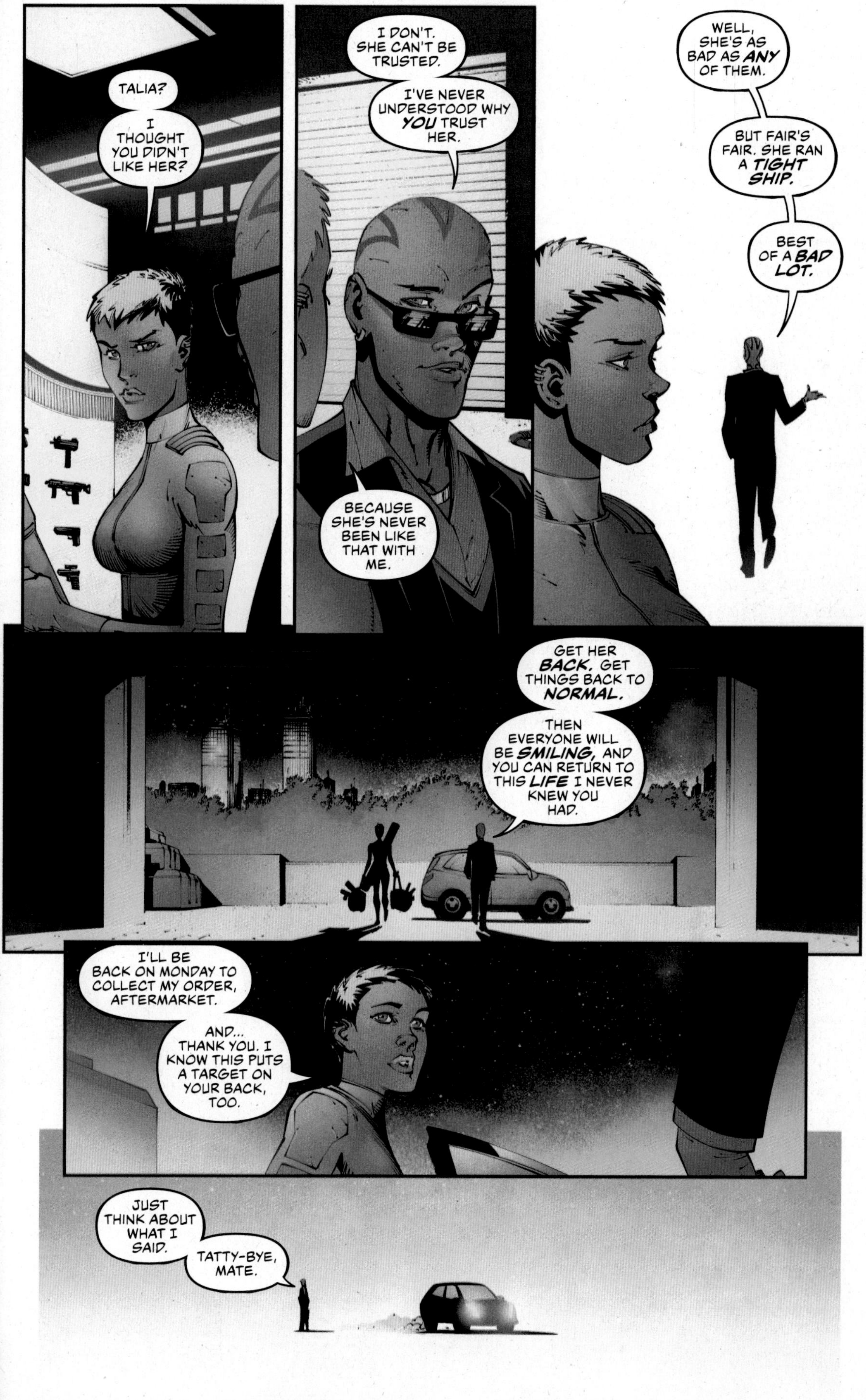
TALIA?
I THOUGHT YOU DIDN'T LIKE HER?
I DON'T. SHE CAN'T BE TRUSTED.
I'VE NEVER UNDERSTOOD WHY YOU TRUST HER.
BECAUSE SHE'S NEVER BEEN LIKE THAT WITH ME.
WELL, SHE'S AS BAD AS ANY OF THEM.
BUT FAIR'S FAIR. SHE RAN A TIGHT SHIP.
BEST OF A BAD LOT.
GET HER BACK. GET THINGS BACK TO NORMAL.
THEN EVERYONE WILL BE SMILING, AND YOU CAN RETURN TO THIS LIFE I NEVER KNEW YOU HAD.
I'LL BE BACK ON MONDAY TO COLLECT MY ORDER, AFTERMARKET.
AND... THANK YOU. I KNOW THIS PUTS A TARGET ON YOUR BACK, TOO.
JUST THINK ABOUT WHAT I SAID.
TATTY-BYE, MATE.

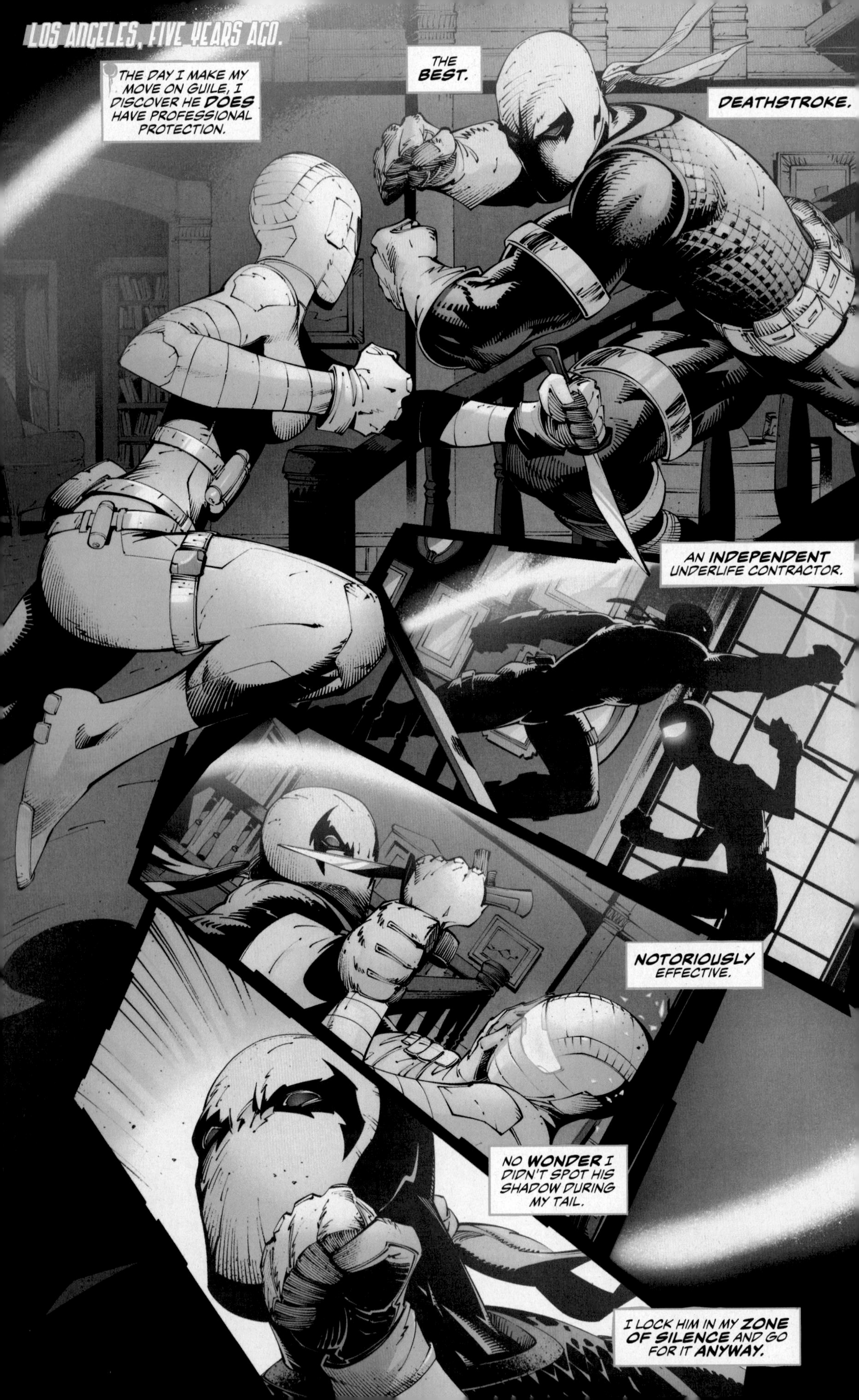
LOS ANGELES, FIVE YEARS AGO.
THE DAY I MAKE MY MOVE ON GUILE, I DISCOVER HE DOES HAVE PROFESSIONAL PROTECTION.
THE BEST.
DEATHSTROKE.
AN INDEPENDENT UNDERLIFE CONTRACTOR.
NOTORIOUSLY EFFECTIVE.
NO WONDER I DIDN'T SPOT HIS SHADOW DURING MY TAIL.
I LOCK HIM IN MY ZONE OF SILENCE AND GO FOR IT ANYWAY.

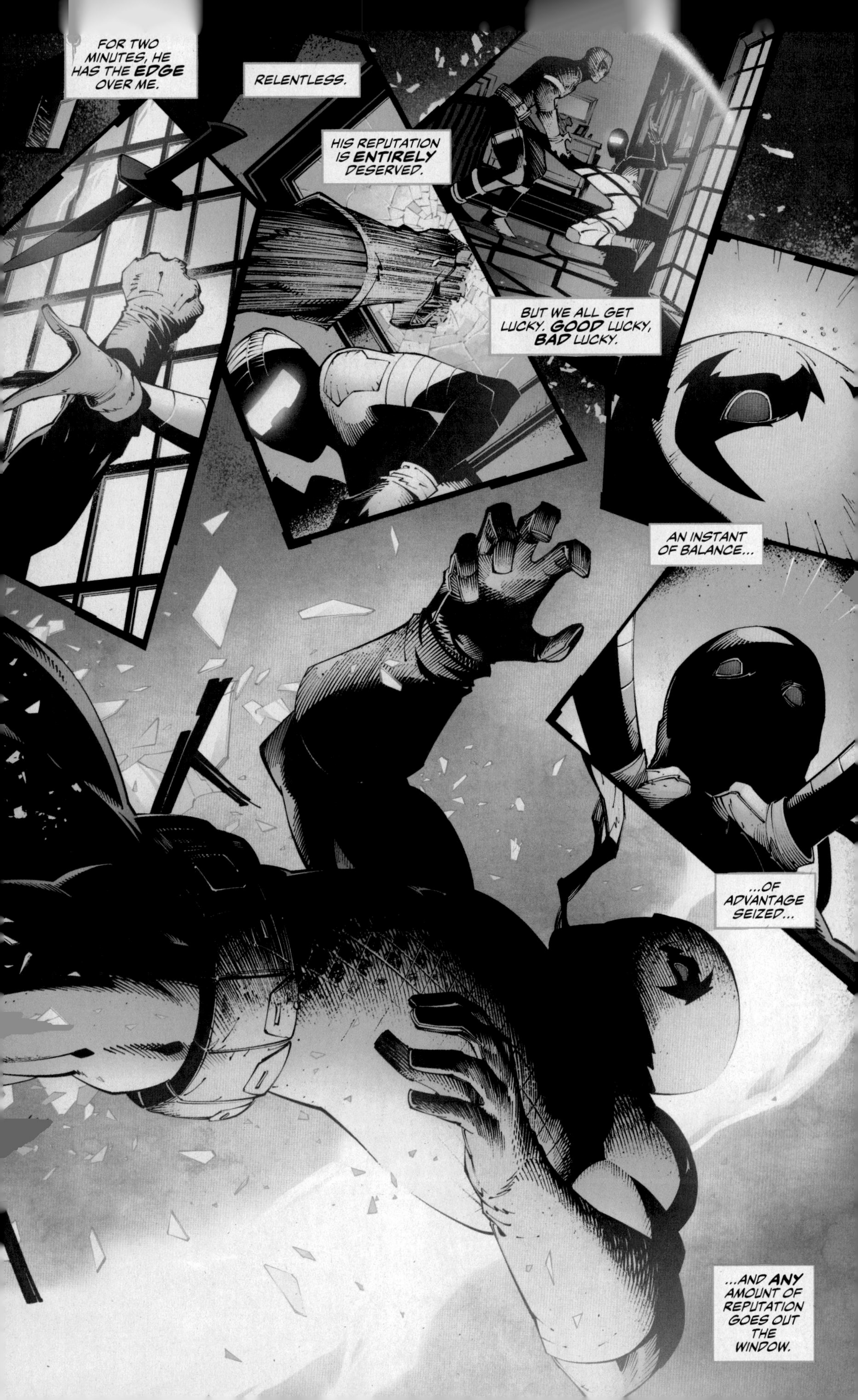
FOR TWO MINUTES, HE HAS THE EDGE OVER ME.
RELENTLESS.
HIS REPUTATION IS ENTIRELY DESERVED.
BUT WE ALL GET LUCKY. GOOD LUCKY, BAD LUCKY.
AN INSTANT OF BALANCE...
...OF ADVANTAGE SEIZED...
...AND ANY AMOUNT OF REPUTATION GOES OUT THE WINDOW.

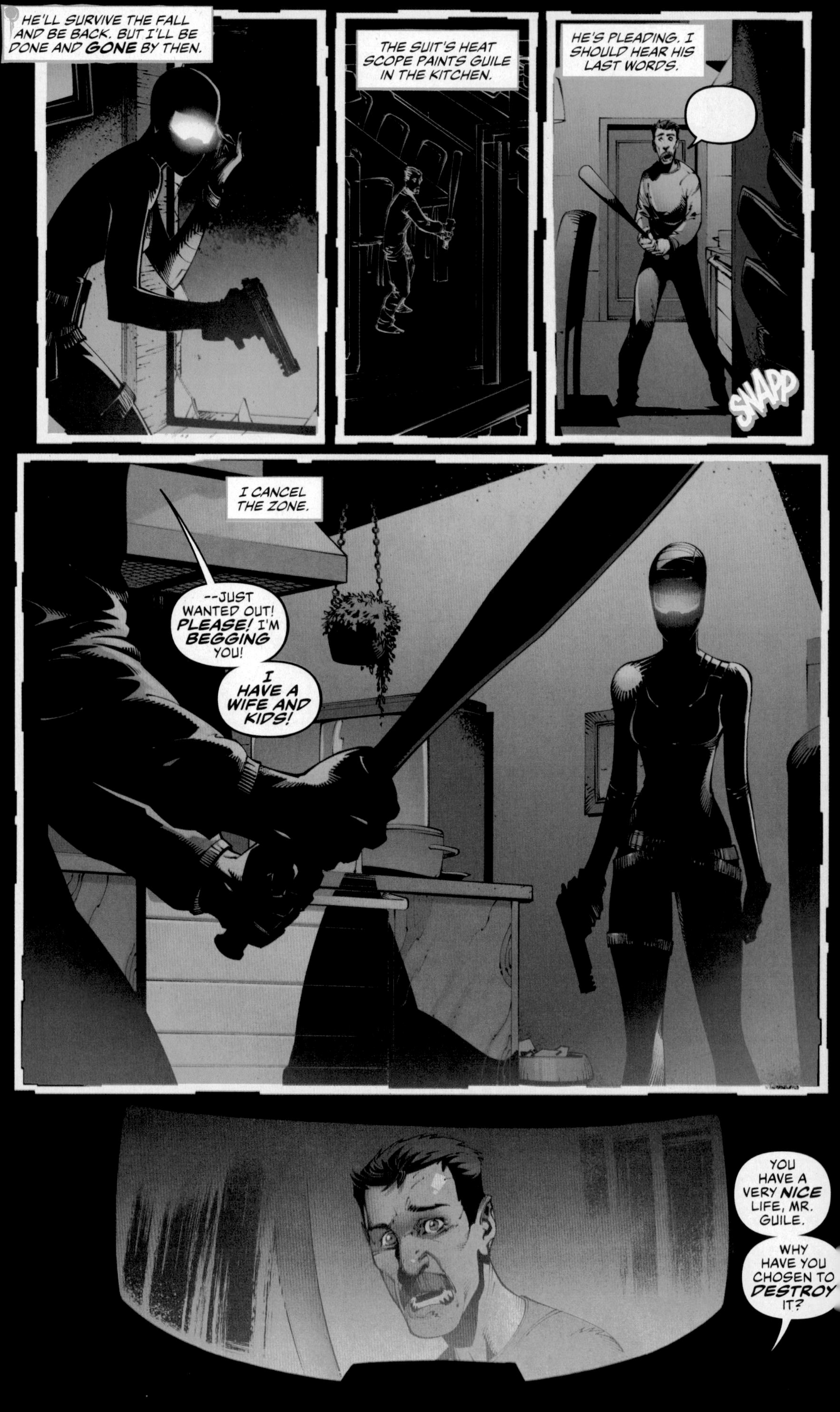
HE'LL SURVIVE THE FALL AND BE BACK. BUT I'LL BE DONE AND GONE BY THEN.
THE SUIT'S HEAT SCOPE PAINTS GUILE IN THE KITCHEN.
HE'S PLEADING. I SHOULD HEAR HIS LAST WORDS.
SNAPP
I CANCEL THE ZONE.
--JUST WANTED OUT! PLEASE! I'M BEGGING YOU!
I HAVE A WIFE AND KIDS!
YOU HAVE A VERY NICE LIFE, MR. GUILE.
WHY HAVE YOU CHOSEN TO DESTROY IT?

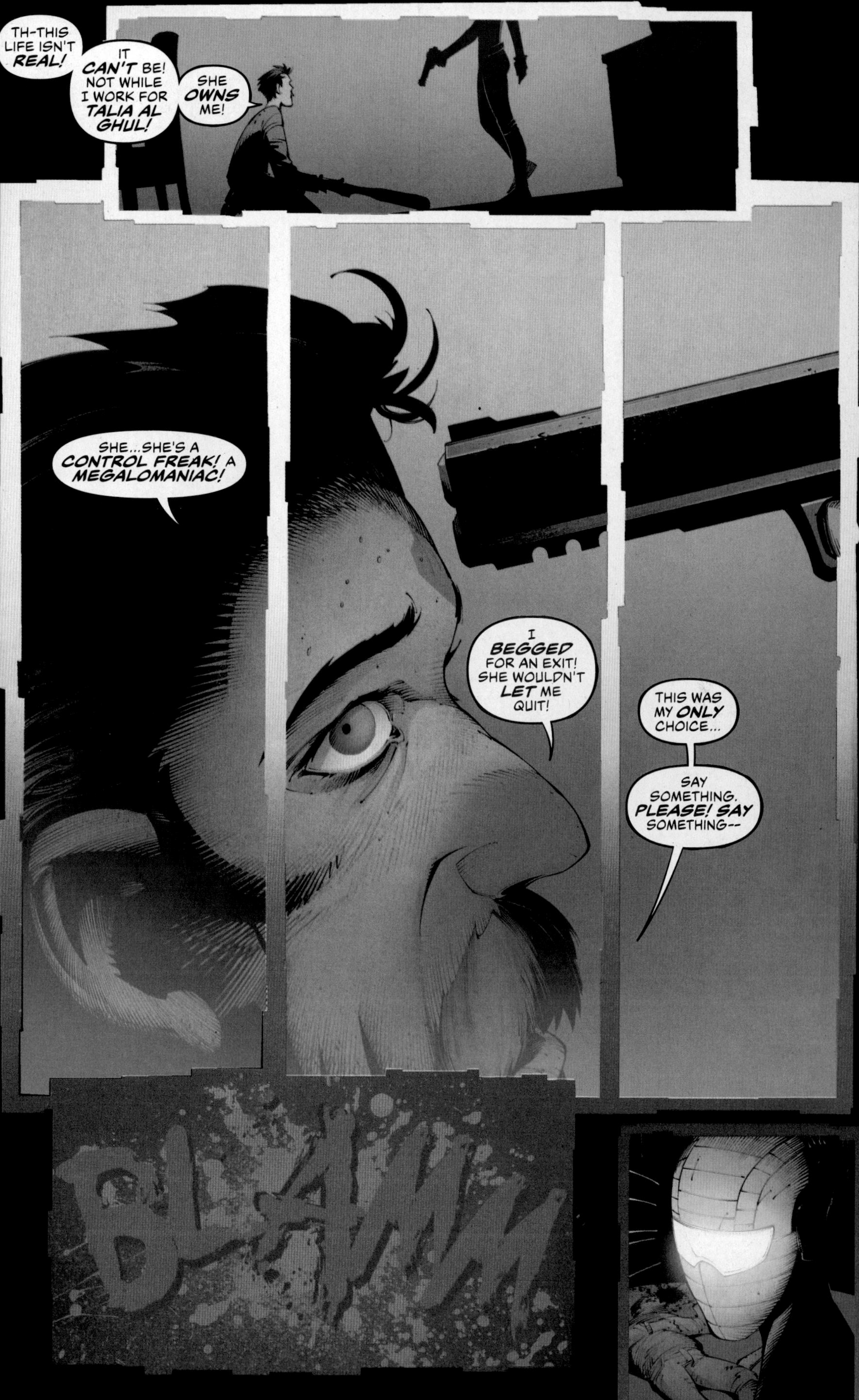
TH-THIS LIFE ISN'T REAL!
IT CAN'T BE! NOT WHILE I WORK FOR TALIA AL GHUL!
SHE OWNS ME!
SHE...SHE'S A CONTROL FREAK! A MEGALOMANIAC!
I BEGGED FOR AN EXIT! SHE WOULDN'T LET ME QUIT!
THIS WAS MY ONLY CHOICE...
SAY SOMETHING. PLEASE! SAY SOMETHING--

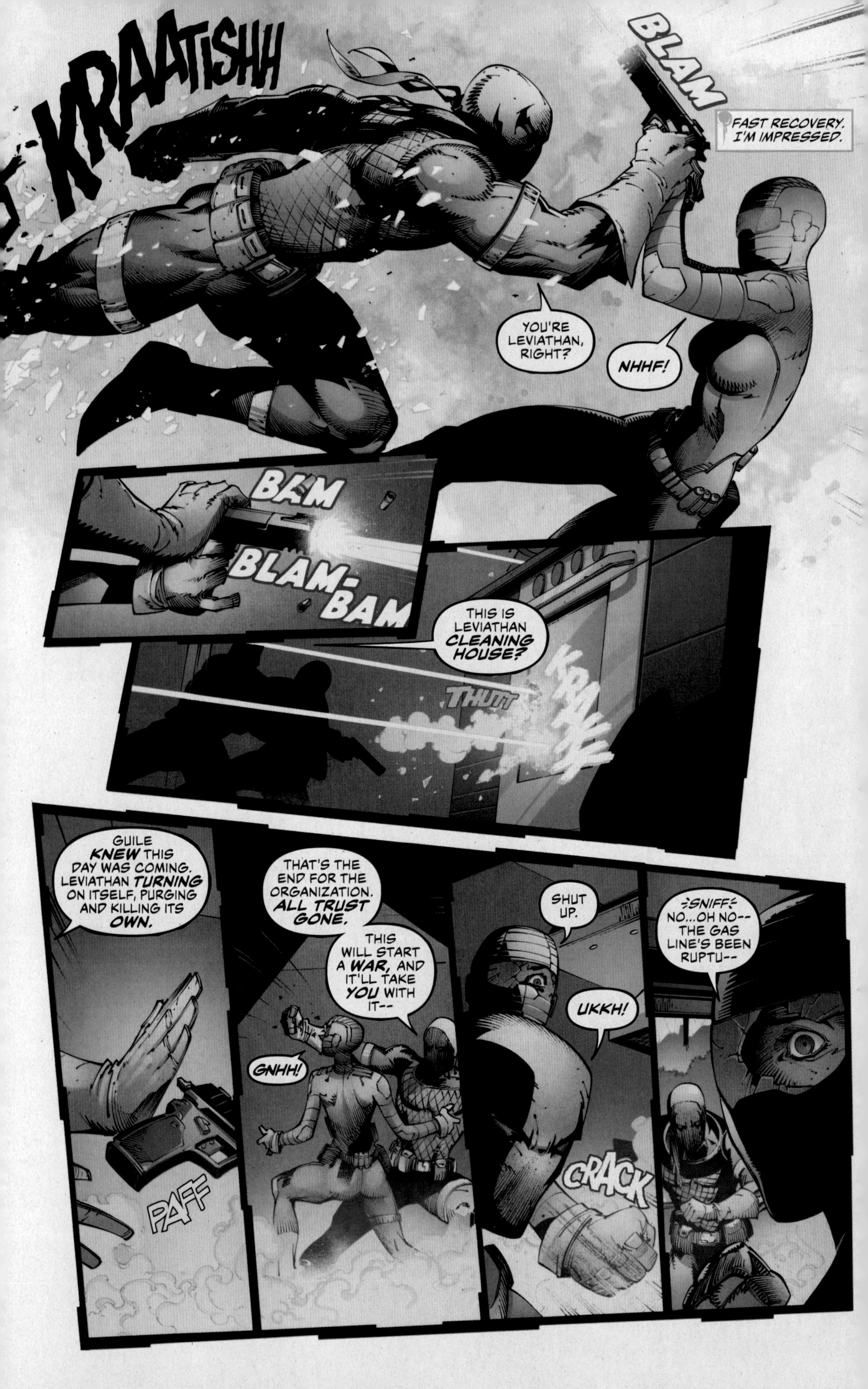
KRAATISHH
BLAM
FAST RECOVERY. I'M IMPRESSED.
YOU'RE LEVIATHAN, RIGHT?
NHHF!
BAM
BLAM-BAM
THIS IS LEVIATHAN CLEANING HOUSE?
THUTT
GUILE KNEW THIS DAY WAS COMING. LEVIATHAN TURNING ON ITSELF, PURGING AND KILLING ITS OWN.
PAFF
THAT'S THE END FOR THE ORGANIZATION. ALL TRUST GONE.
THIS WILL START A WAR, AND IT'LL TAKE YOU WITH IT--
GNHH!
SHUT UP.
UKKH!
CRACK
=SNIFF= NO...OH NO-- THE GAS LINE'S BEEN RUPTU--

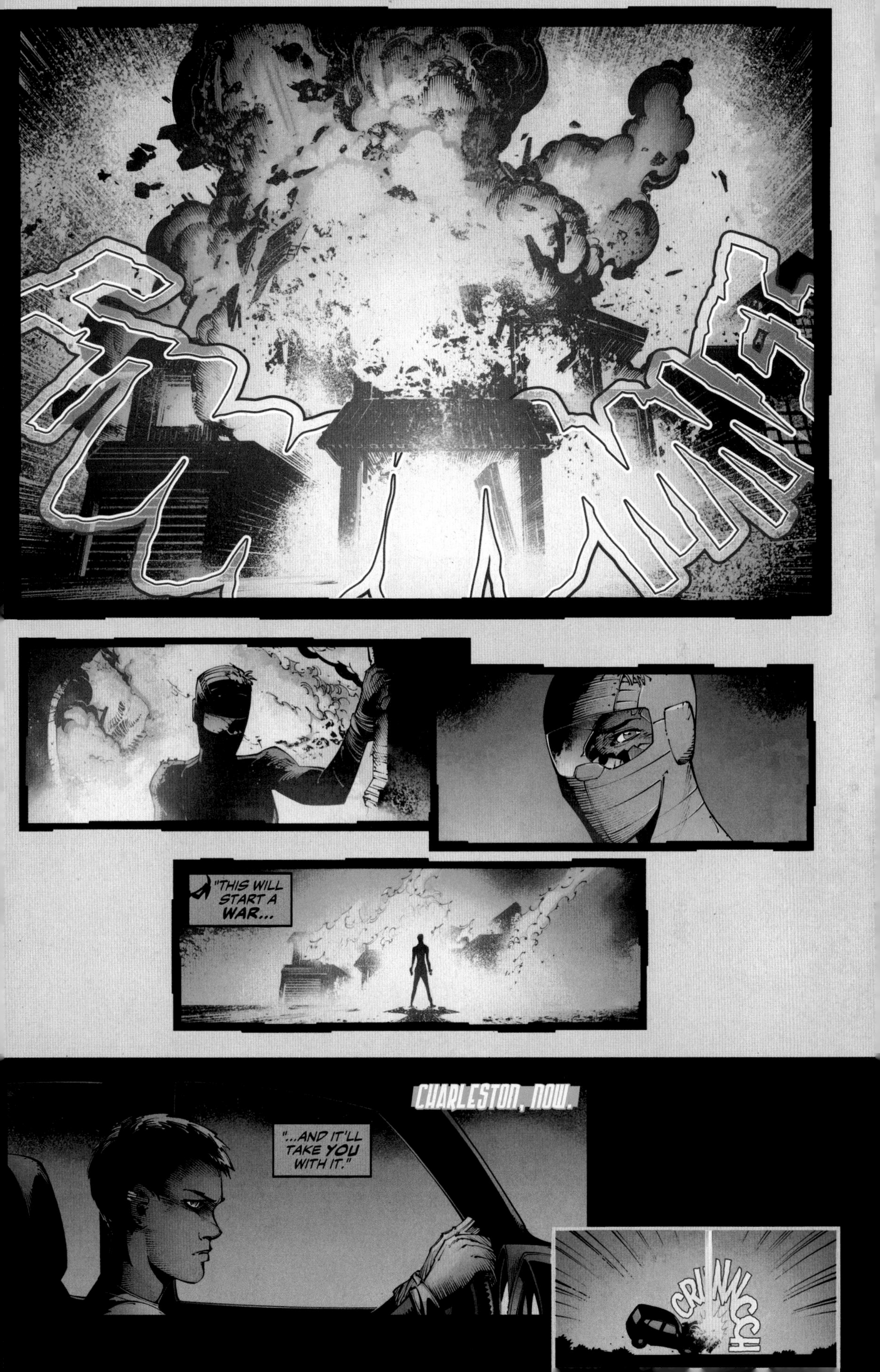
"THIS WILL START A WAR...
CHARLESTON, NOW.
"...AND IT'LL TAKE YOU WITH IT."

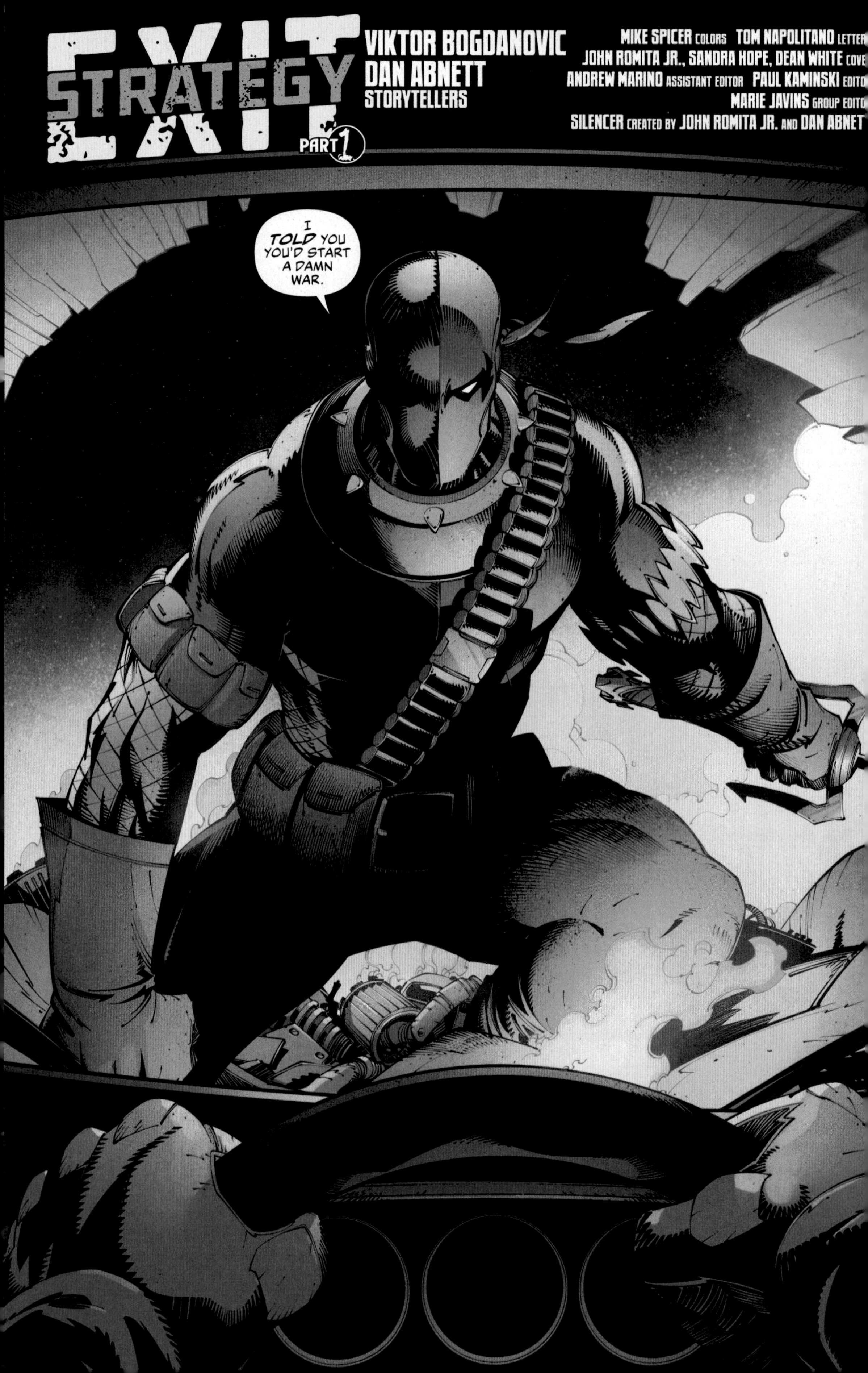
EXIT STRATEGY
PART 1
VIKTOR BOGDANOVIC
DAN ABNETT
STORYTELLERS
MIKE SPICER COLORS TOM NAPOLITANO LETTER
JOHN ROMITA JR., SANDRA HOPE, DEAN WHITE COVE
ANDREW MARINO ASSISTANT EDITOR PAUL KAMINSKI EDITO
MARIE JAVINS GROUP EDITO
SILENCER CREATED BY JOHN ROMITA JR. AND DAN ABNET
I TOLD YOU YOU'D START A DAMN WAR.

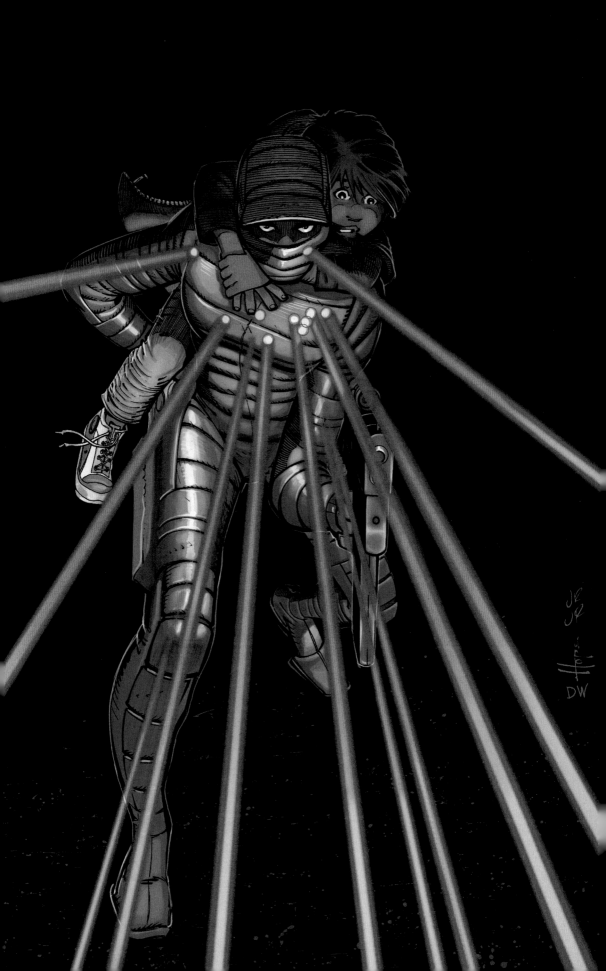

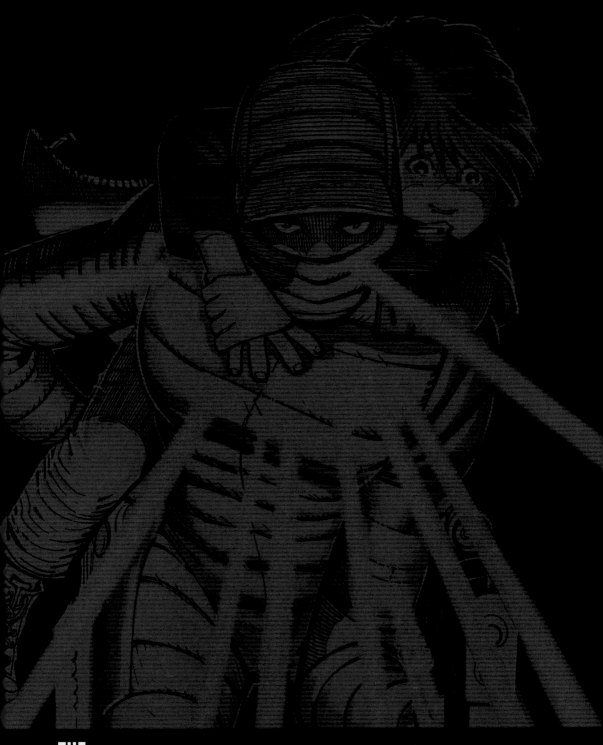

THE
SILENCER
#5

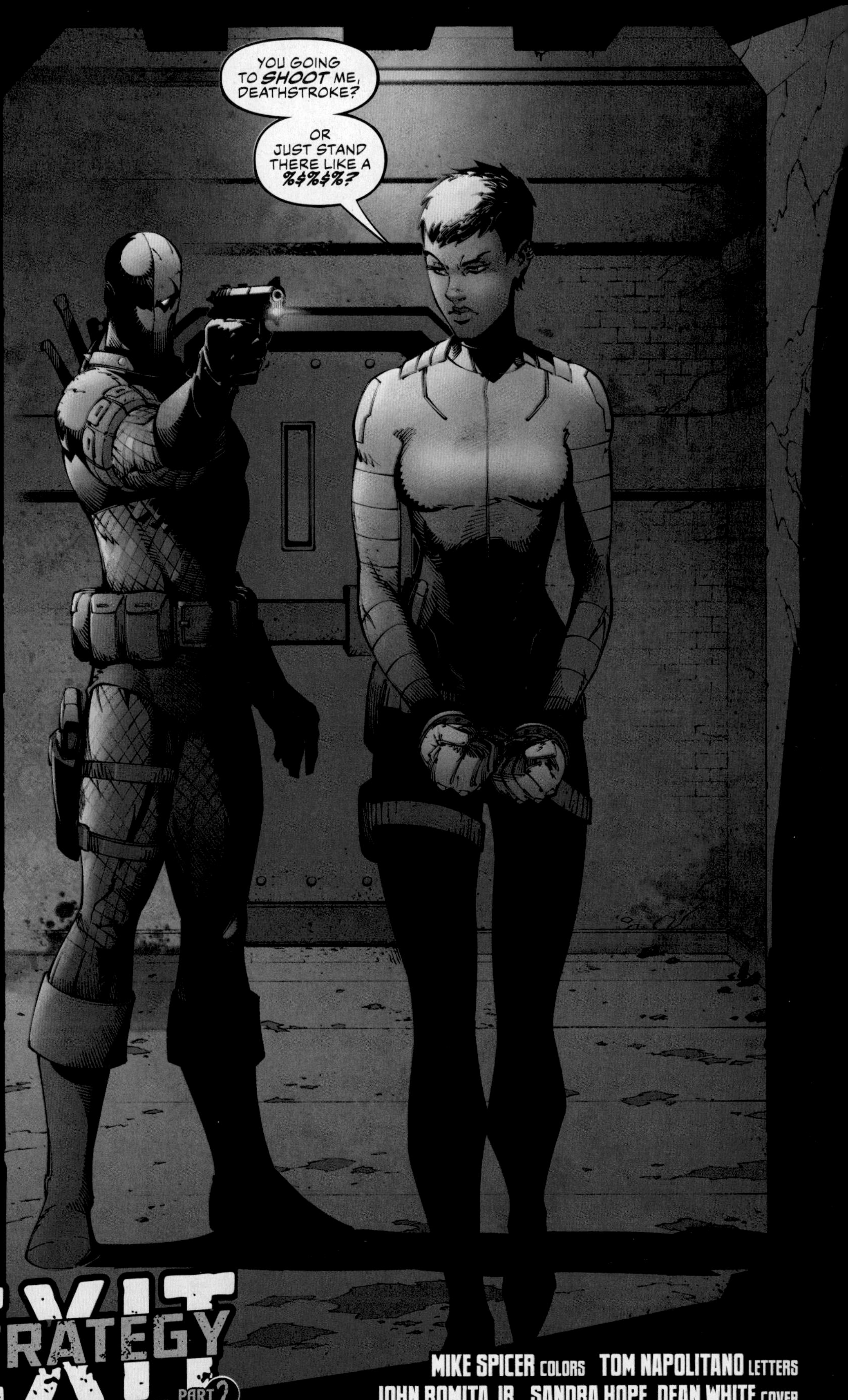
YOU GOING TO *SHOOT* ME, DEATHSTROKE?
OR JUST STAND THERE LIKE A %$%$%?

EXIT STRATEGY

PART 2

VIKTOR BOGDANOVIC
DAN ABNETT
STORYTELLERS

MIKE SPICER COLORS **TOM NAPOLITANO** LETTERS
JOHN ROMITA JR., SANDRA HOPE, DEAN WHITE COVER
ROB LEVIN ASSOCIATE EDITOR **PAUL KAMINSKI** EDITOR
MARIE JAVINS GROUP EDITOR
THE SILENCER CREATED BY **JOHN ROMITA JR.** AND **DAN ABNETT**

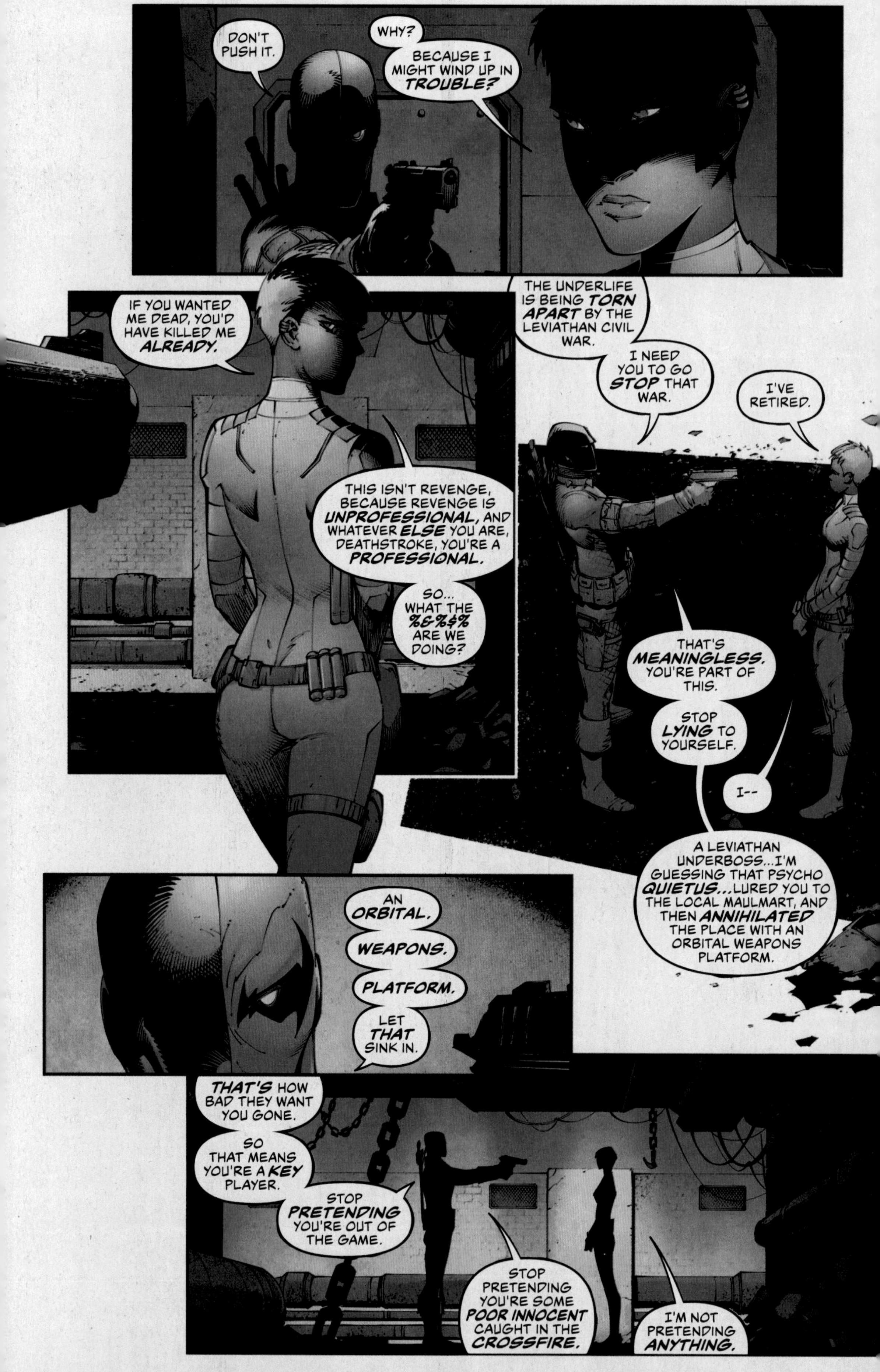

DON'T PUSH IT.
WHY?
BECAUSE I MIGHT WIND UP IN TROUBLE?
IF YOU WANTED ME DEAD, YOU'D HAVE KILLED ME ALREADY.
THIS ISN'T REVENGE, BECAUSE REVENGE IS UNPROFESSIONAL, AND WHATEVER ELSE YOU ARE, DEATHSTROKE, YOU'RE A PROFESSIONAL.
SO... WHAT THE %&%$% ARE WE DOING?
THE UNDERLIFE IS BEING TORN APART BY THE LEVIATHAN CIVIL WAR.
I NEED YOU TO GO STOP THAT WAR.
I'VE RETIRED.
THAT'S MEANINGLESS. YOU'RE PART OF THIS.
STOP LYING TO YOURSELF.
I--
A LEVIATHAN UNDERBOSS...I'M GUESSING THAT PSYCHO QUIETUS...LURED YOU TO THE LOCAL MAULMART, AND THEN ANNIHILATED THE PLACE WITH AN ORBITAL WEAPONS PLATFORM.
AN ORBITAL.
WEAPONS.
PLATFORM.
LET THAT SINK IN.
THAT'S HOW BAD THEY WANT YOU GONE.
SO THAT MEANS YOU'RE A KEY PLAYER.
STOP PRETENDING YOU'RE OUT OF THE GAME.
STOP PRETENDING YOU'RE SOME POOR INNOCENT CAUGHT IN THE CROSSFIRE.
I'M NOT PRETENDING ANYTHING.

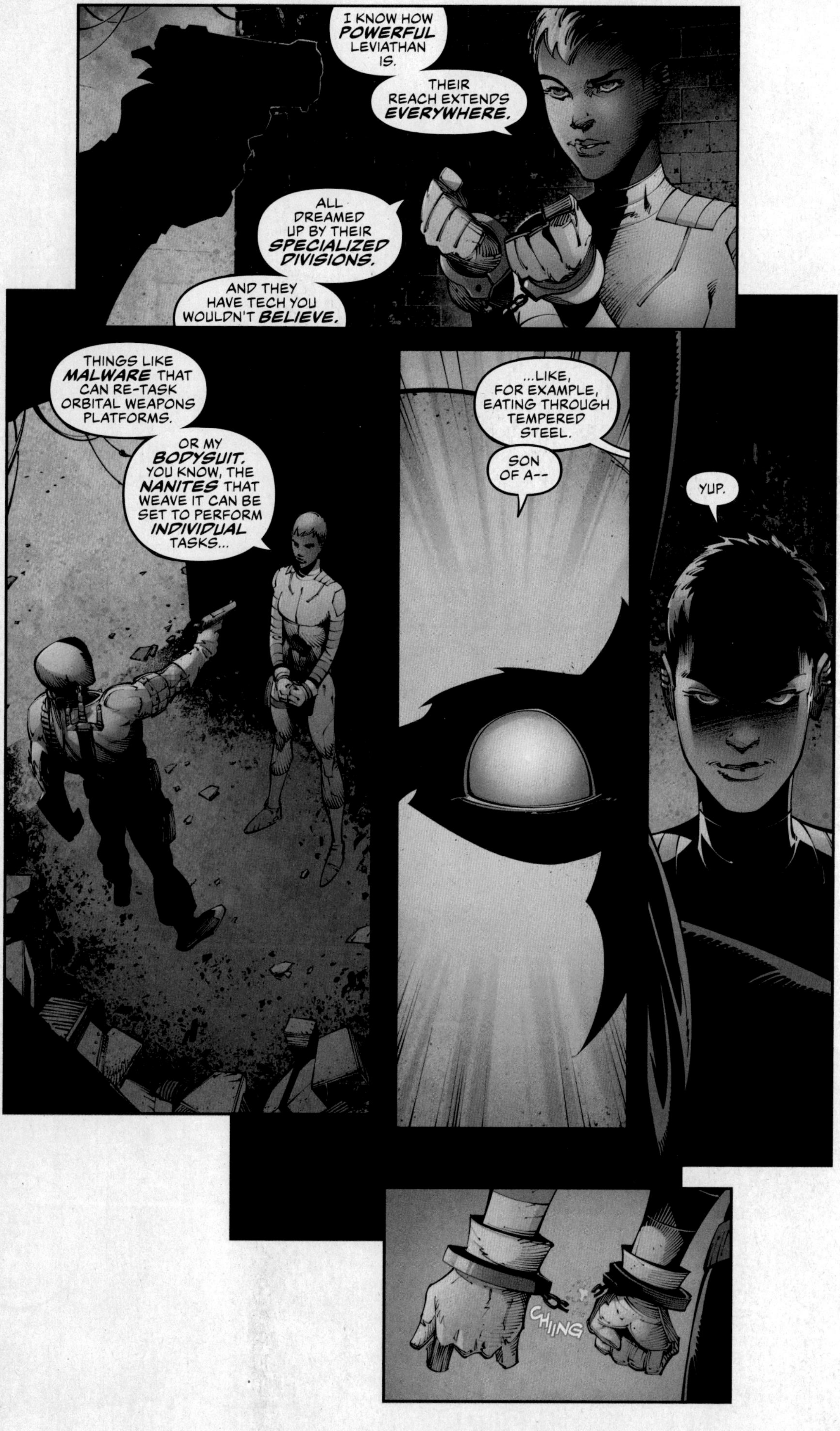

I KNOW HOW POWERFUL LEVIATHAN IS.
THEIR REACH EXTENDS EVERYWHERE.
ALL DREAMED UP BY THEIR SPECIALIZED DIVISIONS.
AND THEY HAVE TECH YOU WOULDN'T BELIEVE.
THINGS LIKE MALWARE THAT CAN RE-TASK ORBITAL WEAPONS PLATFORMS.
OR MY BODYSUIT. YOU KNOW, THE NANITES THAT WEAVE IT CAN BE SET TO PERFORM INDIVIDUAL TASKS...
...LIKE, FOR EXAMPLE, EATING THROUGH TEMPERED STEEL.
SON OF A--
YUP.
CHIING

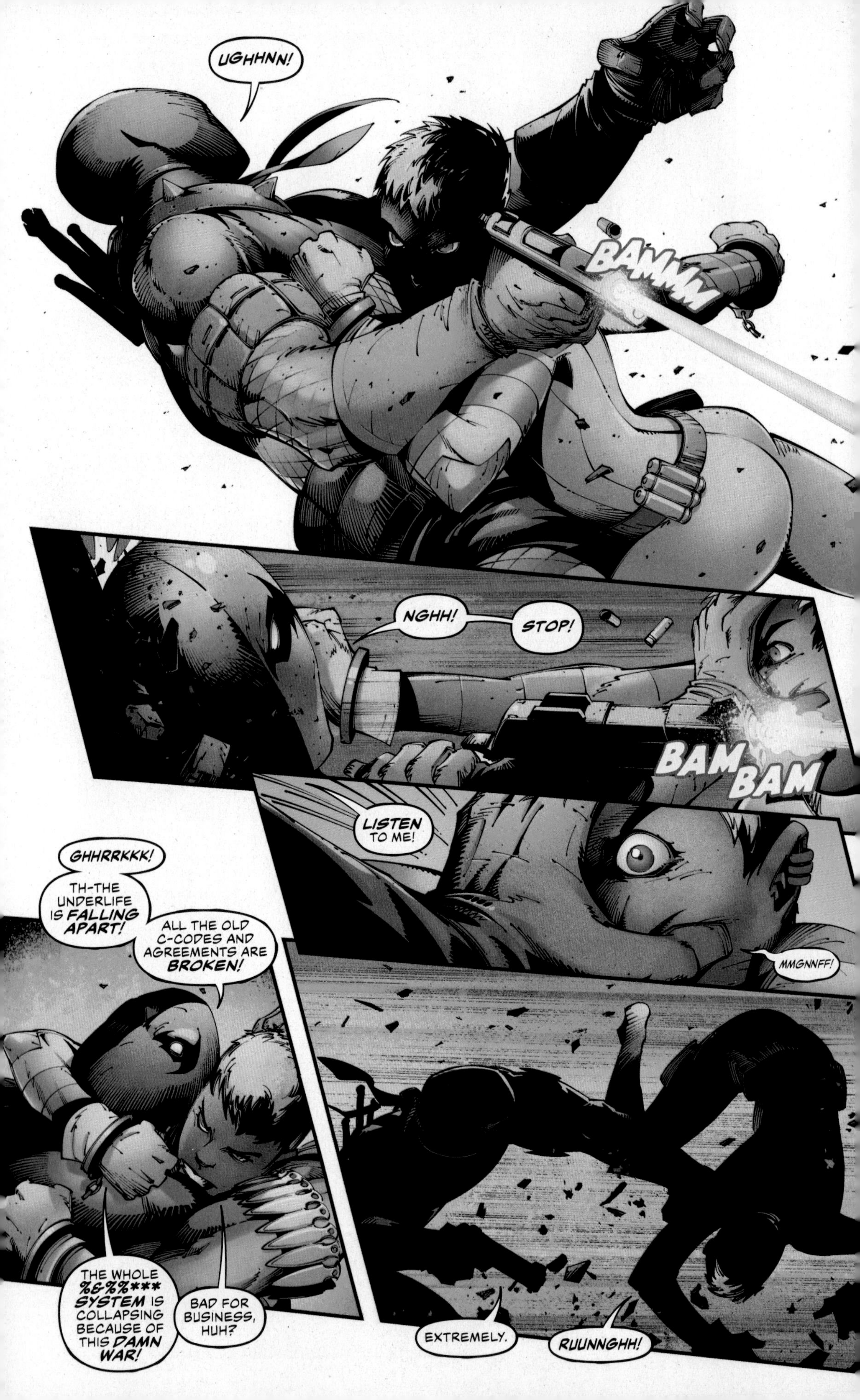
UGHHNN!
BAMMM
NGHH!
STOP!
BAM BAM
LISTEN TO ME!
MMGNNFF!
GHHRRKKK!
TH-THE UNDERLIFE IS FALLING APART!
ALL THE OLD C-CODES AND AGREEMENTS ARE BROKEN!
THE WHOLE %&%%*** SYSTEM IS COLLAPSING BECAUSE OF THIS DAMN WAR!
BAD FOR BUSINESS, HUH?
EXTREMELY.
RUUNNGHH!

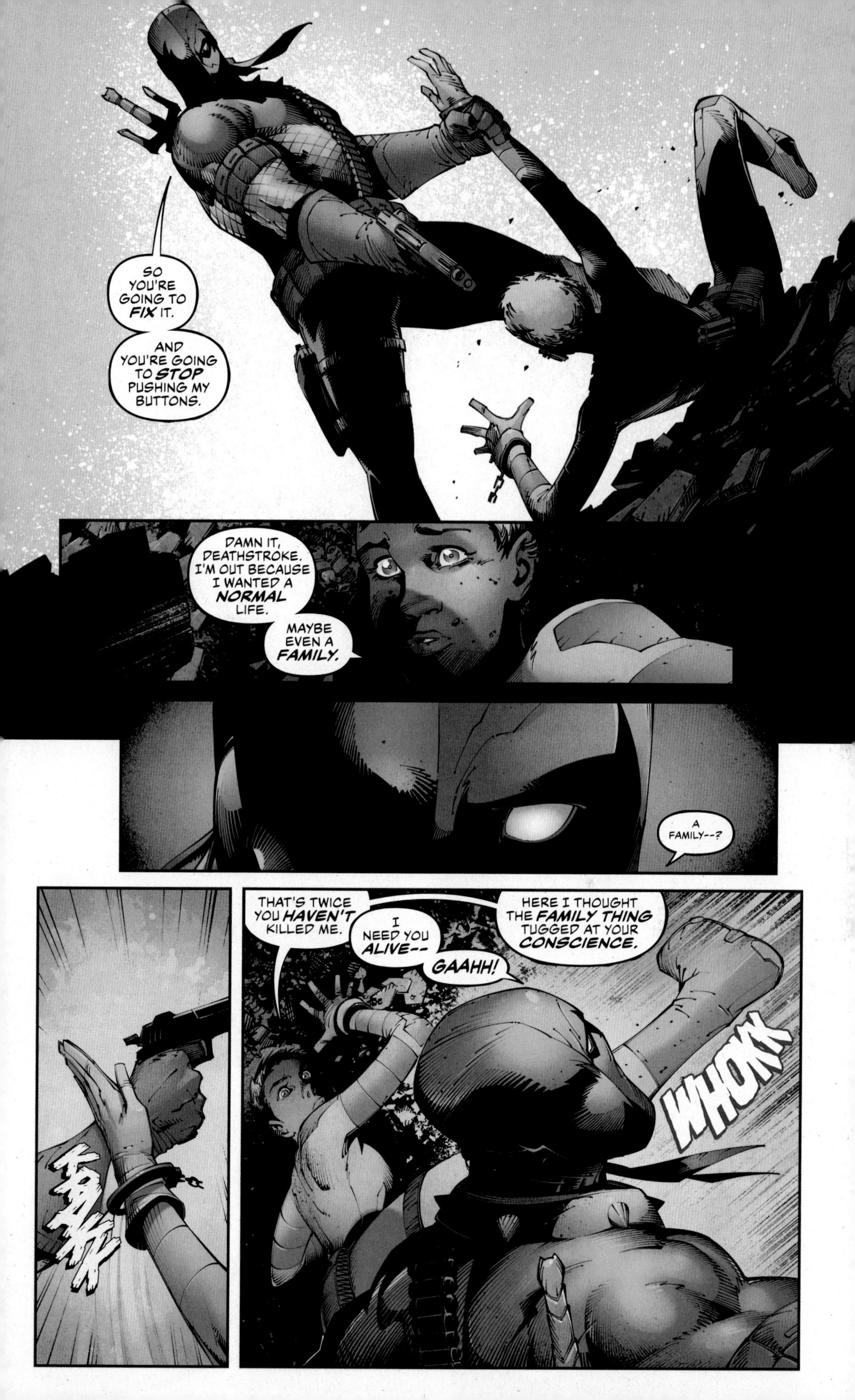

SO YOU'RE GOING TO FIX IT.
AND YOU'RE GOING TO STOP PUSHING MY BUTTONS.
DAMN IT, DEATHSTROKE. I'M OUT BECAUSE I WANTED A NORMAL LIFE.
MAYBE EVEN A FAMILY.
A FAMILY--?
THAT'S TWICE YOU HAVEN'T KILLED ME.
I NEED YOU ALIVE--
GAAHH!
HERE I THOUGHT THE FAMILY THING TUGGED AT YOUR CONSCIENCE.
WHOKK

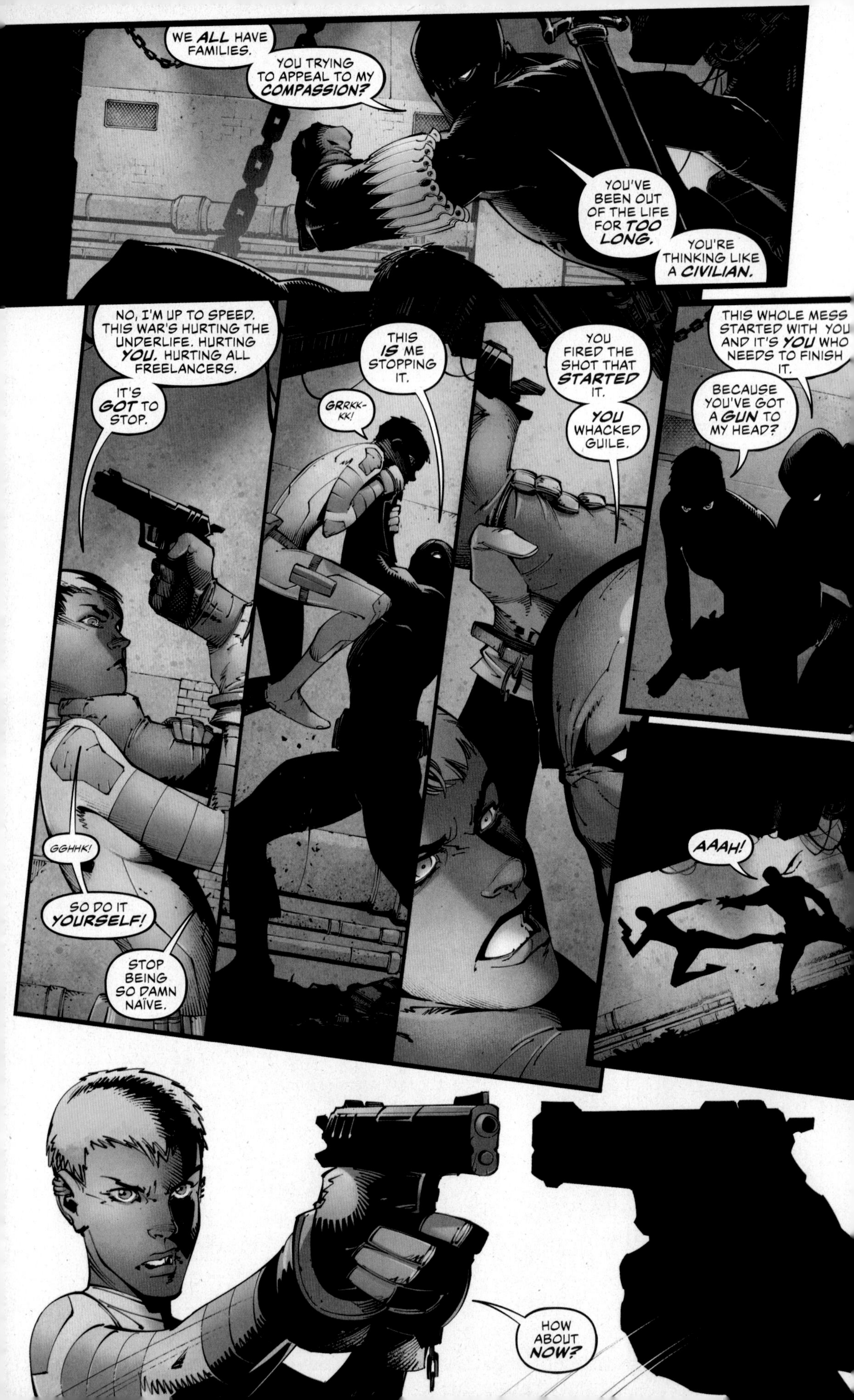
WE ALL HAVE FAMILIES.
YOU TRYING TO APPEAL TO MY COMPASSION?
YOU'VE BEEN OUT OF THE LIFE FOR TOO LONG.
YOU'RE THINKING LIKE A CIVILIAN.
NO, I'M UP TO SPEED. THIS WAR'S HURTING THE UNDERLIFE. HURTING YOU. HURTING ALL FREELANCERS.
IT'S GOT TO STOP.
GGHHK!
SO DO IT YOURSELF!
STOP BEING SO DAMN NAÏVE.
THIS IS ME STOPPING IT.
GRRKK-KK!
YOU FIRED THE SHOT THAT STARTED IT.
YOU WHACKED GUILE.
THIS WHOLE MESS STARTED WITH YOU AND IT'S YOU WHO NEEDS TO FINISH IT.
BECAUSE YOU'VE GOT A GUN TO MY HEAD?
AAAH!
HOW ABOUT NOW?

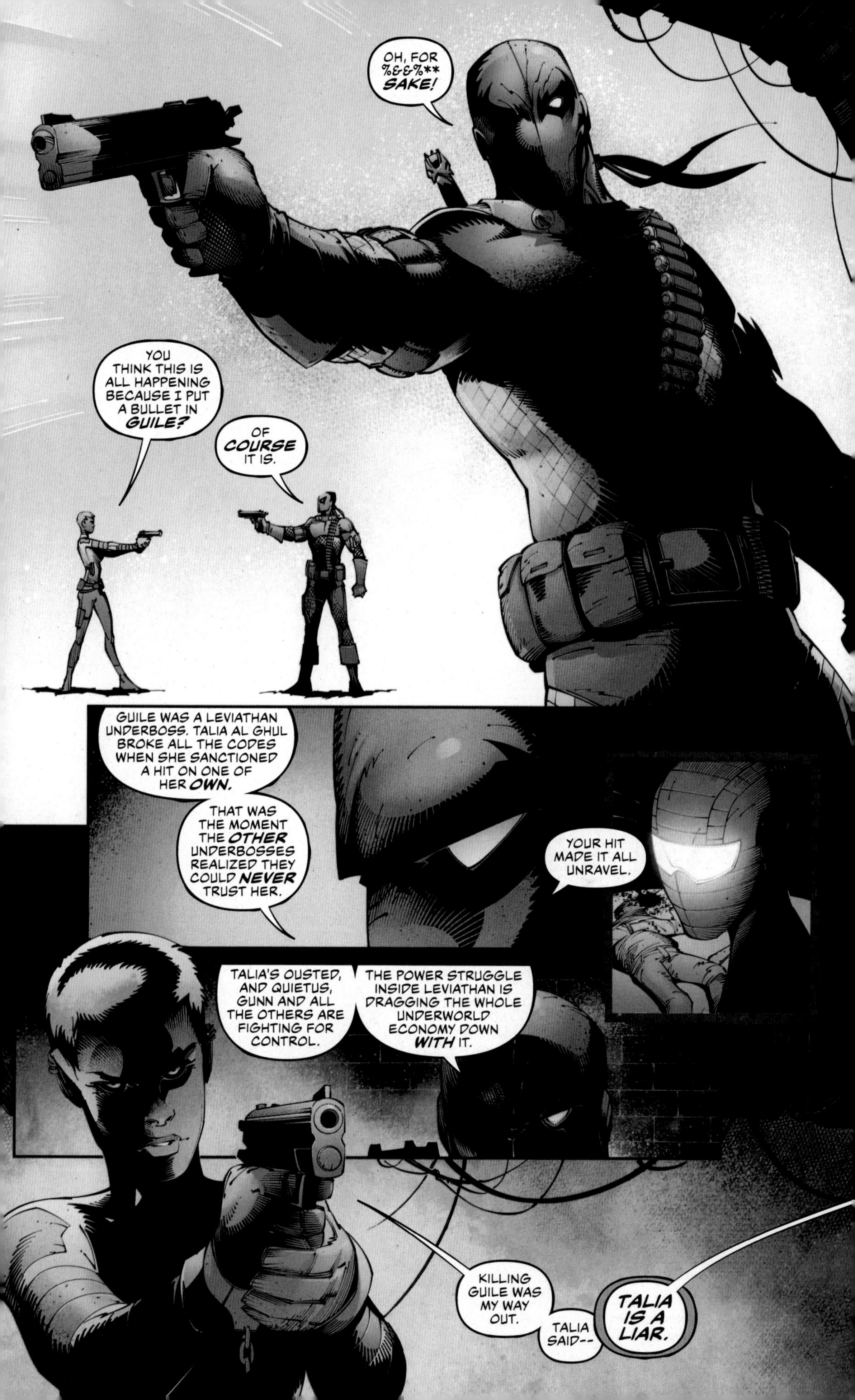
OH, FOR %&&%** SAKE!
YOU THINK THIS IS ALL HAPPENING BECAUSE I PUT A BULLET IN GUILE?
OF COURSE IT IS.
GUILE WAS A LEVIATHAN UNDERBOSS. TALIA AL GHUL BROKE ALL THE CODES WHEN SHE SANCTIONED A HIT ON ONE OF HER OWN.
THAT WAS THE MOMENT THE OTHER UNDERBOSSES REALIZED THEY COULD NEVER TRUST HER.
YOUR HIT MADE IT ALL UNRAVEL.
TALIA'S OUSTED, AND QUIETUS, GUNN AND ALL THE OTHERS ARE FIGHTING FOR CONTROL.
THE POWER STRUGGLE INSIDE LEVIATHAN IS DRAGGING THE WHOLE UNDERWORLD ECONOMY DOWN WITH IT.
KILLING GUILE WAS MY WAY OUT.
TALIA SAID--
TALIA IS A LIAR.

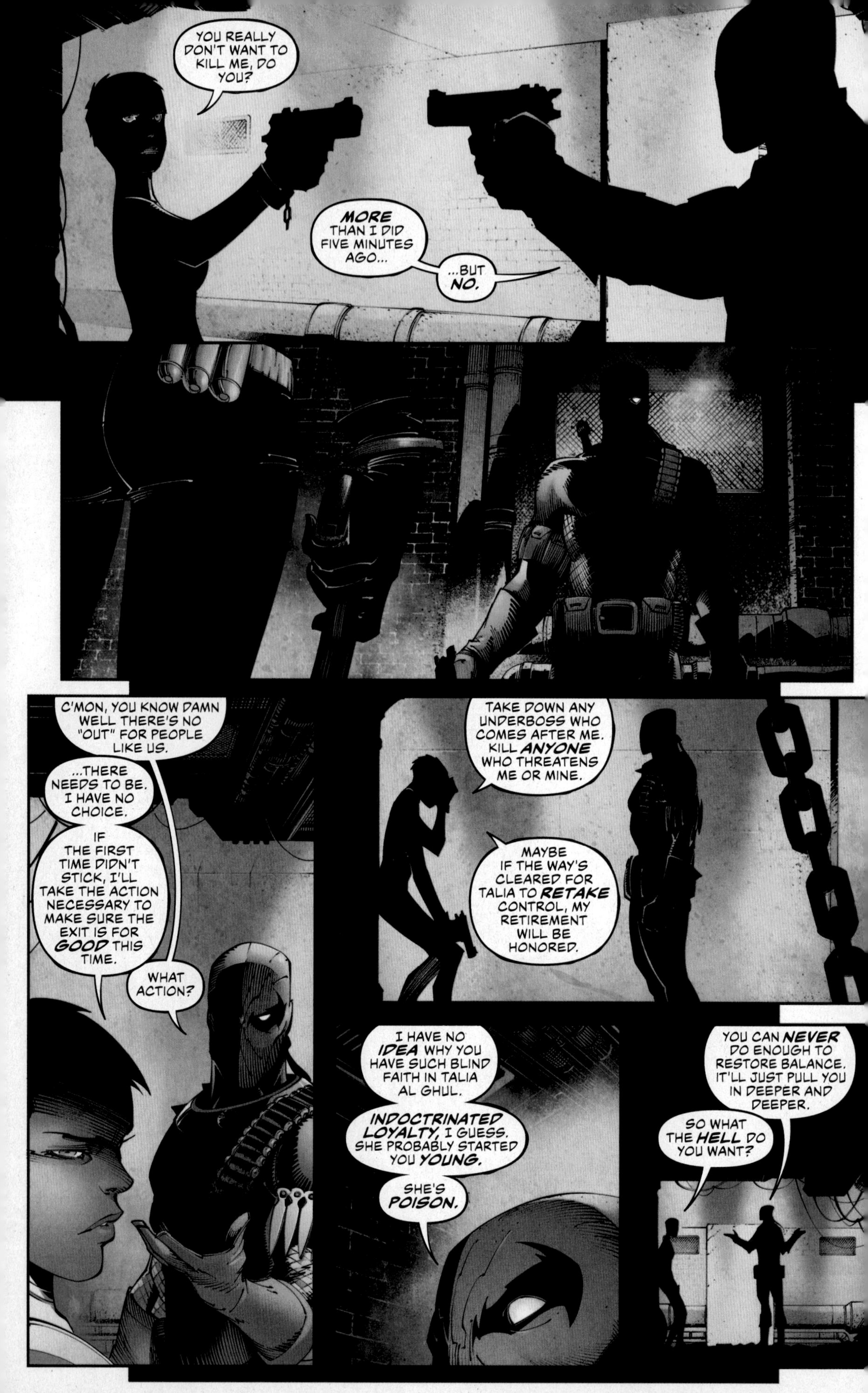
YOU REALLY DON'T WANT TO KILL ME, DO YOU?
MORE THAN I DID FIVE MINUTES AGO...
...BUT NO.
C'MON, YOU KNOW DAMN WELL THERE'S NO "OUT" FOR PEOPLE LIKE US.
...THERE NEEDS TO BE. I HAVE NO CHOICE.
IF THE FIRST TIME DIDN'T STICK, I'LL TAKE THE ACTION NECESSARY TO MAKE SURE THE EXIT IS FOR GOOD THIS TIME.
WHAT ACTION?
TAKE DOWN ANY UNDERBOSS WHO COMES AFTER ME. KILL ANYONE WHO THREATENS ME OR MINE.
MAYBE IF THE WAY'S CLEARED FOR TALIA TO RETAKE CONTROL, MY RETIREMENT WILL BE HONORED.
I HAVE NO IDEA WHY YOU HAVE SUCH BLIND FAITH IN TALIA AL GHUL.
INDOCTRINATED LOYALTY, I GUESS. SHE PROBABLY STARTED YOU YOUNG.
SHE'S POISON.
YOU CAN NEVER DO ENOUGH TO RESTORE BALANCE. IT'LL JUST PULL YOU IN DEEPER AND DEEPER.
SO WHAT THE HELL DO YOU WANT?

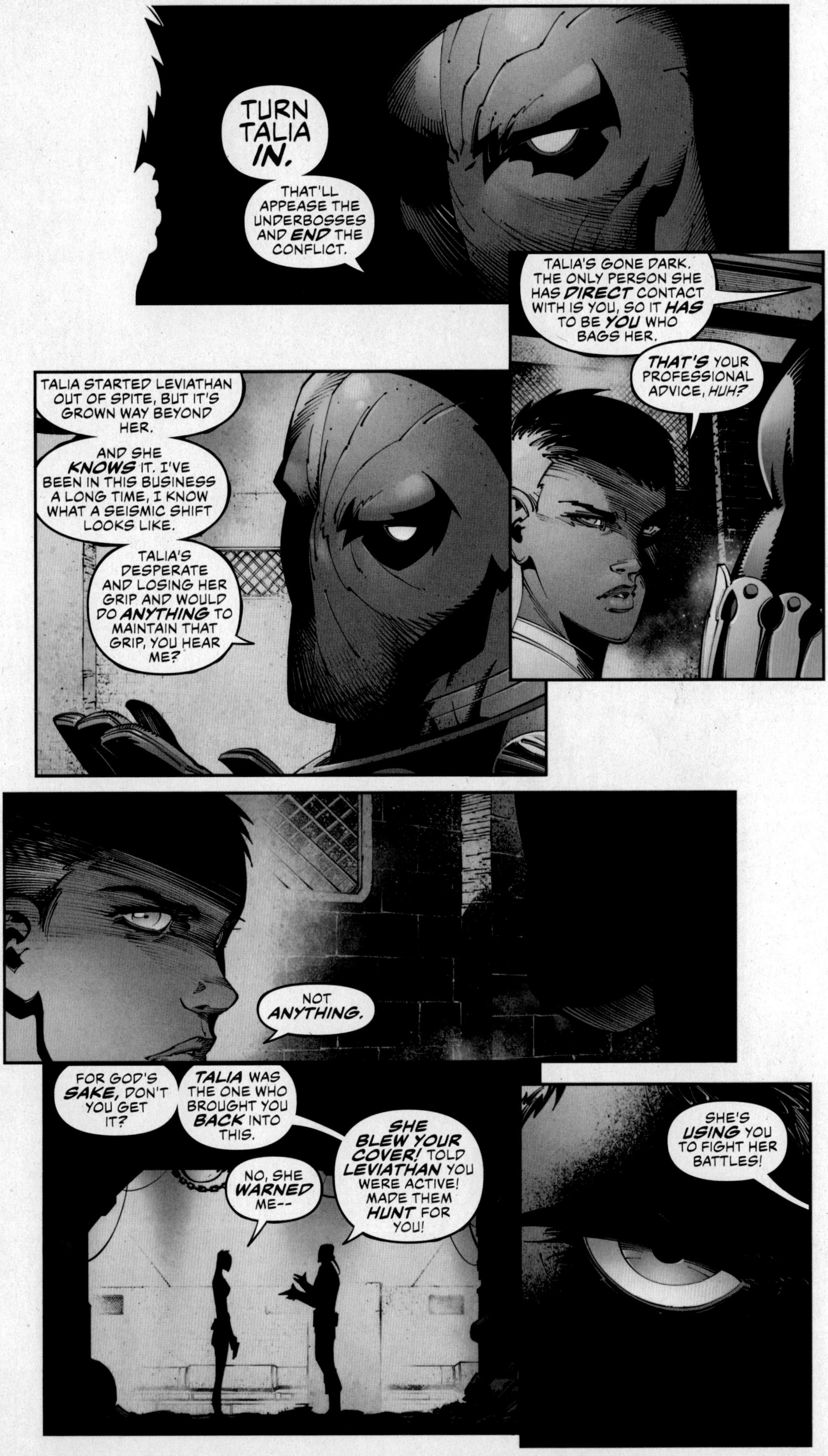

TURN TALIA IN.
THAT'LL APPEASE THE UNDERBOSSES AND END THE CONFLICT.
TALIA'S GONE DARK. THE ONLY PERSON SHE HAS DIRECT CONTACT WITH IS YOU, SO IT HAS TO BE YOU WHO BAGS HER.
THAT'S YOUR PROFESSIONAL ADVICE, HUH?
TALIA STARTED LEVIATHAN OUT OF SPITE, BUT IT'S GROWN WAY BEYOND HER.
AND SHE KNOWS IT. I'VE BEEN IN THIS BUSINESS A LONG TIME, I KNOW WHAT A SEISMIC SHIFT LOOKS LIKE.
TALIA'S DESPERATE AND LOSING HER GRIP AND WOULD DO ANYTHING TO MAINTAIN THAT GRIP, YOU HEAR ME?
NOT ANYTHING.
FOR GOD'S SAKE, DON'T YOU GET IT?
TALIA WAS THE ONE WHO BROUGHT YOU BACK INTO THIS.
NO, SHE WARNED ME--
SHE BLEW YOUR COVER! TOLD LEVIATHAN YOU WERE ACTIVE! MADE THEM HUNT FOR YOU!
SHE'S USING YOU TO FIGHT HER BATTLES!

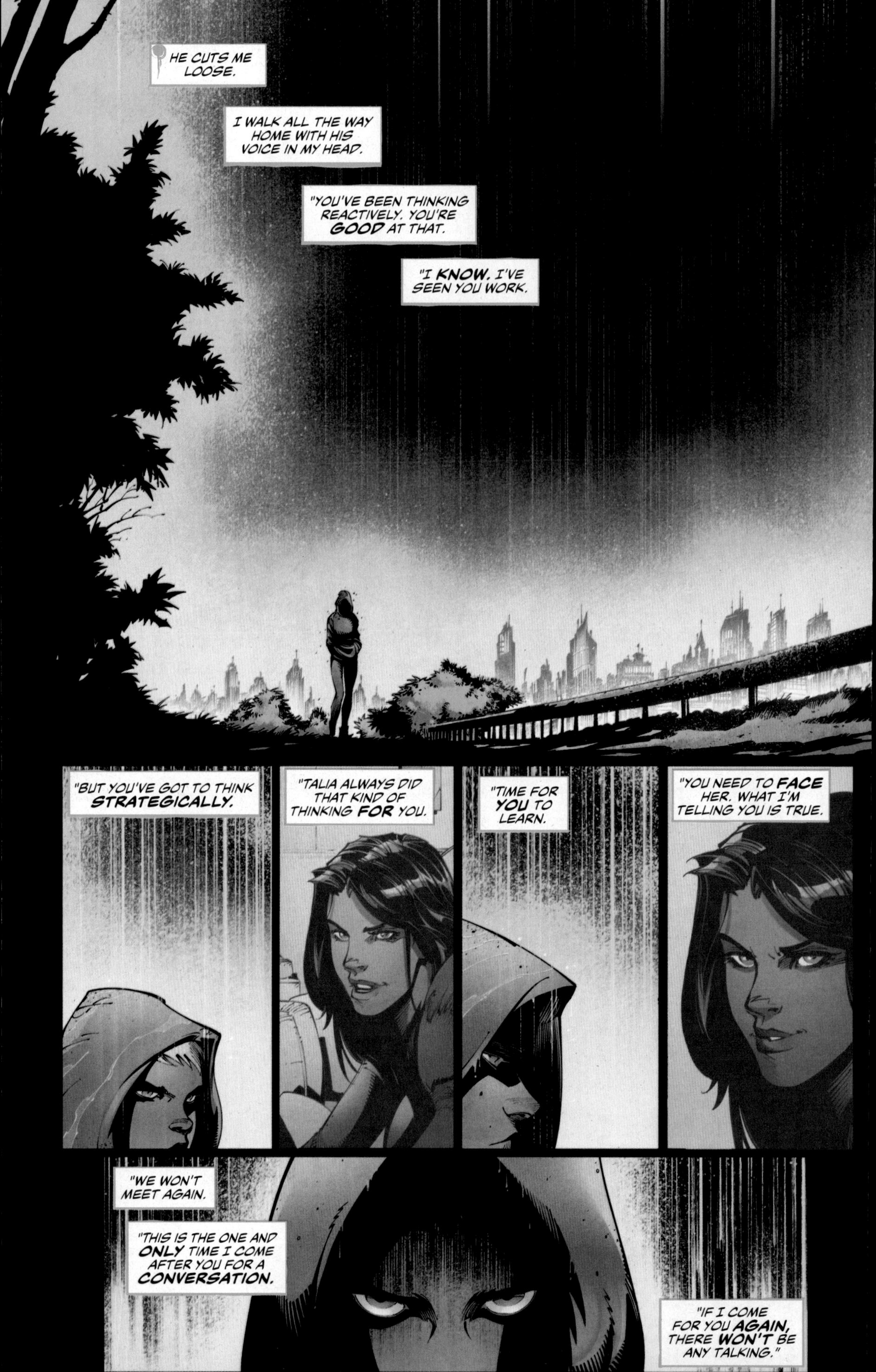
HE CUTS ME LOOSE.
I WALK ALL THE WAY HOME WITH HIS VOICE IN MY HEAD.
"YOU'VE BEEN THINKING REACTIVELY. YOU'RE GOOD AT THAT.
"I KNOW. I'VE SEEN YOU WORK.
"BUT YOU'VE GOT TO THINK STRATEGICALLY.
"TALIA ALWAYS DID THAT KIND OF THINKING FOR YOU.
"TIME FOR YOU TO LEARN.
"YOU NEED TO FACE HER. WHAT I'M TELLING YOU IS TRUE.
"WE WON'T MEET AGAIN.
"THIS IS THE ONE AND ONLY TIME I COME AFTER YOU FOR A CONVERSATION.
"IF I COME FOR YOU AGAIN, THERE WON'T BE ANY TALKING."

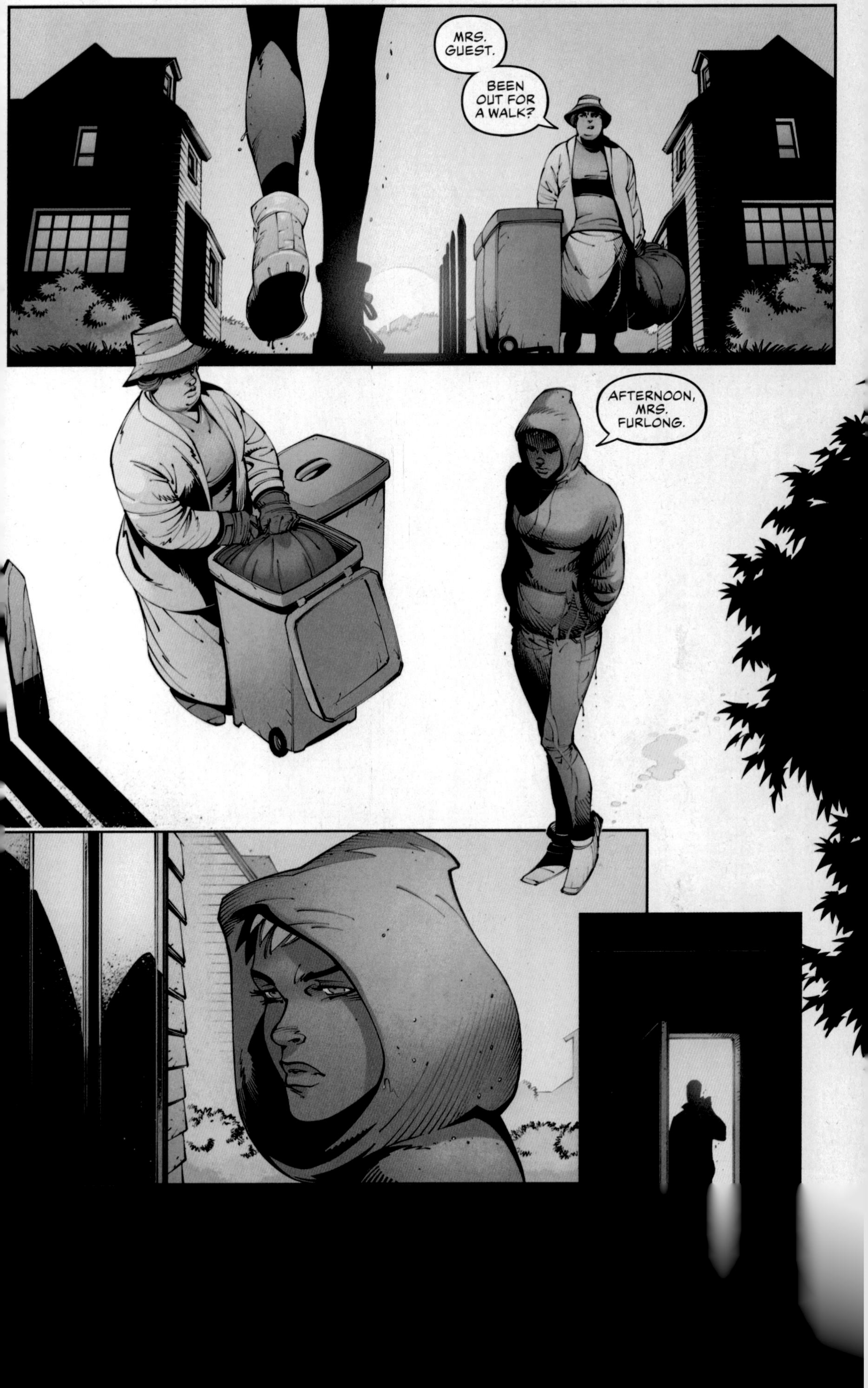
MRS. GUEST.
BEEN OUT FOR A WALK?
AFTERNOON, MRS. FURLONG.

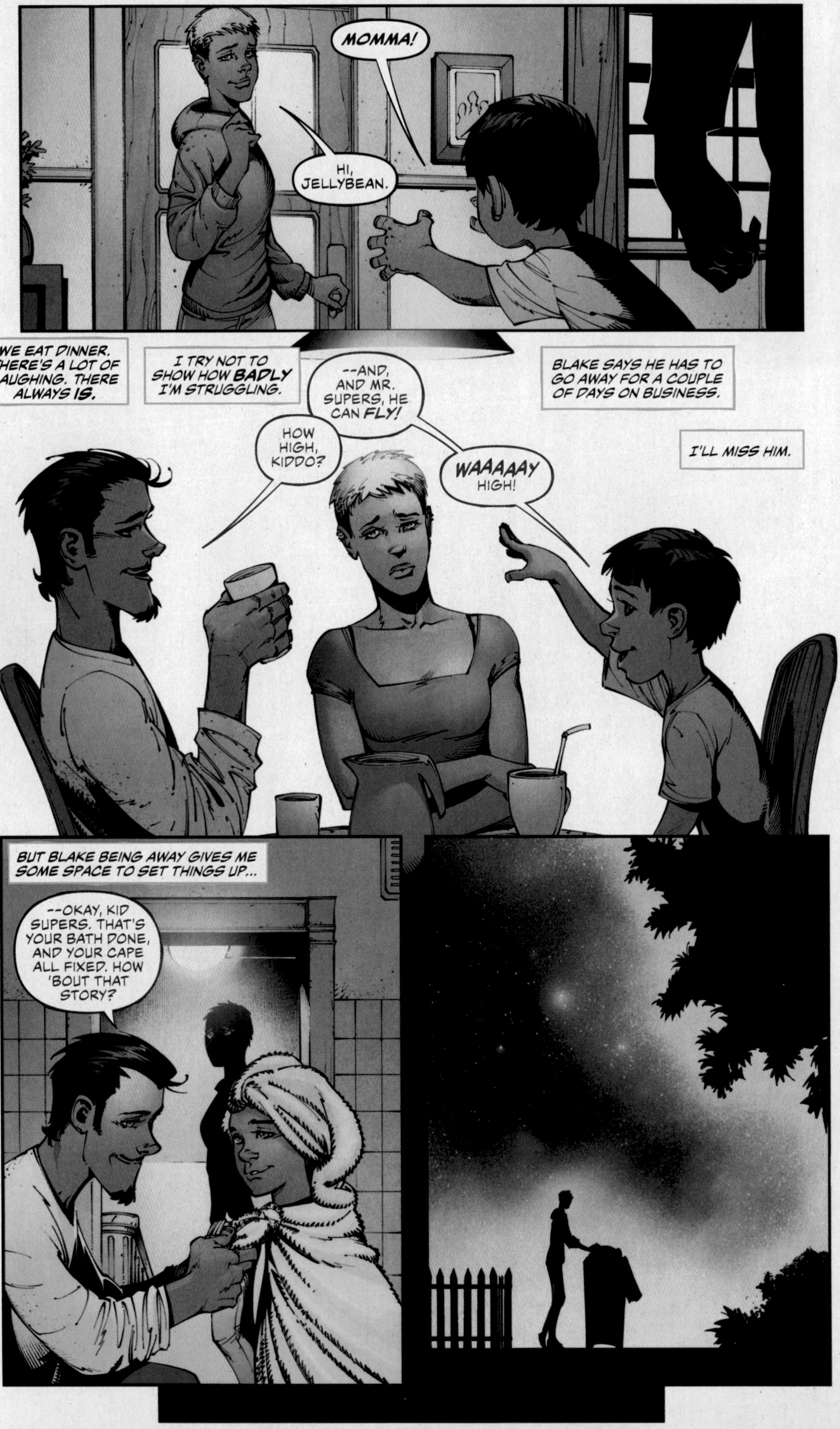
MOMMA!
HI, JELLYBEAN.
WE EAT DINNER. THERE'S A LOT OF LAUGHING. THERE ALWAYS IS.
I TRY NOT TO SHOW HOW BADLY I'M STRUGGLING.
--AND, AND MR. SUPERS, HE CAN FLY!
HOW HIGH, KIDDO?
WAAAAAY HIGH!
BLAKE SAYS HE HAS TO GO AWAY FOR A COUPLE OF DAYS ON BUSINESS.
I'LL MISS HIM.
BUT BLAKE BEING AWAY GIVES ME SOME SPACE TO SET THINGS UP...
--OKAY, KID SUPERS. THAT'S YOUR BATH DONE, AND YOUR CAPE ALL FIXED. HOW 'BOUT THAT STORY?

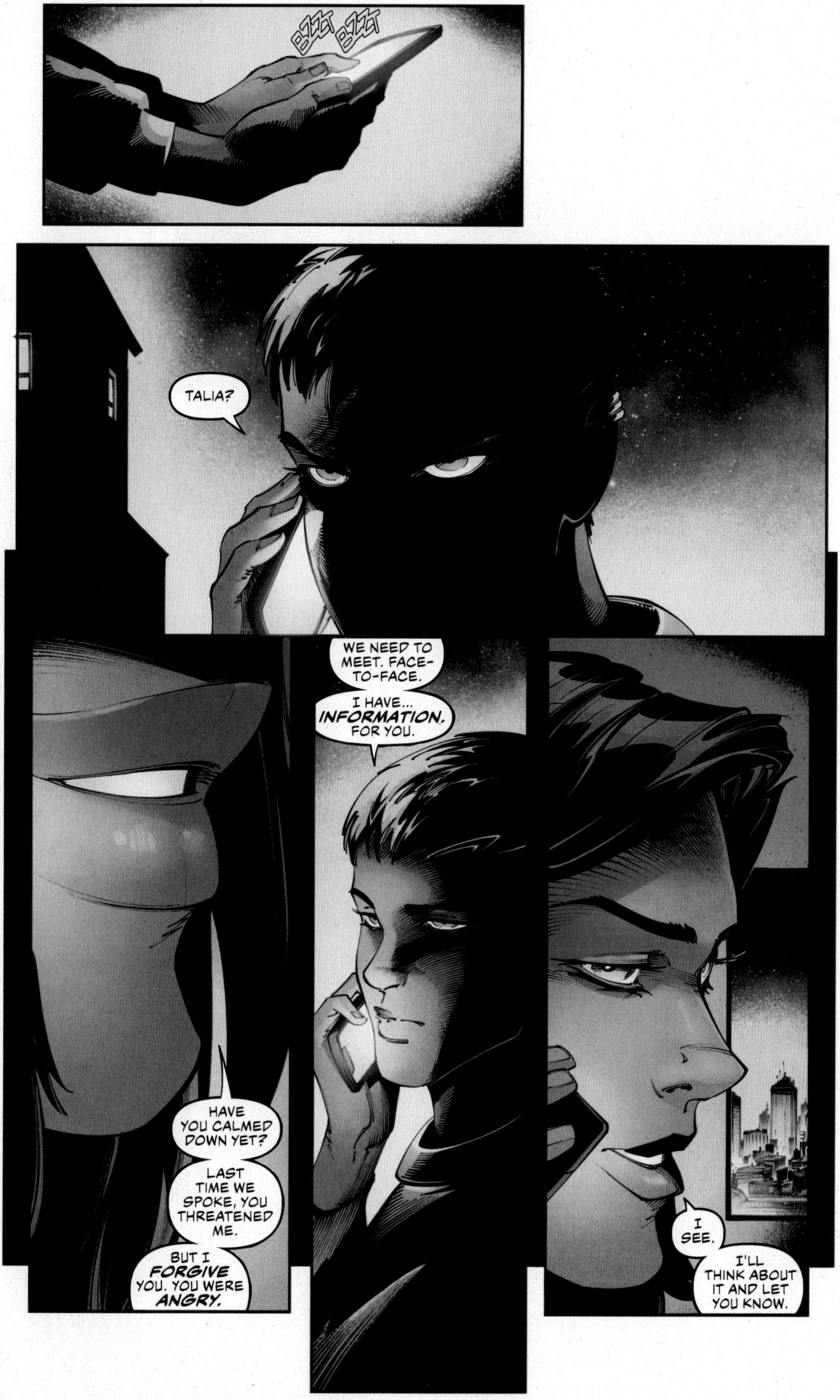
BZZT BZZT
TALIA?
HAVE YOU CALMED DOWN YET?
LAST TIME WE SPOKE, YOU THREATENED ME.
BUT I **FORGIVE** YOU. YOU WERE **ANGRY.**
WE NEED TO MEET. FACE-TO-FACE.
I HAVE... ***INFORMATION.*** FOR YOU.
I SEE.
I'LL THINK ABOUT IT AND LET YOU KNOW.

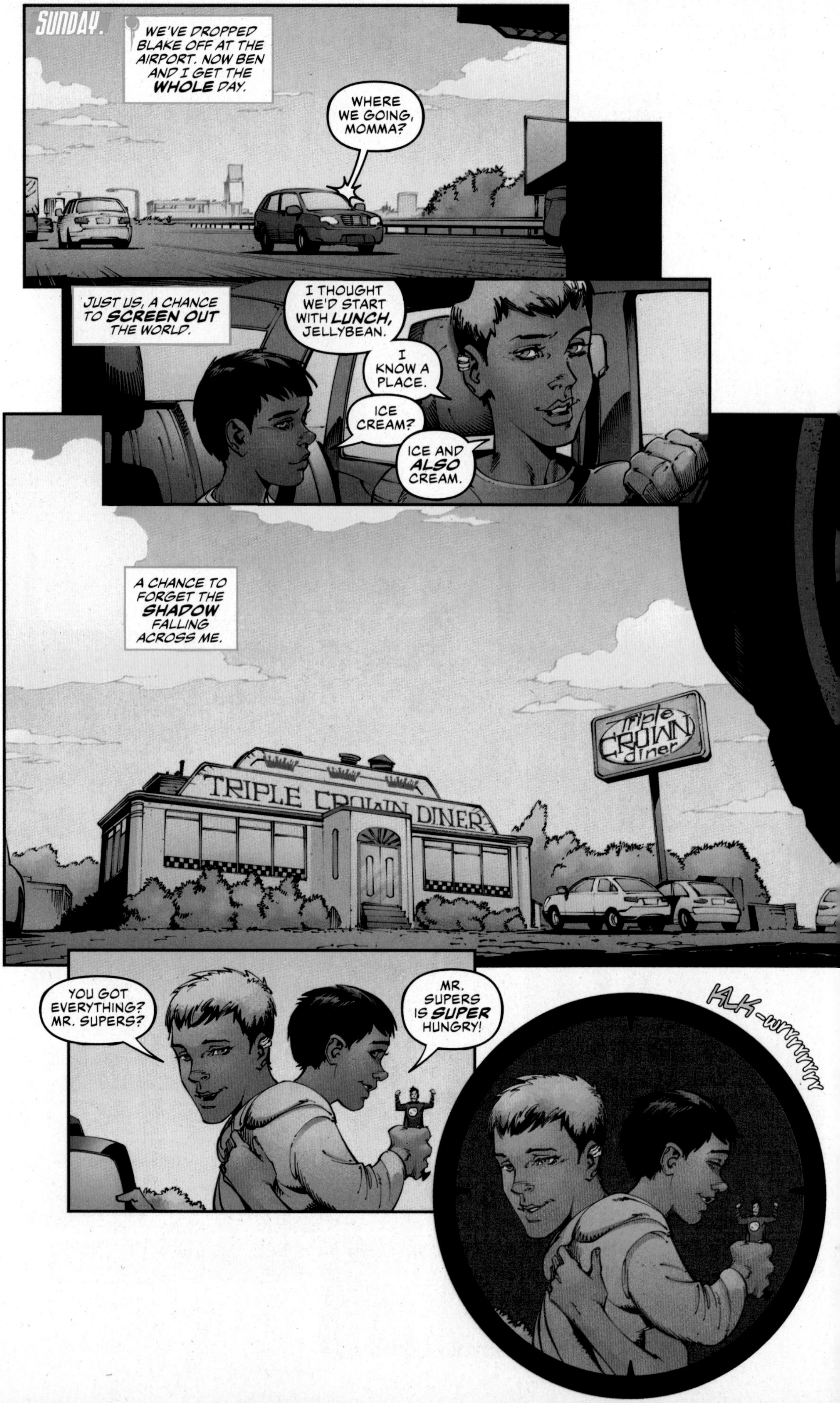
SUNDAY.
WE'VE DROPPED BLAKE OFF AT THE AIRPORT. NOW BEN AND I GET THE WHOLE DAY.
WHERE WE GOING, MOMMA?
JUST US, A CHANCE TO SCREEN OUT THE WORLD.
I THOUGHT WE'D START WITH LUNCH, JELLYBEAN.
I KNOW A PLACE.
ICE CREAM?
ICE AND ALSO CREAM.
A CHANCE TO FORGET THE SHADOW FALLING ACROSS ME.
TRIPLE CROWN DINER
Triple CROWN diner
YOU GOT EVERYTHING? MR. SUPERS?
MR. SUPERS IS SUPER HUNGRY!
KLK-wrrrrrrr

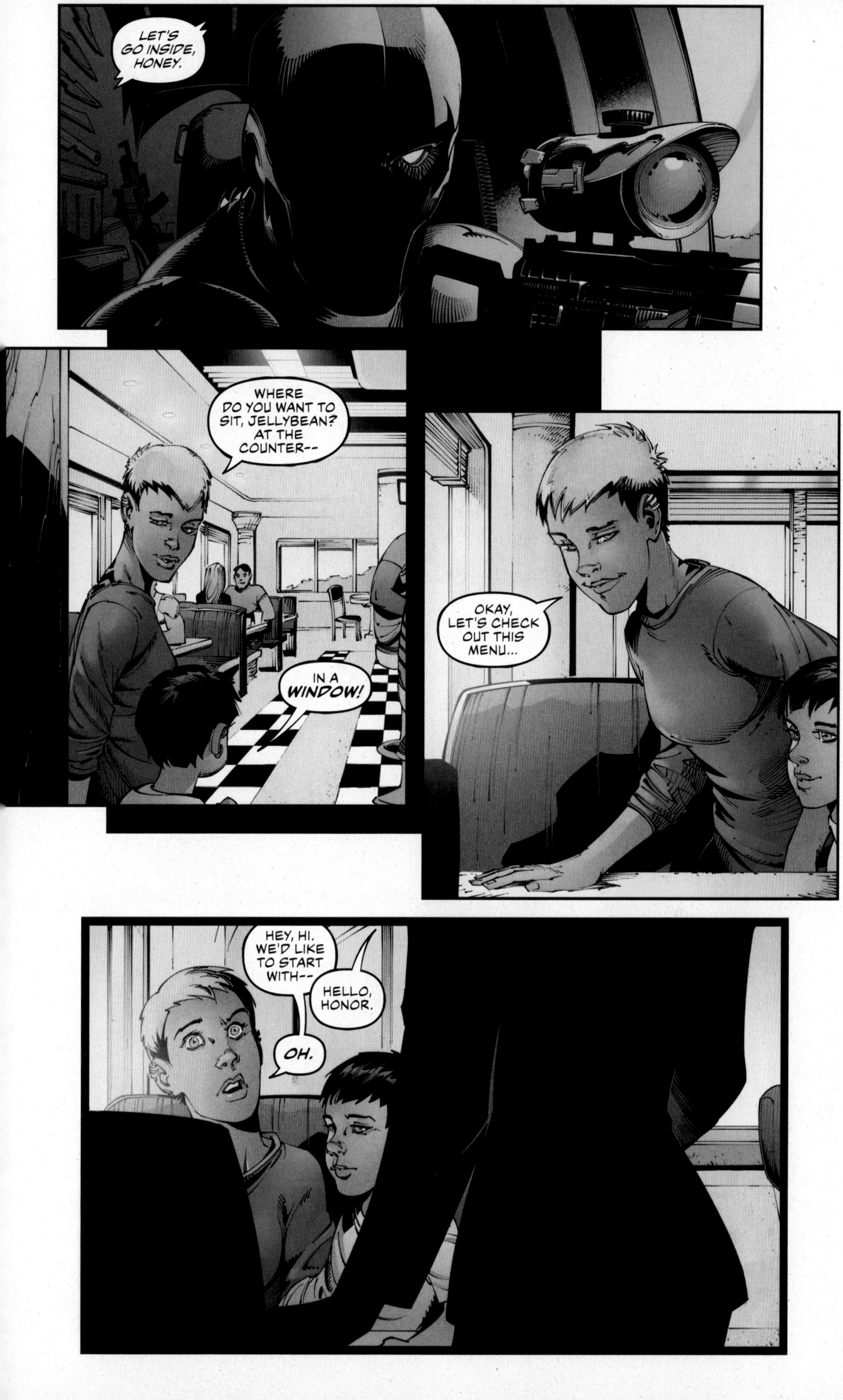
LET'S GO INSIDE, HONEY.
WHERE DO YOU WANT TO SIT, JELLYBEAN? AT THE COUNTER--
IN A WINDOW!
OKAY, LET'S CHECK OUT THIS MENU...
HEY, HI. WE'D LIKE TO START WITH--
HELLO, HONOR.
OH.

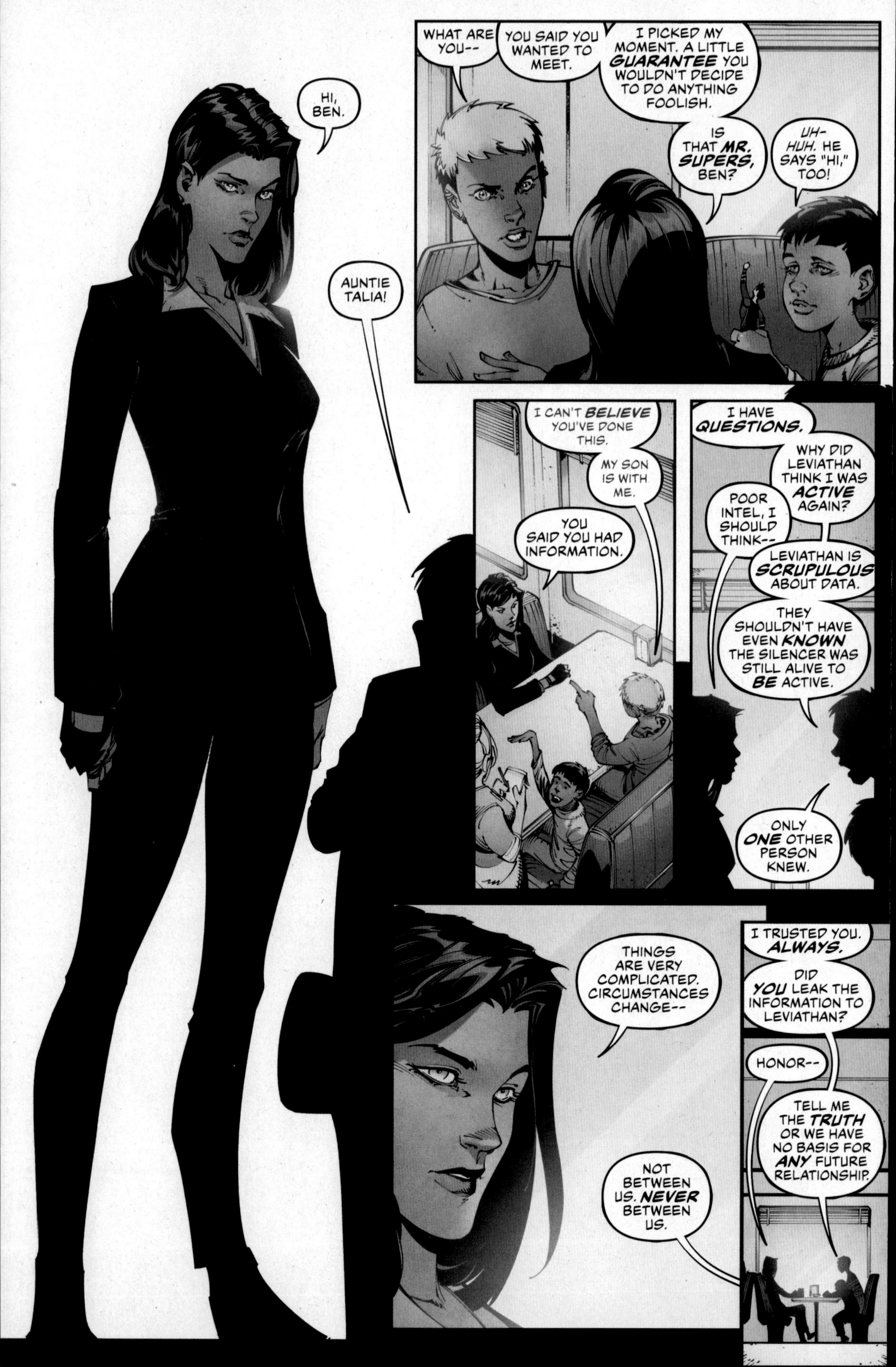
HI, BEN.
AUNTIE TALIA!
WHAT ARE YOU--
YOU SAID YOU WANTED TO MEET.
I PICKED MY MOMENT. A LITTLE GUARANTEE YOU WOULDN'T DECIDE TO DO ANYTHING FOOLISH.
IS THAT MR. SUPERS, BEN?
UH-HUH. HE SAYS "HI," TOO!
I CAN'T BELIEVE YOU'VE DONE THIS.
MY SON IS WITH ME.
YOU SAID YOU HAD INFORMATION.
I HAVE QUESTIONS.
WHY DID LEVIATHAN THINK I WAS ACTIVE AGAIN?
POOR INTEL, I SHOULD THINK--
LEVIATHAN IS SCRUPULOUS ABOUT DATA.
THEY SHOULDN'T HAVE EVEN KNOWN THE SILENCER WAS STILL ALIVE TO BE ACTIVE.
ONLY ONE OTHER PERSON KNEW.
THINGS ARE VERY COMPLICATED. CIRCUMSTANCES CHANGE--
I TRUSTED YOU. ALWAYS.
DID YOU LEAK THE INFORMATION TO LEVIATHAN?
HONOR--
TELL ME THE TRUTH OR WE HAVE NO BASIS FOR ANY FUTURE RELATIONSHIP.
NOT BETWEEN US. NEVER BETWEEN US.

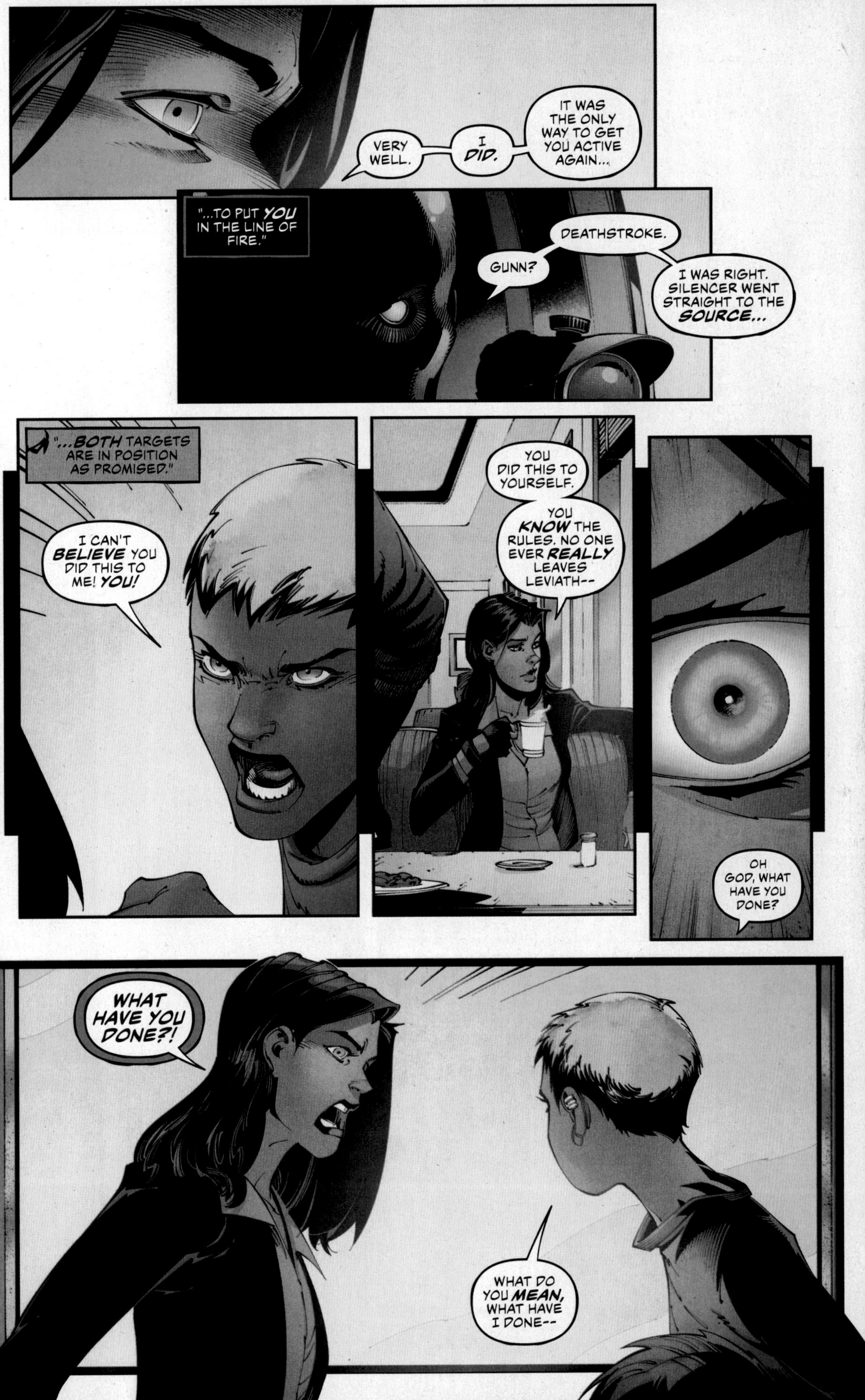

VERY WELL.
I DID.
IT WAS THE ONLY WAY TO GET YOU ACTIVE AGAIN...
"...TO PUT YOU IN THE LINE OF FIRE."
GUNN?
DEATHSTROKE.
I WAS RIGHT. SILENCER WENT STRAIGHT TO THE SOURCE...
"...BOTH TARGETS ARE IN POSITION AS PROMISED."
I CAN'T BELIEVE YOU DID THIS TO ME! YOU!
YOU DID THIS TO YOURSELF.
YOU KNOW THE RULES. NO ONE EVER REALLY LEAVES LEVIATH--
OH GOD, WHAT HAVE YOU DONE?
WHAT HAVE YOU DONE?!
WHAT DO YOU MEAN, WHAT HAVE I DONE--

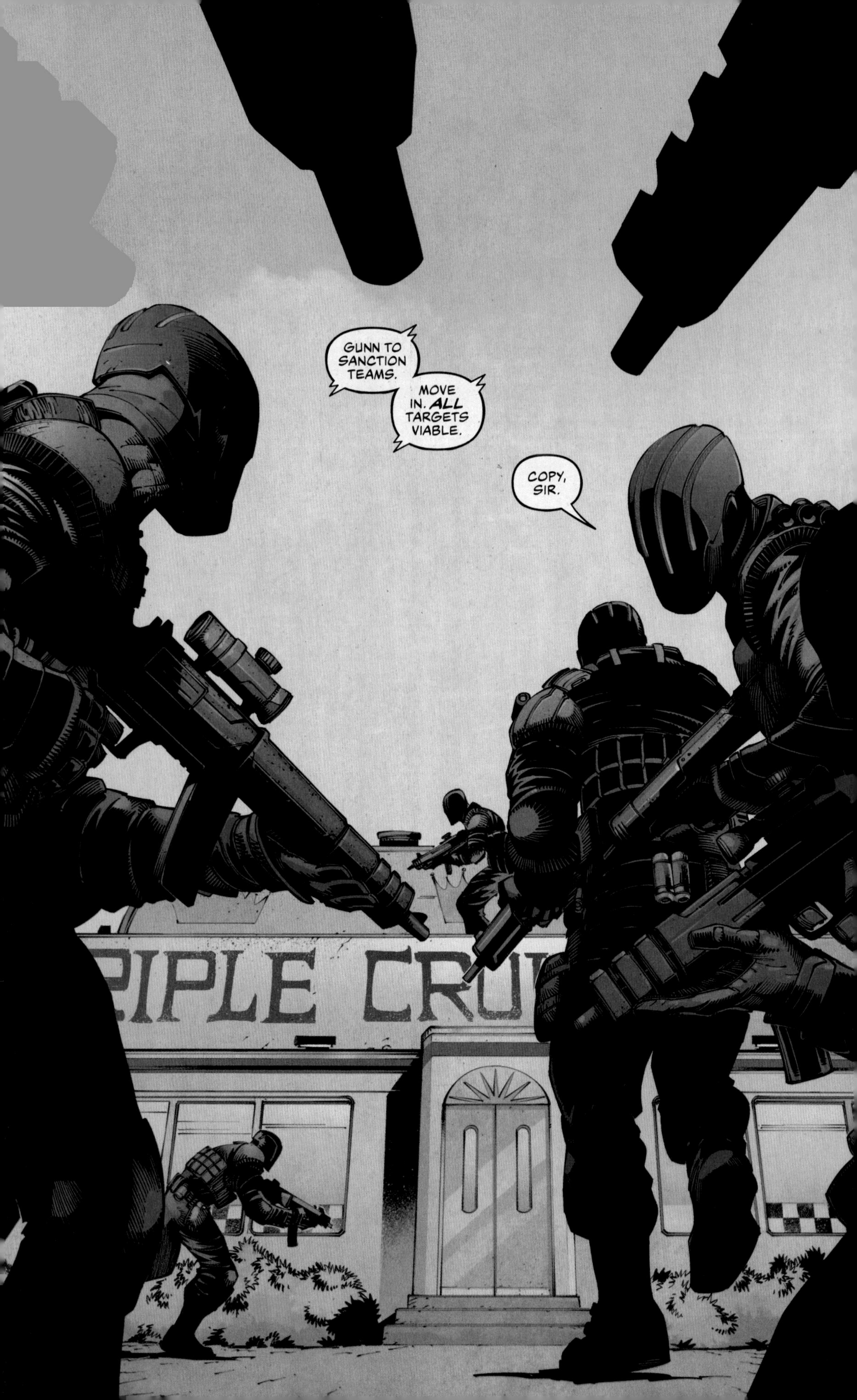
GUNN TO SANCTION TEAMS.
MOVE IN. ALL TARGETS VIABLE.
COPY, SIR.
IPLE CRU

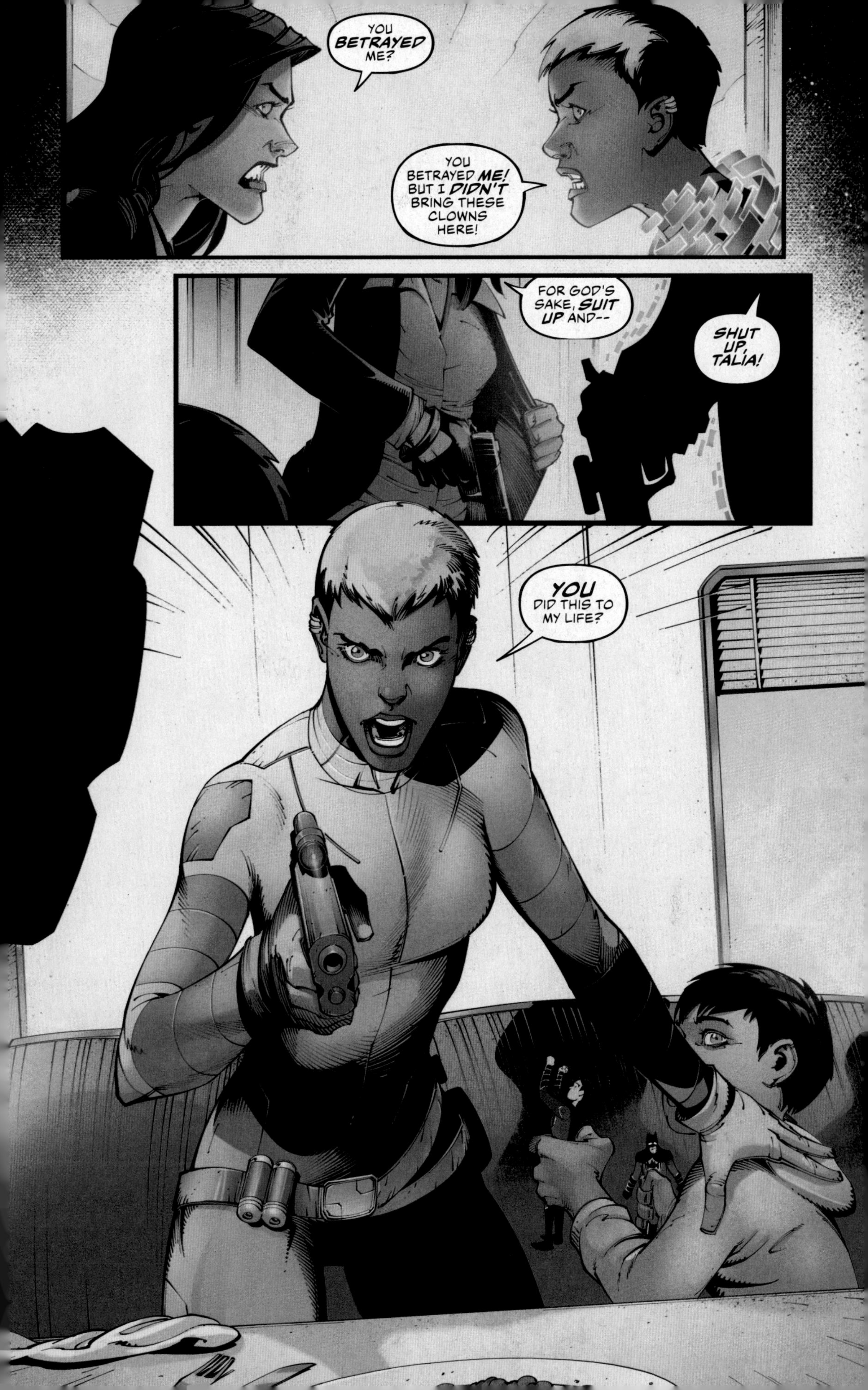
YOU BETRAYED ME?
YOU BETRAYED ME! BUT I DIDN'T BRING THESE CLOWNS HERE!
FOR GOD'S SAKE, SUIT UP AND--
SHUT UP, TALIA!
YOU DID THIS TO MY LIFE?

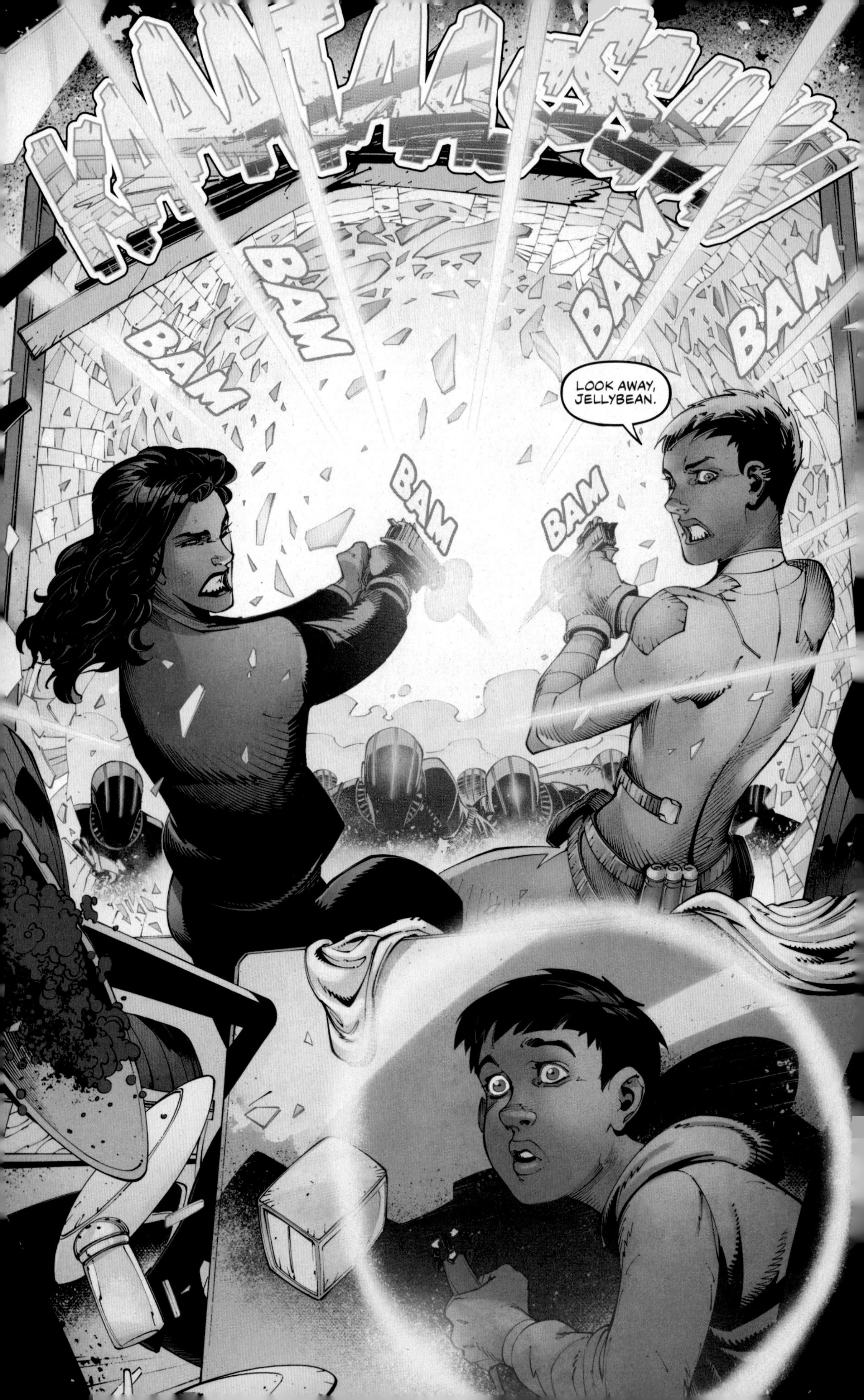
BAM
BAM
BAM
BAM
LOOK AWAY, JELLYBEAN.
BAM
BAM
BAM

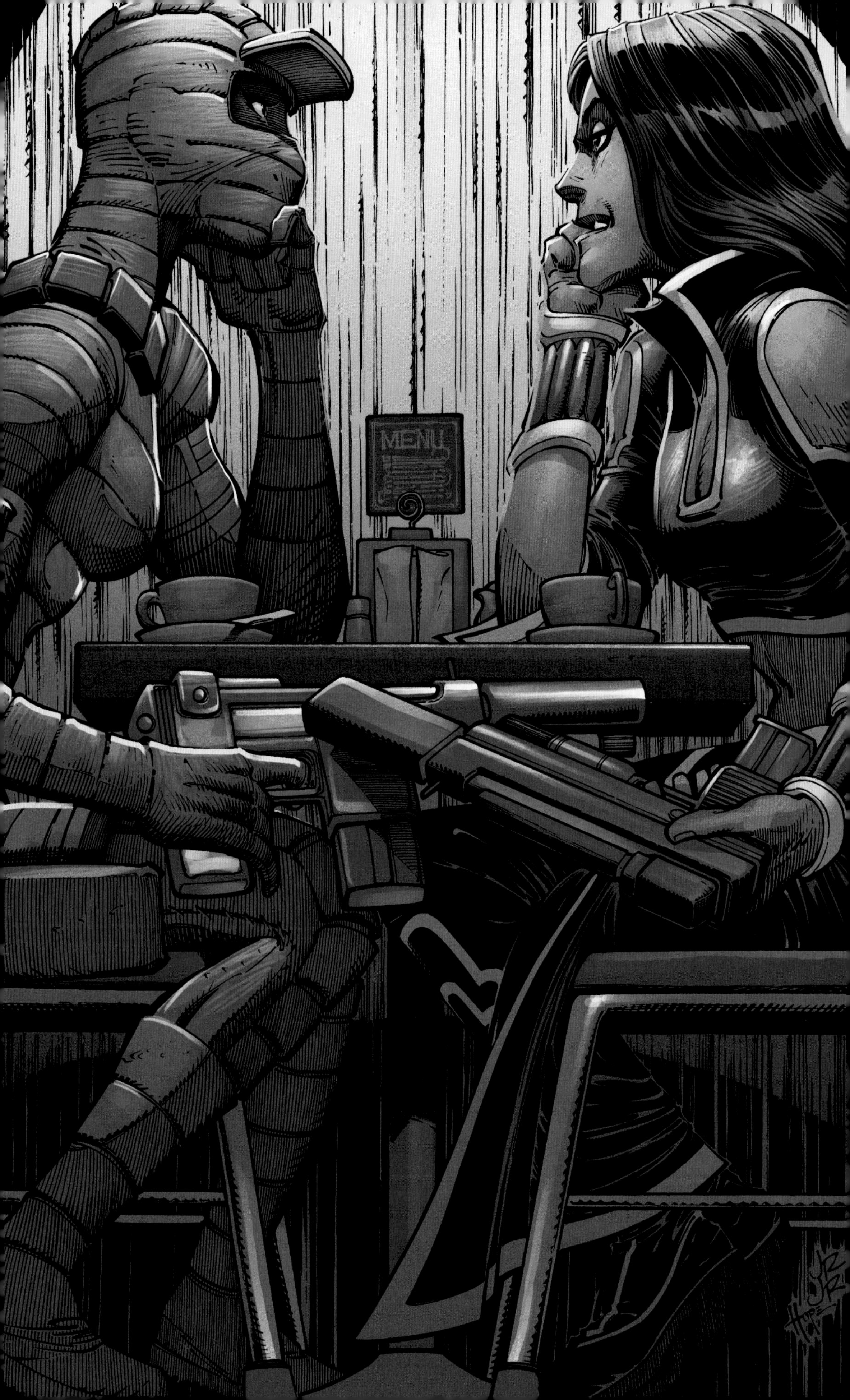
MENU

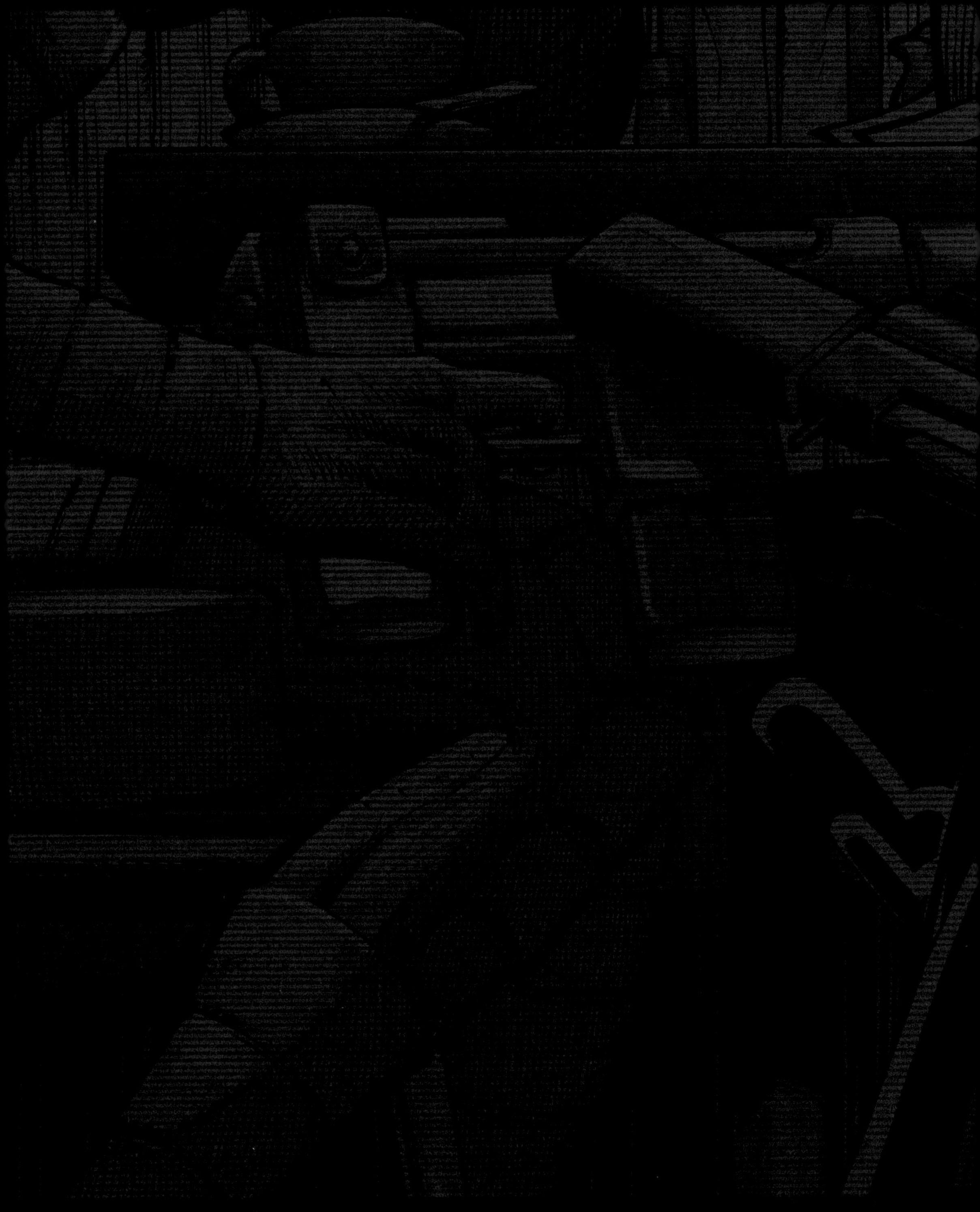

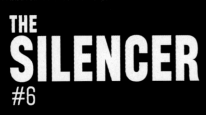

THE SILENCER
#6

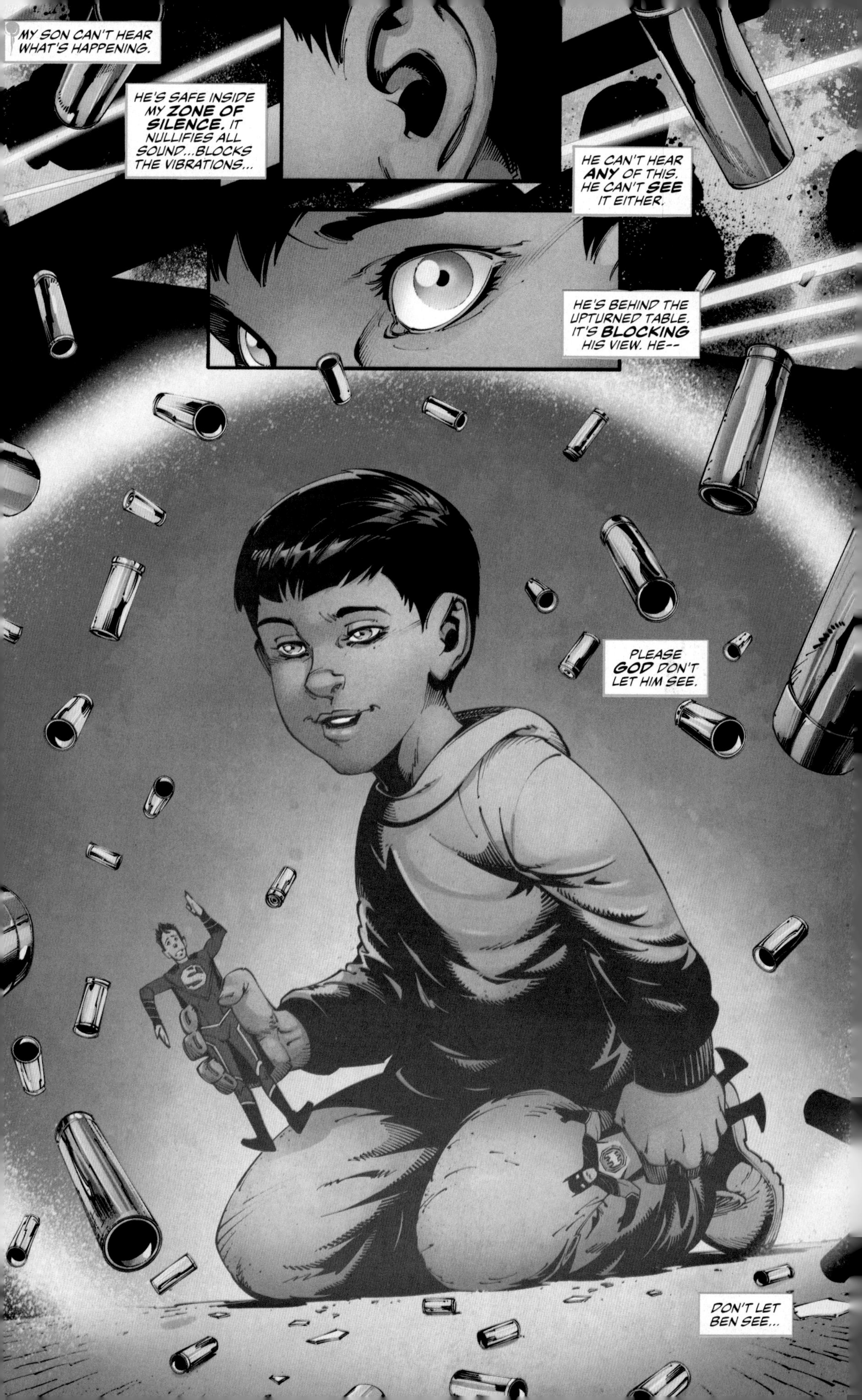
MY SON CAN'T HEAR WHAT'S HAPPENING.
HE'S SAFE INSIDE MY **ZONE OF SILENCE.** IT NULLIFIES ALL SOUND...BLOCKS THE VIBRATIONS...
HE CAN'T HEAR **ANY** OF THIS. HE CAN'T **SEE** IT EITHER.
HE'S BEHIND THE UPTURNED TABLE. IT'S **BLOCKING** HIS VIEW. HE--
PLEASE **GOD** DON'T LET HIM SEE.
DON'T LET BEN SEE...

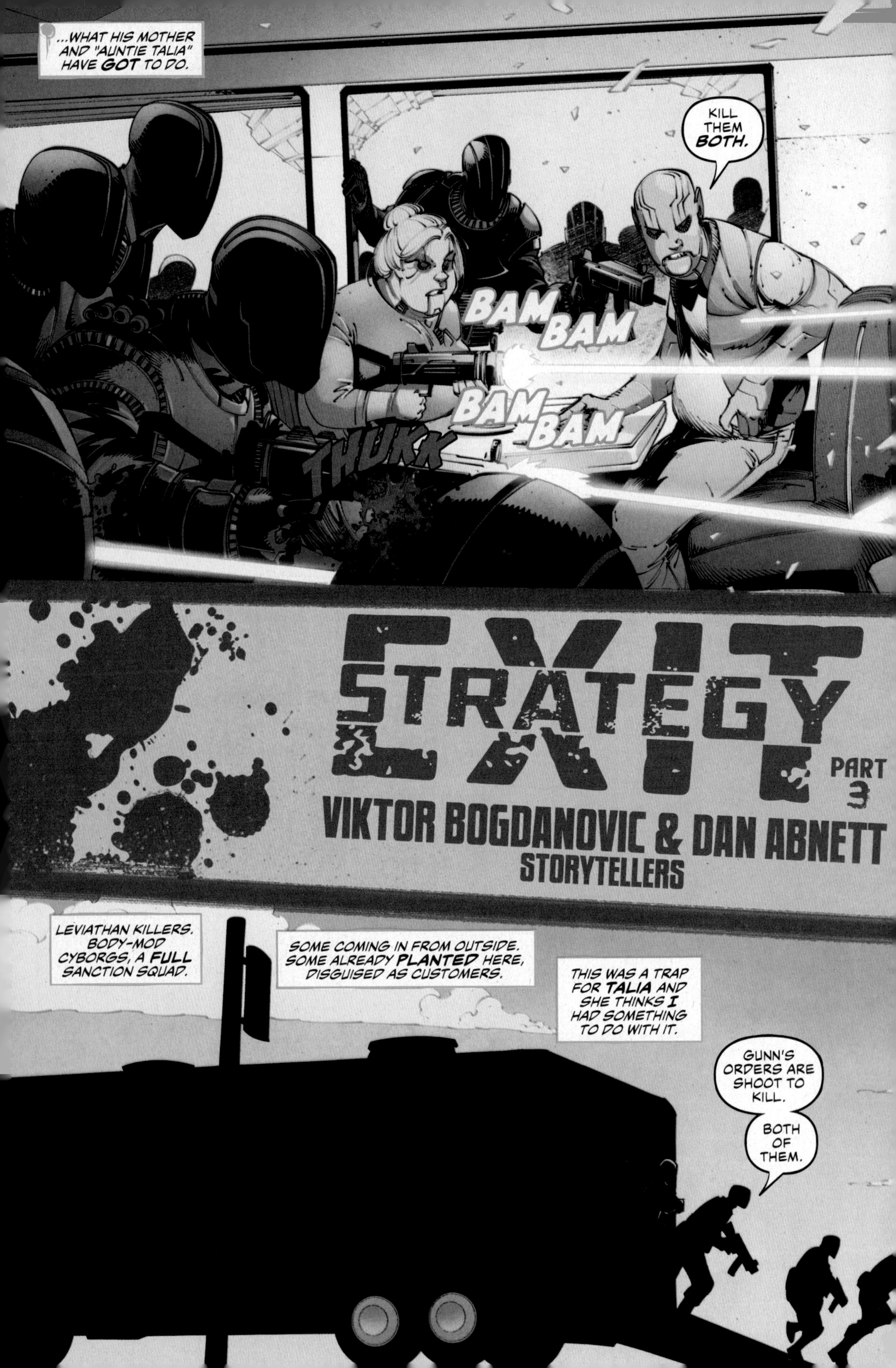
...WHAT HIS MOTHER AND "AUNTIE TALIA" HAVE GOT TO DO.
KILL THEM BOTH.
BAM BAM
BAM BAM
THUKK
STRATEGY
EXIT
PART 3
VIKTOR BOGDANOVIC & DAN ABNETT
STORYTELLERS
LEVIATHAN KILLERS. BODY-MOD CYBORGS, A FULL SANCTION SQUAD.
SOME COMING IN FROM OUTSIDE. SOME ALREADY PLANTED HERE, DISGUISED AS CUSTOMERS.
THIS WAS A TRAP FOR TALIA AND SHE THINKS I HAD SOMETHING TO DO WITH IT.
GUNN'S ORDERS ARE SHOOT TO KILL.
BOTH OF THEM.

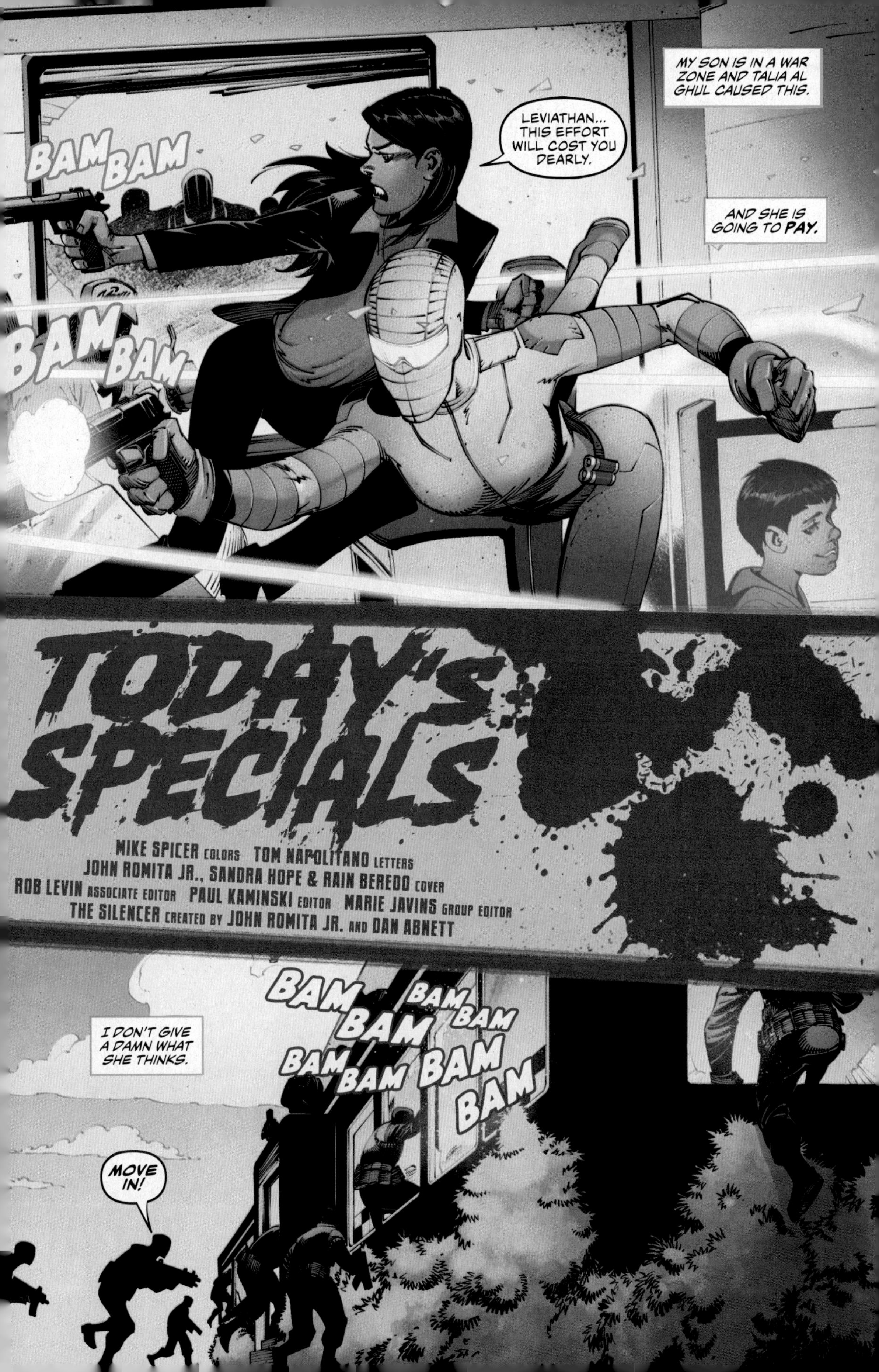
MY SON IS IN A WAR ZONE AND TALIA AL GHUL CAUSED THIS.
LEVIATHAN... THIS EFFORT WILL COST YOU DEARLY.
BAM BAM
AND SHE IS GOING TO PAY.
BAM BAM
TODAY'S SPECIALS
MIKE SPICER COLORS TOM NAPOLITANO LETTERS
JOHN ROMITA JR., SANDRA HOPE & RAIN BEREDO COVER
ROB LEVIN ASSOCIATE EDITOR PAUL KAMINSKI EDITOR MARIE JAVINS GROUP EDITOR
THE SILENCER CREATED BY JOHN ROMITA JR. AND DAN ABNETT
I DON'T GIVE A DAMN WHAT SHE THINKS.
BAM BAM BAM BAM BAM BAM BAM BAM BAM
MOVE IN!

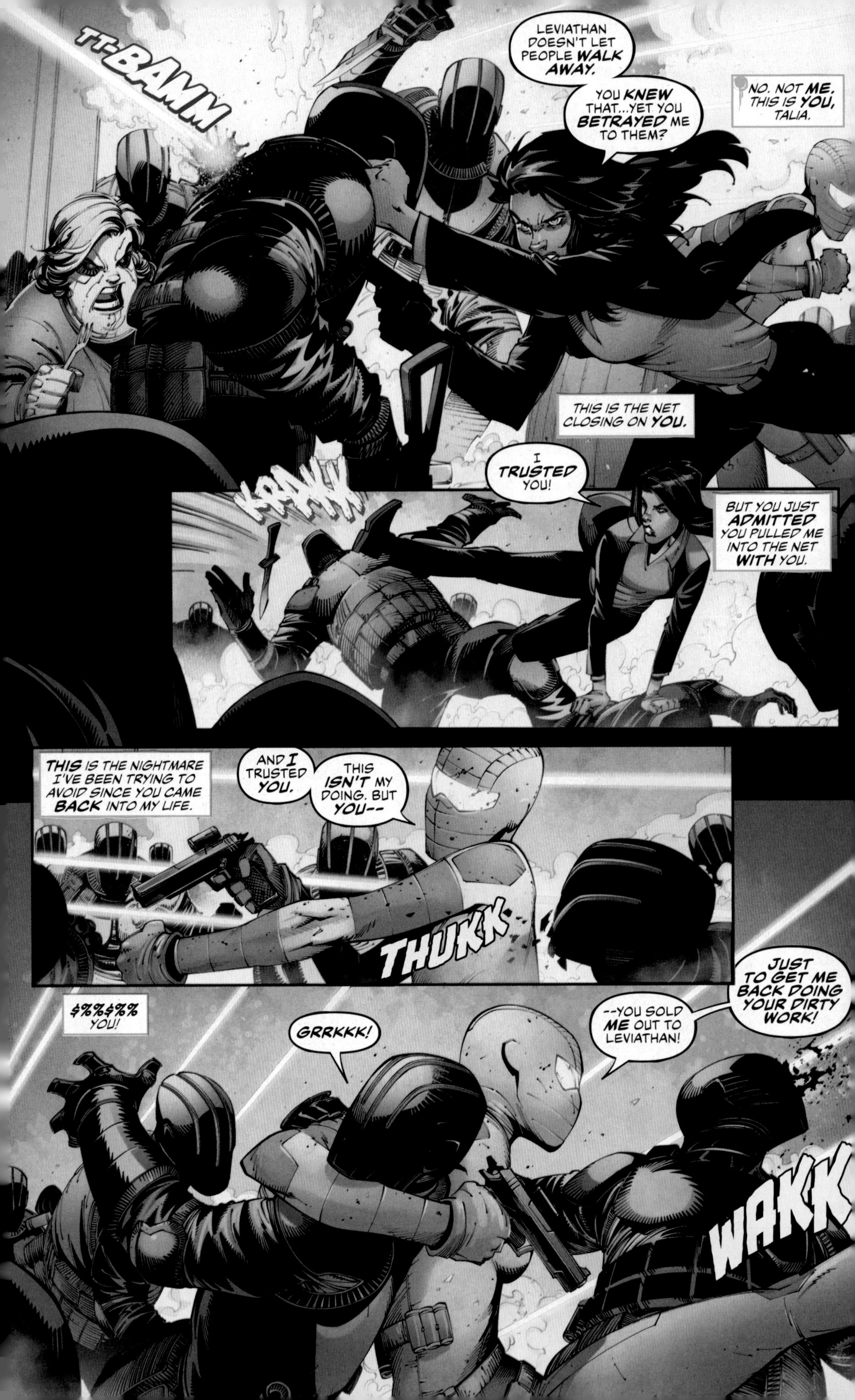
TT-BAMM
LEVIATHAN DOESN'T LET PEOPLE WALK AWAY.
YOU KNEW THAT...YET YOU BETRAYED ME TO THEM?
NO. NOT ME. THIS IS YOU, TALIA.
THIS IS THE NET CLOSING ON YOU.
I TRUSTED YOU!
BUT YOU JUST ADMITTED YOU PULLED ME INTO THE NET WITH YOU.
THIS IS THE NIGHTMARE I'VE BEEN TRYING TO AVOID SINCE YOU CAME BACK INTO MY LIFE.
AND I TRUSTED YOU.
THIS ISN'T MY DOING. BUT YOU--
THUKK
$%%$%% YOU!
GRRKKK!
--YOU SOLD ME OUT TO LEVIATHAN!
JUST TO GET ME BACK DOING YOUR DIRTY WORK!
WAKK

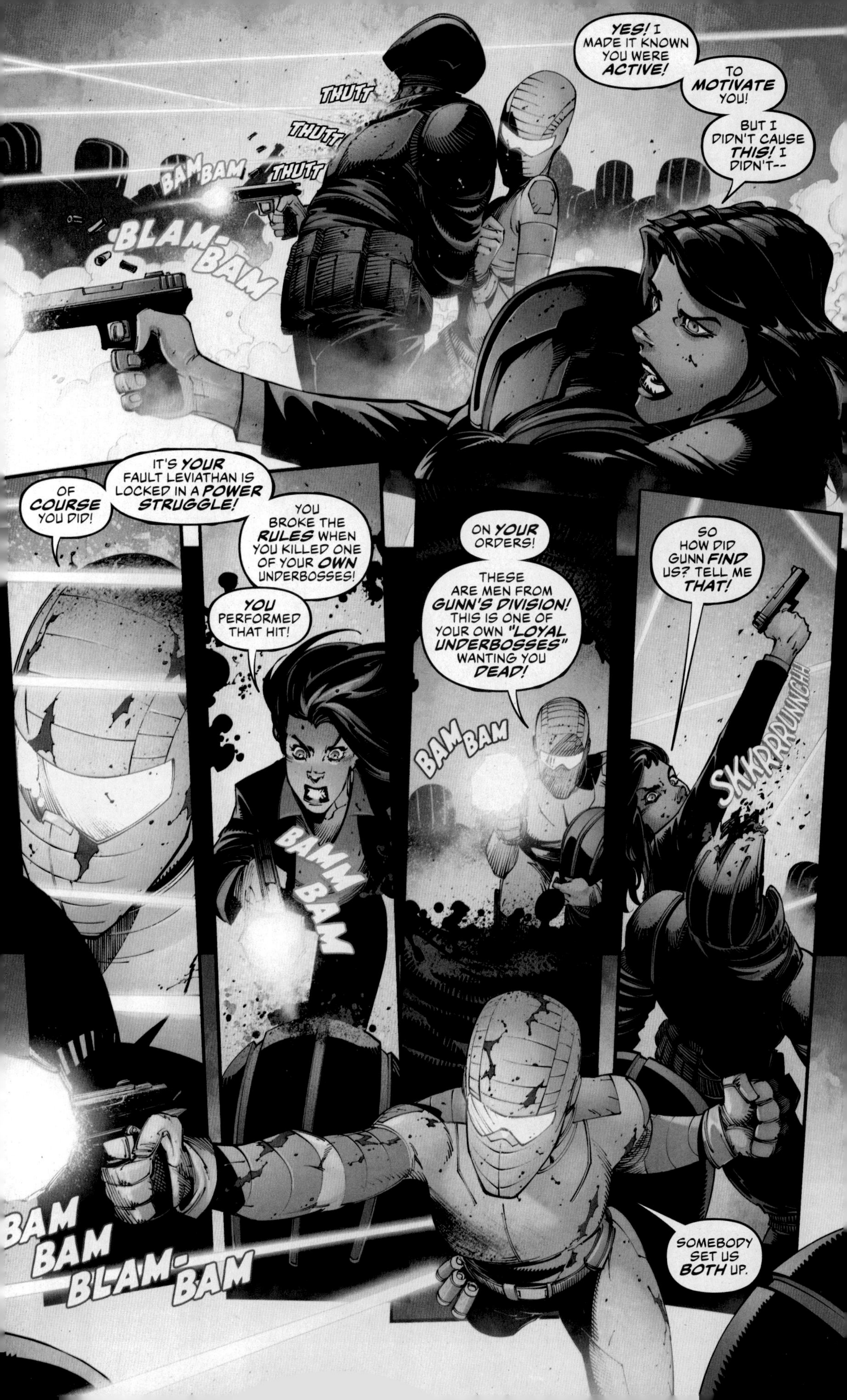

THUTT
THUTT
THUTT
BAM BAM
BLAM-BAM
YES! I MADE IT KNOWN YOU WERE ACTIVE!
TO MOTIVATE YOU!
BUT I DIDN'T CAUSE THIS! I DIDN'T--
OF COURSE YOU DID!
IT'S YOUR FAULT LEVIATHAN IS LOCKED IN A POWER STRUGGLE!
YOU BROKE THE RULES WHEN YOU KILLED ONE OF YOUR OWN UNDERBOSSES!
YOU PERFORMED THAT HIT!
BAMM BAM
ON YOUR ORDERS!
THESE ARE MEN FROM GUNN'S DIVISION! THIS IS ONE OF YOUR OWN "LOYAL UNDERBOSSES" WANTING YOU DEAD!
BAM BAM
SO HOW DID GUNN FIND US? TELL ME THAT!
SKKRRUNCH!!
BAM BAM BLAM-BAM
SOMEBODY SET US BOTH UP.

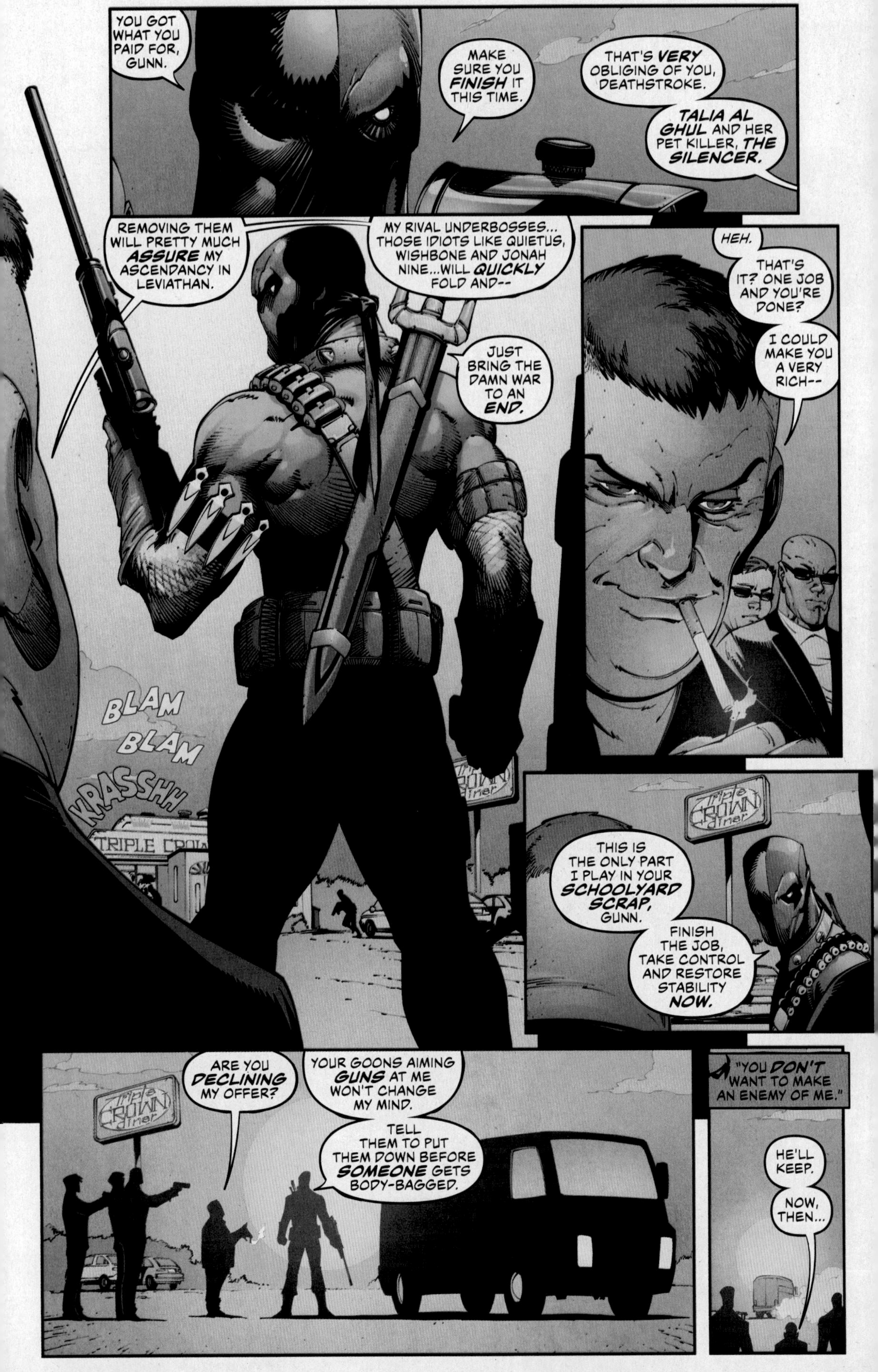
YOU GOT WHAT YOU PAID FOR, GUNN.
MAKE SURE YOU FINISH IT THIS TIME.
THAT'S VERY OBLIGING OF YOU, DEATHSTROKE.
TALIA AL GHUL AND HER PET KILLER, THE SILENCER.
REMOVING THEM WILL PRETTY MUCH ASSURE MY ASCENDANCY IN LEVIATHAN.
MY RIVAL UNDERBOSSES... THOSE IDIOTS LIKE QUIETUS, WISHBONE AND JONAH NINE...WILL QUICKLY FOLD AND--
JUST BRING THE DAMN WAR TO AN END.
BLAM
BLAM
KRASSHH
TRIPLE CROW
HEH.
THAT'S IT? ONE JOB AND YOU'RE DONE?
I COULD MAKE YOU A VERY RICH--
Triple CROWN diner
THIS IS THE ONLY PART I PLAY IN YOUR SCHOOLYARD SCRAP, GUNN.
FINISH THE JOB, TAKE CONTROL AND RESTORE STABILITY NOW.
Triple CROWN diner
ARE YOU DECLINING MY OFFER?
YOUR GOONS AIMING GUNS AT ME WON'T CHANGE MY MIND.
TELL THEM TO PUT THEM DOWN BEFORE SOMEONE GETS BODY-BAGGED.
"YOU DON'T WANT TO MAKE AN ENEMY OF ME."
HE'LL KEEP.
NOW, THEN...

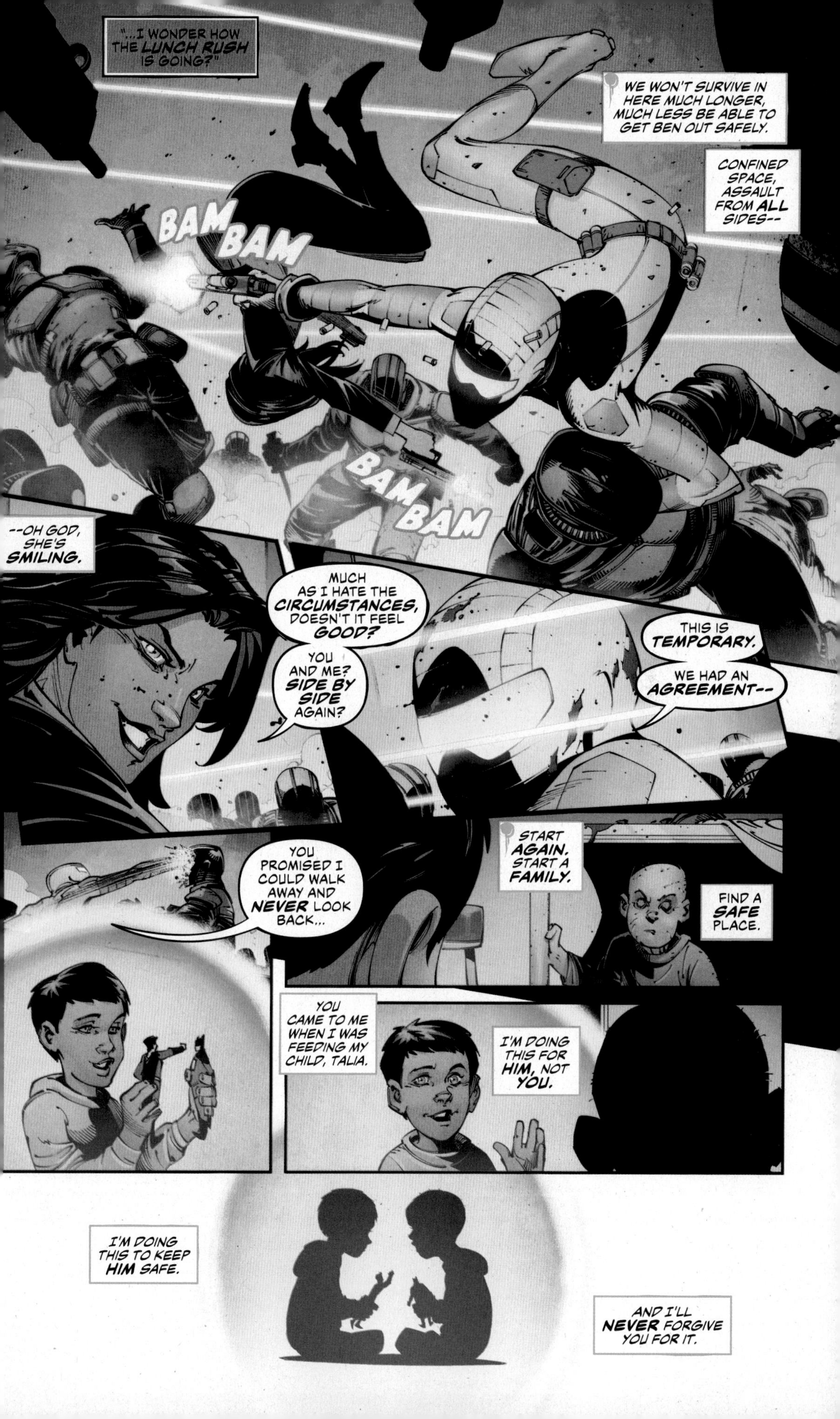
"...I WONDER HOW THE LUNCH RUSH IS GOING?"
WE WON'T SURVIVE IN HERE MUCH LONGER, MUCH LESS BE ABLE TO GET BEN OUT SAFELY.
CONFINED SPACE, ASSAULT FROM ALL SIDES--
BAM BAM
BAM BAM
--OH GOD, SHE'S SMILING.
MUCH AS I HATE THE CIRCUMSTANCES, DOESN'T IT FEEL GOOD?
YOU AND ME? SIDE BY SIDE AGAIN?
THIS IS TEMPORARY.
WE HAD AN AGREEMENT--
YOU PROMISED I COULD WALK AWAY AND NEVER LOOK BACK...
START AGAIN. START A FAMILY.
FIND A SAFE PLACE.
YOU CAME TO ME WHEN I WAS FEEDING MY CHILD, TALIA.
I'M DOING THIS FOR HIM, NOT YOU.
I'M DOING THIS TO KEEP HIM SAFE.
AND I'LL NEVER FORGIVE YOU FOR IT.

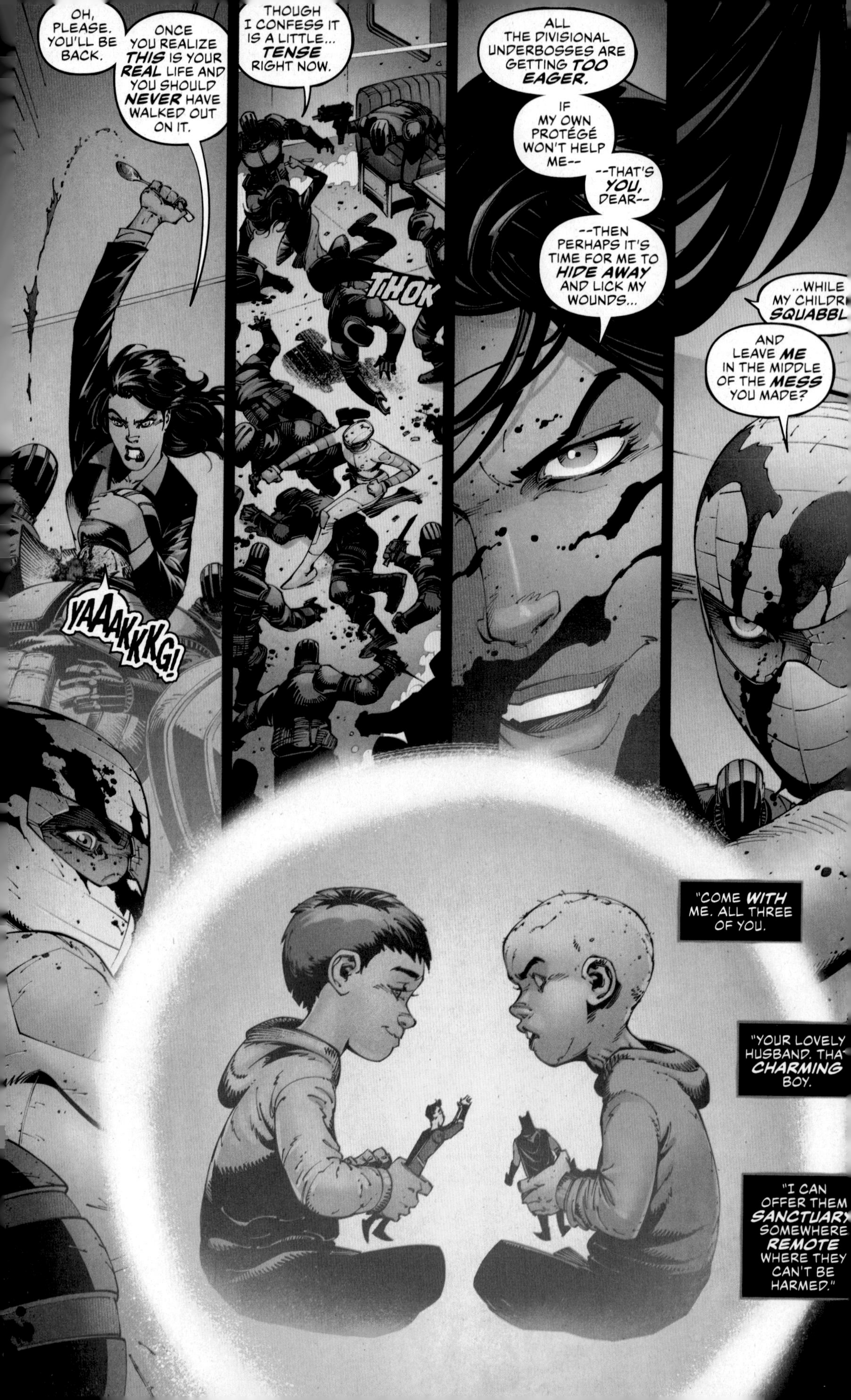
OH, PLEASE. YOU'LL BE BACK.
ONCE YOU REALIZE THIS IS YOUR REAL LIFE AND YOU SHOULD NEVER HAVE WALKED OUT ON IT.
YAAAKKKG!
THOUGH I CONFESS IT IS A LITTLE... TENSE RIGHT NOW.
THOK
ALL THE DIVISIONAL UNDERBOSSES ARE GETTING TOO EAGER.
IF MY OWN PROTÉGÉ WON'T HELP ME--
--THAT'S YOU, DEAR--
--THEN PERHAPS IT'S TIME FOR ME TO HIDE AWAY AND LICK MY WOUNDS...
...WHILE MY CHILDR SQUABBL
AND LEAVE ME IN THE MIDDLE OF THE MESS YOU MADE?
"COME WITH ME. ALL THREE OF YOU.
"YOUR LOVELY HUSBAND. THA CHARMING BOY.
"I CAN OFFER THEM SANCTUARY SOMEWHERE REMOTE WHERE THEY CAN'T BE HARMED."

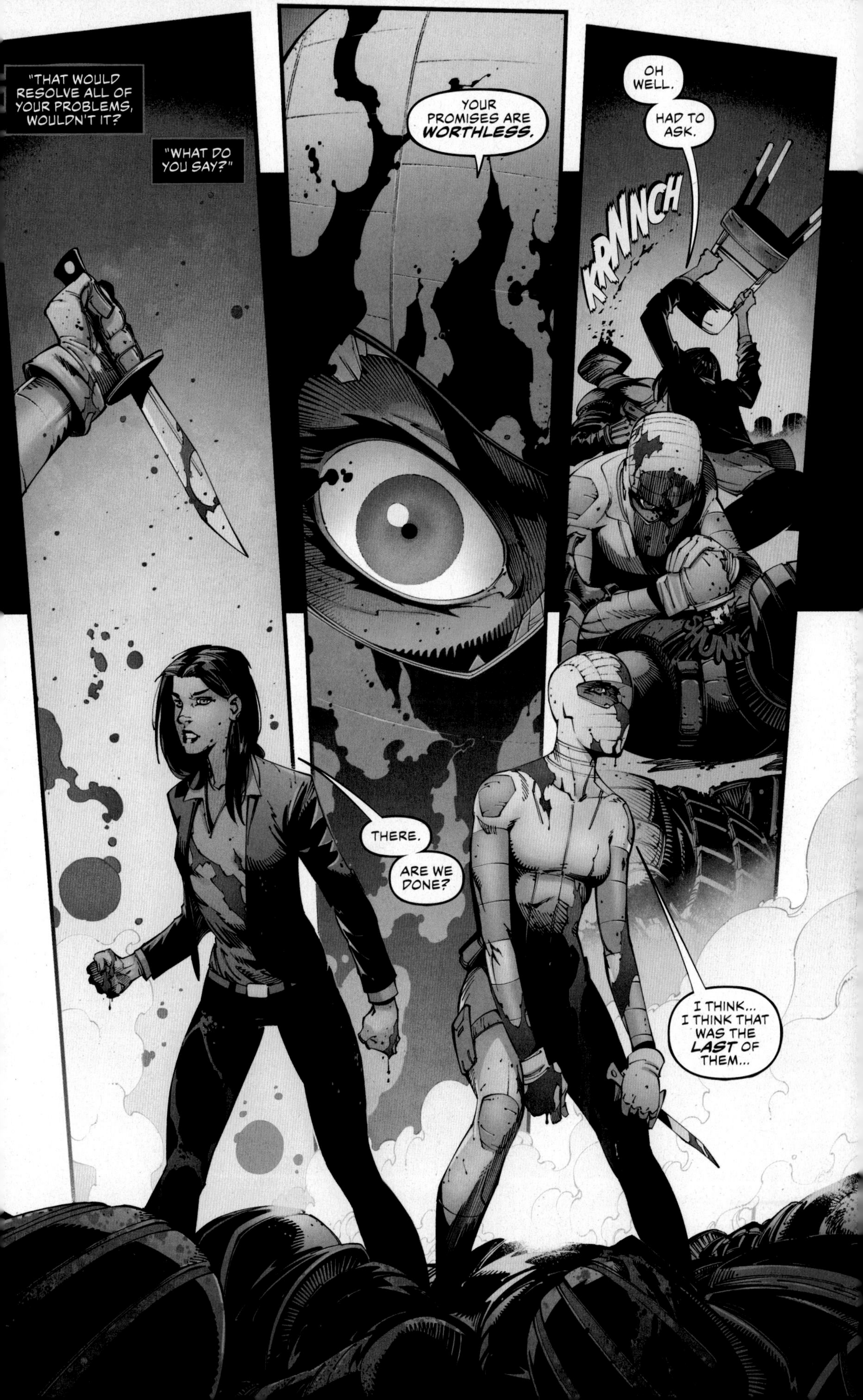
"THAT WOULD RESOLVE ALL OF YOUR PROBLEMS, WOULDN'T IT?
"WHAT DO YOU SAY?"
YOUR PROMISES ARE WORTHLESS.
OH WELL.
HAD TO ASK.
KRNNCH
SHUNK
THERE.
ARE WE DONE?
I THINK... I THINK THAT WAS THE LAST OF THEM...

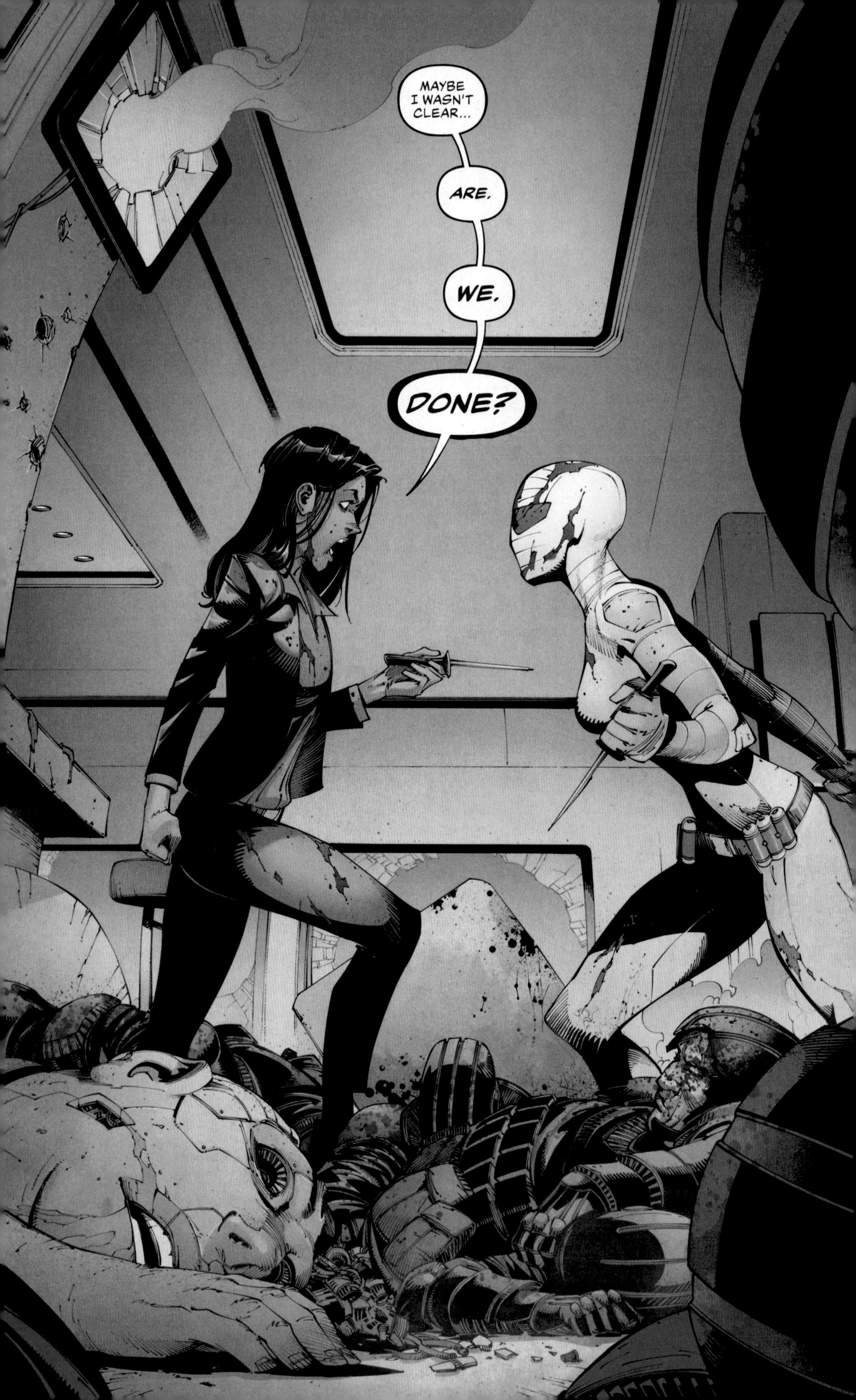
MAYBE I WASN'T CLEAR...
ARE.
WE.
DONE?

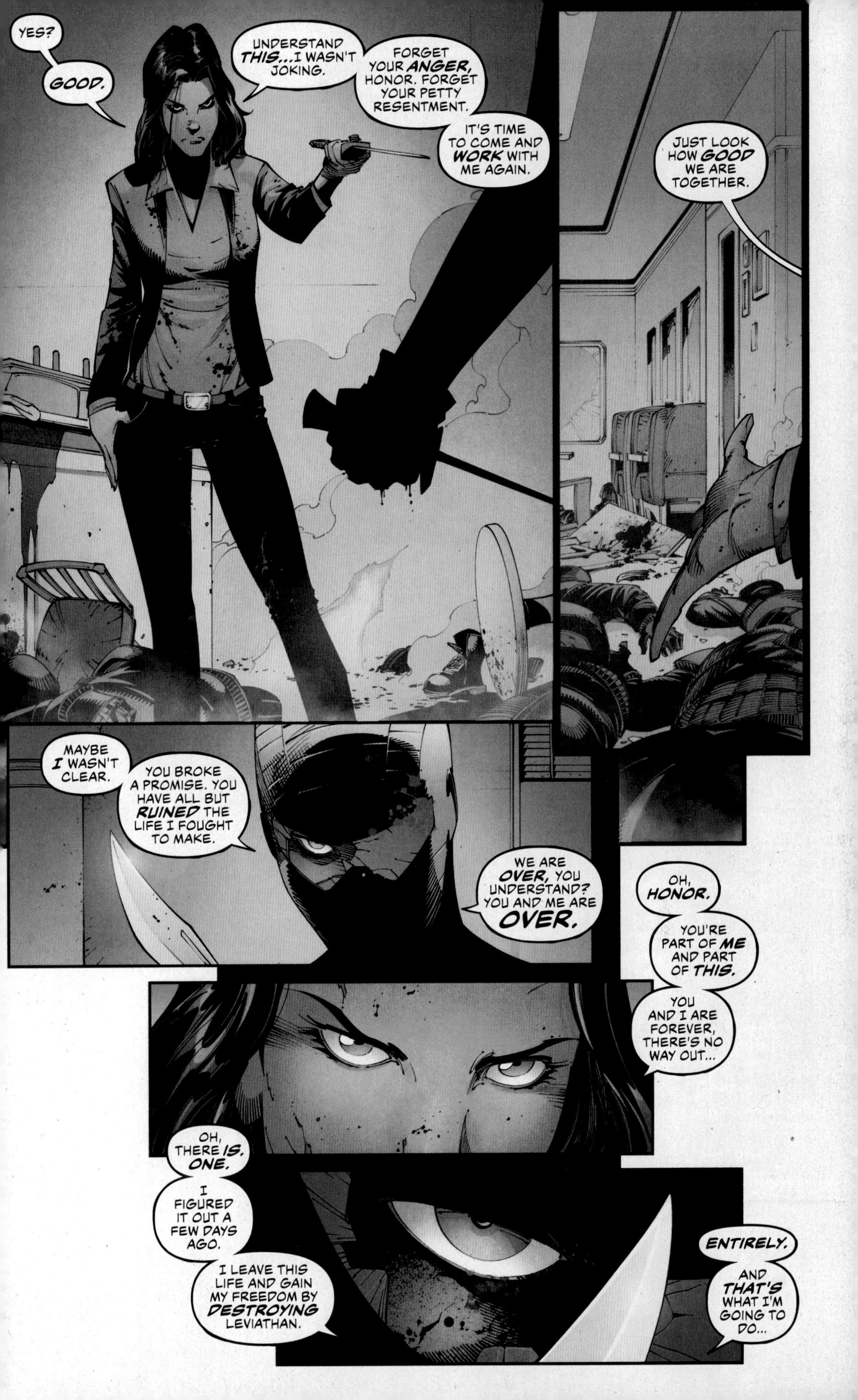
YES?
GOOD.
UNDERSTAND THIS...I WASN'T JOKING.
FORGET YOUR ANGER, HONOR. FORGET YOUR PETTY RESENTMENT.
IT'S TIME TO COME AND WORK WITH ME AGAIN.
JUST LOOK HOW GOOD WE ARE TOGETHER.
MAYBE I WASN'T CLEAR.
YOU BROKE A PROMISE. YOU HAVE ALL BUT RUINED THE LIFE I FOUGHT TO MAKE.
WE ARE OVER, YOU UNDERSTAND? YOU AND ME ARE OVER.
OH, HONOR.
YOU'RE PART OF ME AND PART OF THIS.
YOU AND I ARE FOREVER, THERE'S NO WAY OUT...
OH, THERE IS. ONE.
I FIGURED IT OUT A FEW DAYS AGO.
I LEAVE THIS LIFE AND GAIN MY FREEDOM BY DESTROYING LEVIATHAN.
ENTIRELY.
AND THAT'S WHAT I'M GOING TO DO...

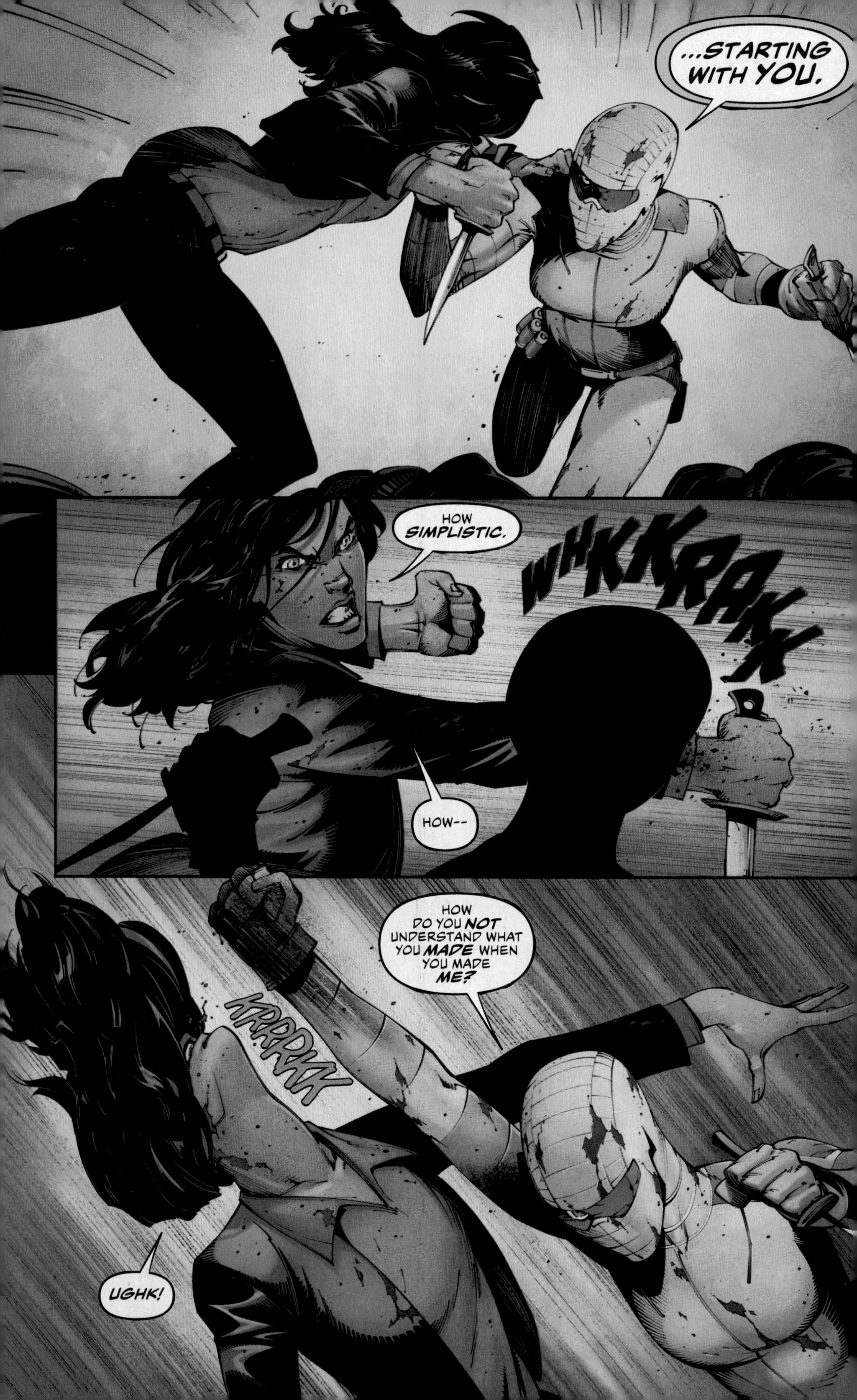
...STARTING WITH YOU.
HOW SIMPLISTIC.
WHKKRAKK
HOW--
HOW DO YOU NOT UNDERSTAND WHAT YOU MADE WHEN YOU MADE ME?
KRRRKK
UGHK!

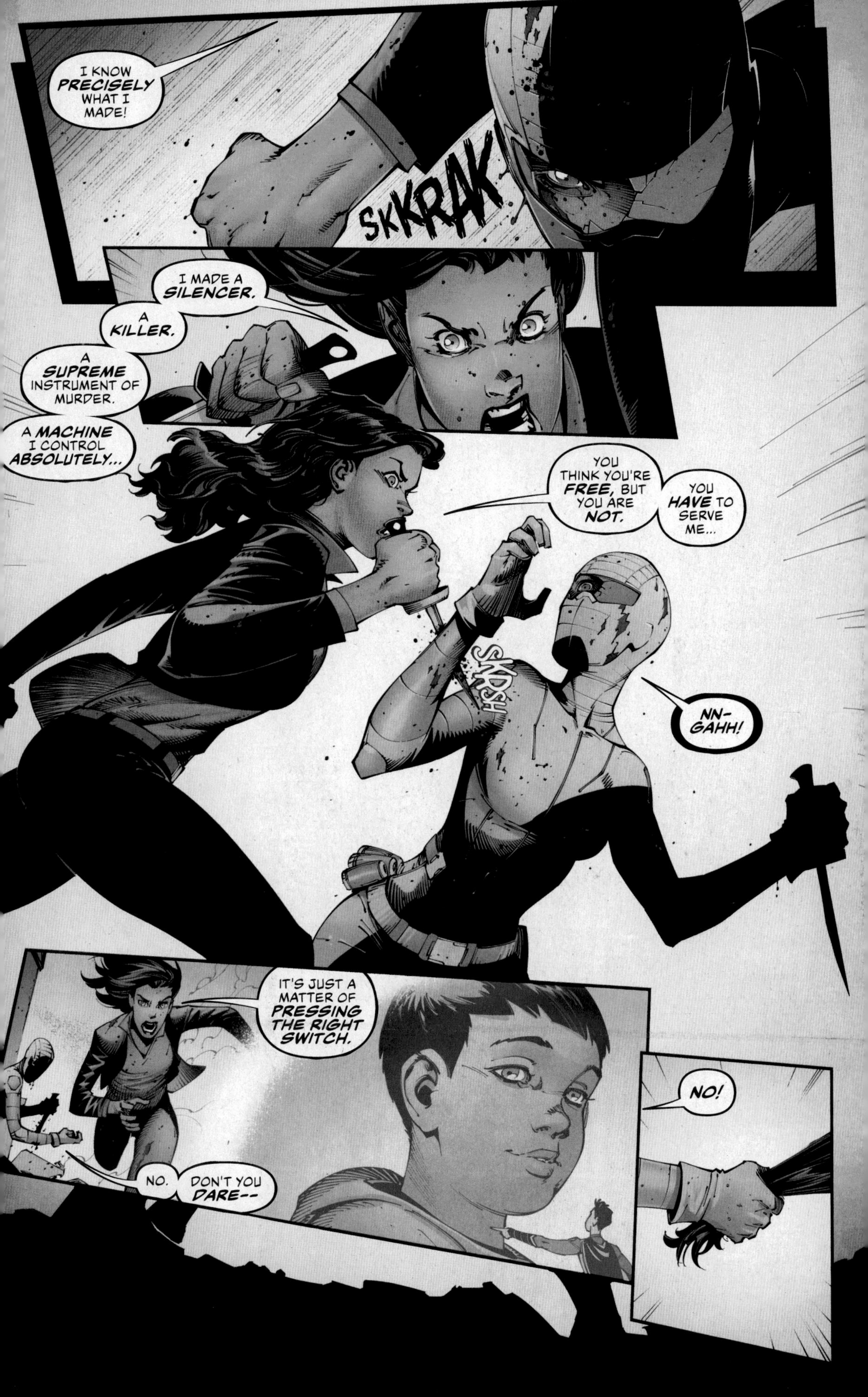
I KNOW PRECISELY WHAT I MADE!
SKKRAK
I MADE A SILENCER.
A KILLER.
A SUPREME INSTRUMENT OF MURDER.
A MACHINE I CONTROL ABSOLUTELY...
YOU THINK YOU'RE FREE, BUT YOU ARE NOT.
YOU HAVE TO SERVE ME...
SKRSH
NN-GAHH!
IT'S JUST A MATTER OF PRESSING THE RIGHT SWITCH.
NO.
DON'T YOU DARE--
NO!

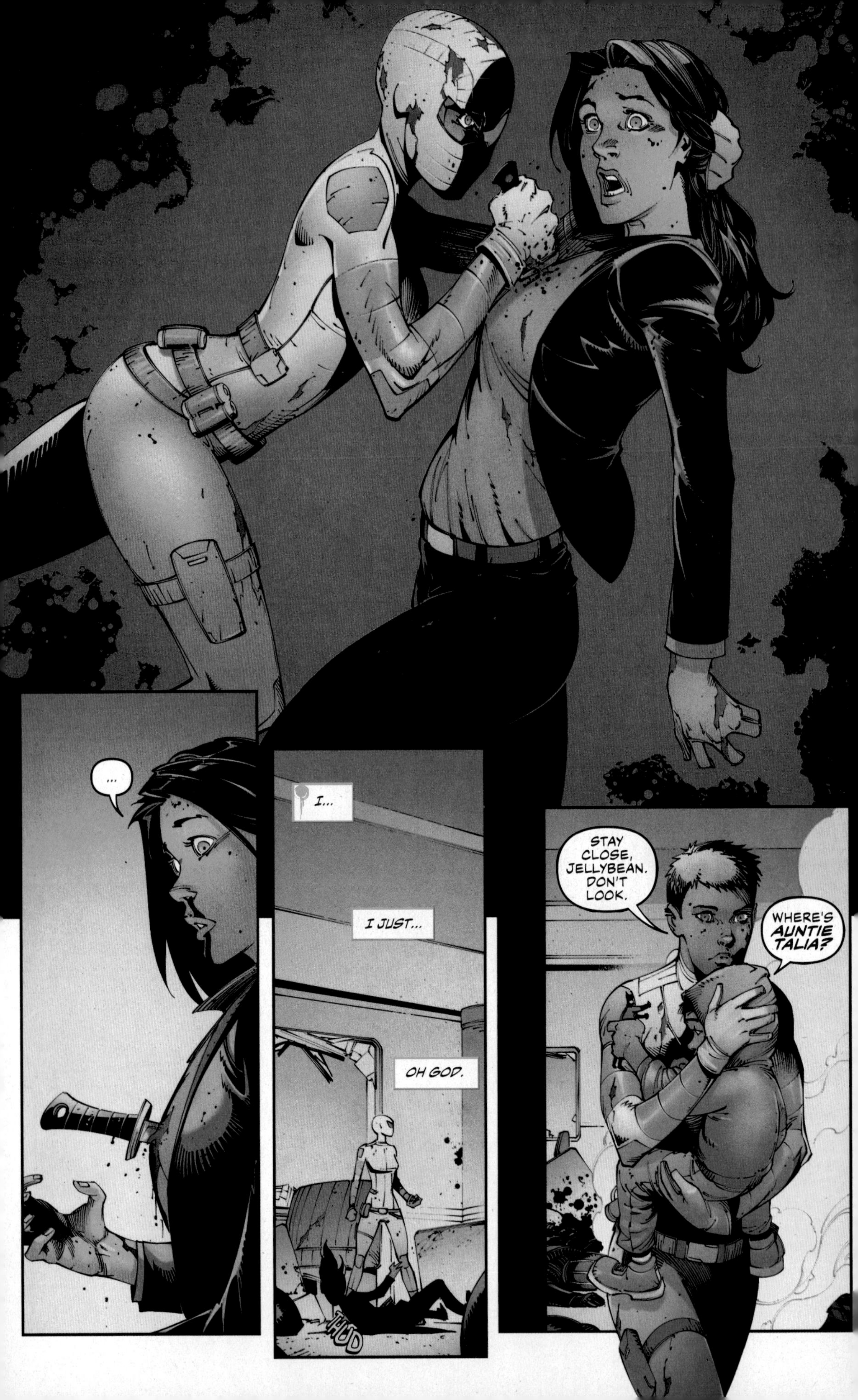
...
I...
I JUST...
OH GOD.
THUD
STAY CLOSE, JELLYBEAN. DON'T LOOK.
WHERE'S AUNTIE TALIA?

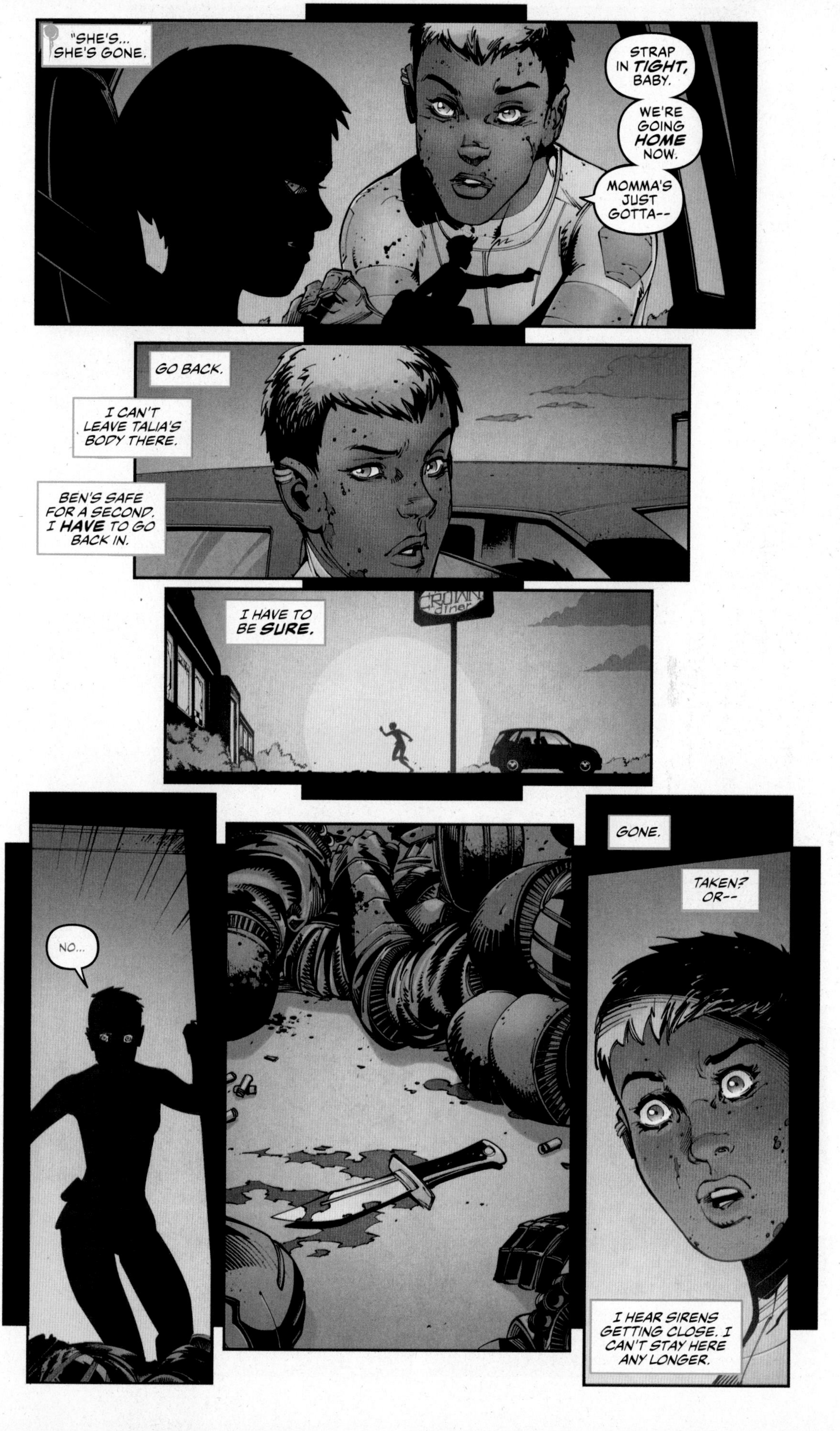
"SHE'S... SHE'S GONE.
STRAP IN TIGHT, BABY.
WE'RE GOING HOME NOW.
MOMMA'S JUST GOTTA--
GO BACK.
I CAN'T LEAVE TALIA'S BODY THERE.
BEN'S SAFE FOR A SECOND. I HAVE TO GO BACK IN.
I HAVE TO BE SURE.
NO...
GONE.
TAKEN? OR--
I HEAR SIRENS GETTING CLOSE. I CAN'T STAY HERE ANY LONGER.

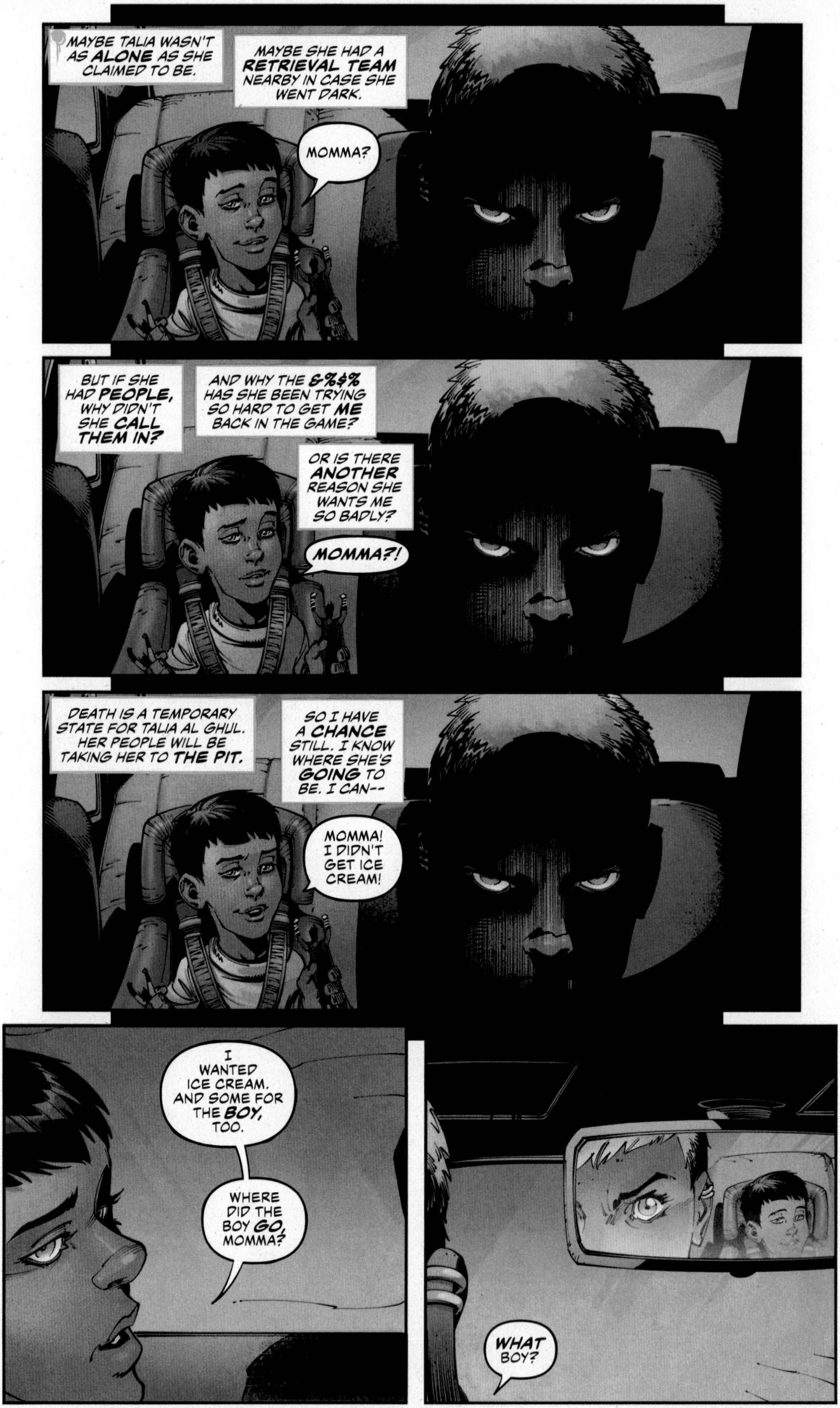
MAYBE TALIA WASN'T AS ALONE AS SHE CLAIMED TO BE.
MAYBE SHE HAD A RETRIEVAL TEAM NEARBY IN CASE SHE WENT DARK.
MOMMA?
BUT IF SHE HAD PEOPLE, WHY DIDN'T SHE CALL THEM IN?
AND WHY THE &%$% HAS SHE BEEN TRYING SO HARD TO GET ME BACK IN THE GAME?
OR IS THERE ANOTHER REASON SHE WANTS ME SO BADLY?
MOMMA?!
DEATH IS A TEMPORARY STATE FOR TALIA AL GHUL. HER PEOPLE WILL BE TAKING HER TO THE PIT.
SO I HAVE A CHANCE STILL. I KNOW WHERE SHE'S GOING TO BE. I CAN--
MOMMA! I DIDN'T GET ICE CREAM!
I WANTED ICE CREAM. AND SOME FOR THE BOY, TOO.
WHERE DID THE BOY GO, MOMMA?
WHAT BOY?

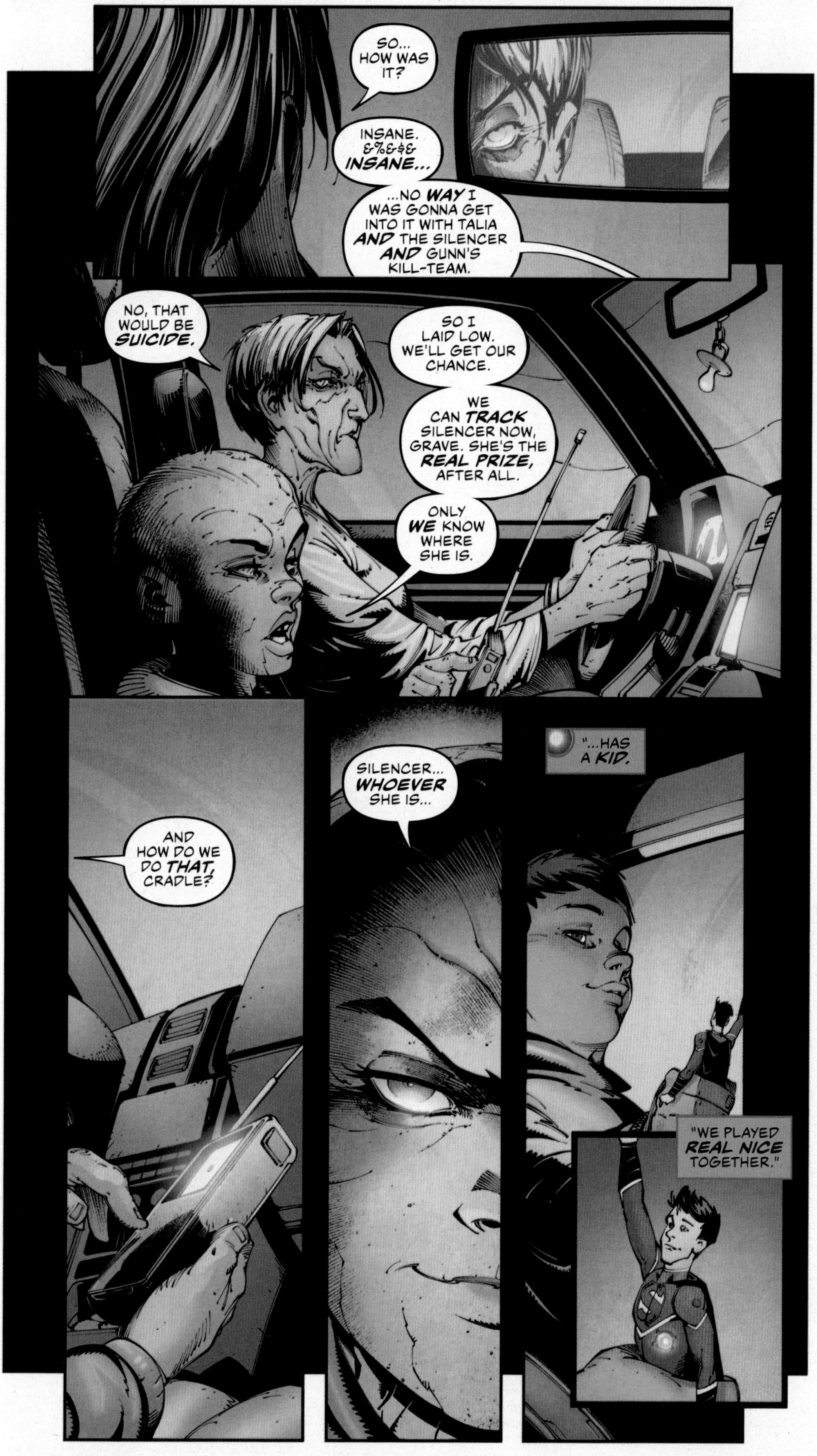
SO... HOW WAS IT?
INSANE. &%&$& INSANE...
...NO WAY I WAS GONNA GET INTO IT WITH TALIA AND THE SILENCER AND GUNN'S KILL-TEAM.
NO, THAT WOULD BE SUICIDE.
SO I LAID LOW. WE'LL GET OUR CHANCE.
WE CAN TRACK SILENCER NOW, GRAVE. SHE'S THE REAL PRIZE, AFTER ALL.
ONLY WE KNOW WHERE SHE IS.
AND HOW DO WE DO THAT, CRADLE?
SILENCER... WHOEVER SHE IS...
"...HAS A KID.
"WE PLAYED REAL NICE TOGETHER."

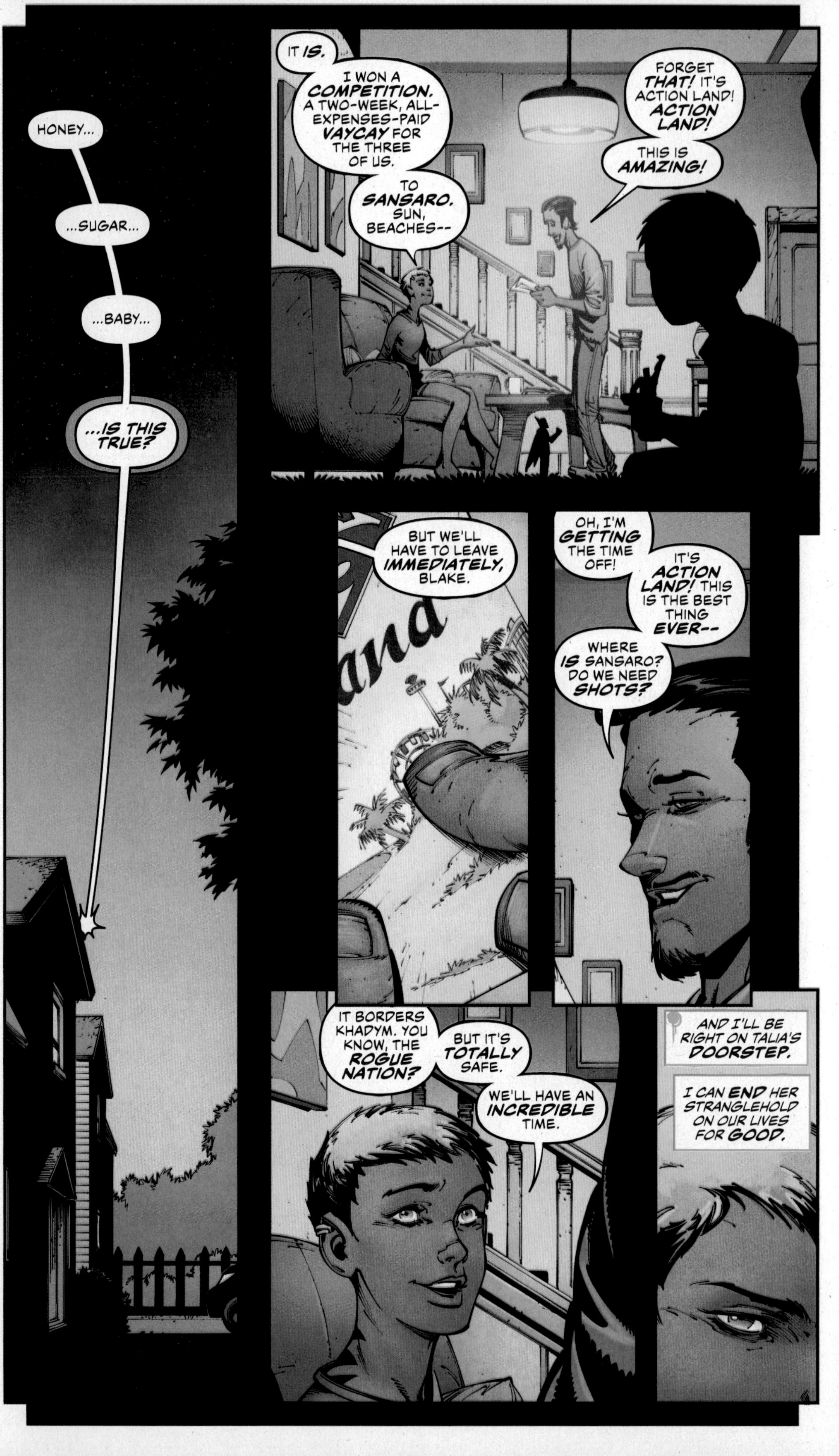
HONEY...
...SUGAR...
...BABY...
...IS THIS TRUE?
IT IS.
I WON A COMPETITION. A TWO-WEEK, ALL-EXPENSES-PAID VAYCAY FOR THE THREE OF US.
TO SANSARO. SUN, BEACHES--
FORGET THAT! IT'S ACTION LAND! ACTION LAND!
THIS IS AMAZING!
BUT WE'LL HAVE TO LEAVE IMMEDIATELY, BLAKE.
OH, I'M GETTING THE TIME OFF!
IT'S ACTION LAND! THIS IS THE BEST THING EVER--
WHERE IS SANSARO? DO WE NEED SHOTS?
IT BORDERS KHADYM. YOU KNOW, THE ROGUE NATION?
BUT IT'S TOTALLY SAFE.
WE'LL HAVE AN INCREDIBLE TIME.
AND I'LL BE RIGHT ON TALIA'S DOORSTEP.
I CAN END HER STRANGLEHOLD ON OUR LIVES FOR GOOD.

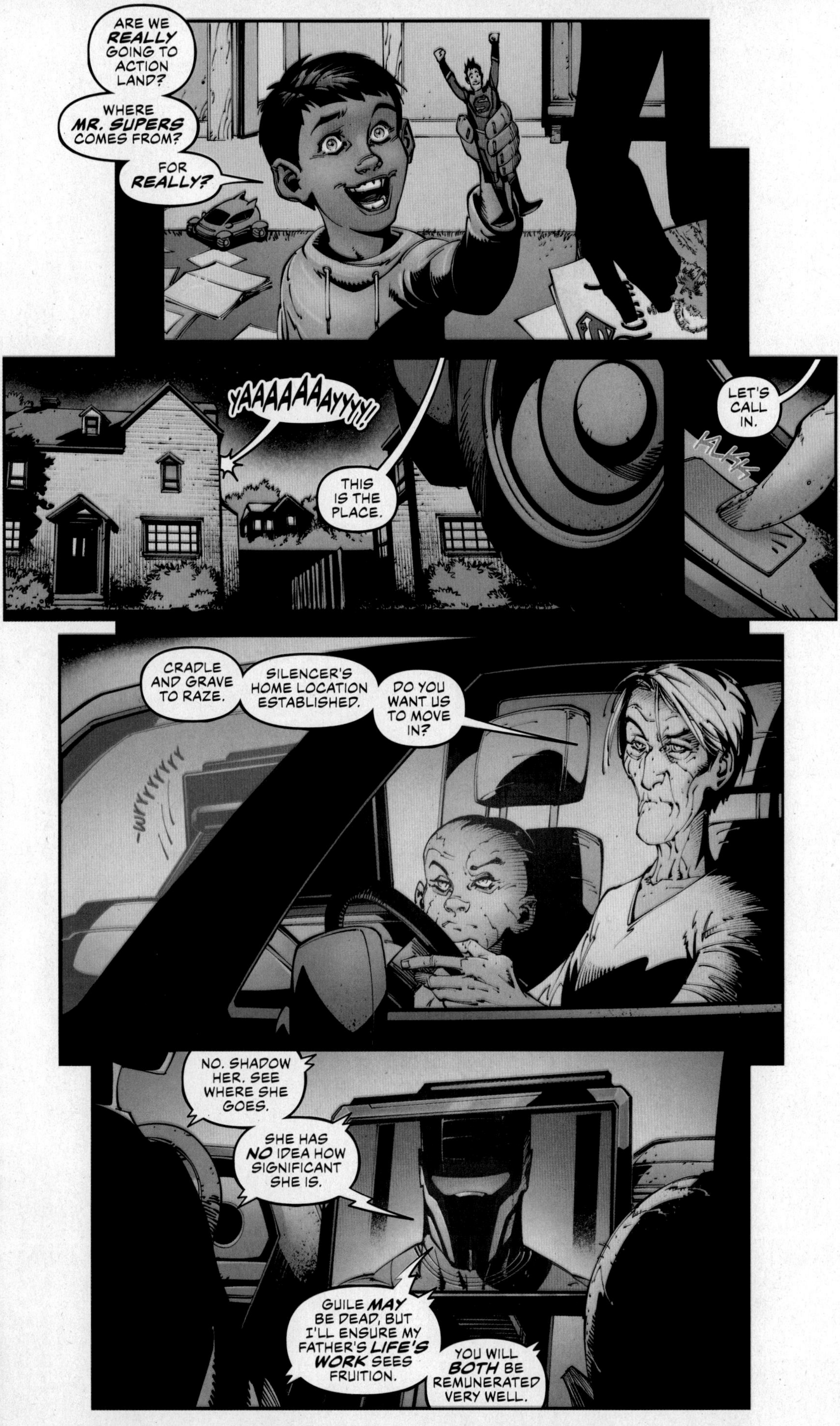

ARE WE REALLY GOING TO ACTION LAND?
WHERE MR. SUPERS COMES FROM?
FOR REALLY?
YAAAAAAAYYYY!
THIS IS THE PLACE.
LET'S CALL IN.
CRADLE AND GRAVE TO RAZE.
SILENCER'S HOME LOCATION ESTABLISHED.
DO YOU WANT US TO MOVE IN?
-WRYYYYYYY
NO. SHADOW HER. SEE WHERE SHE GOES.
SHE HAS NO IDEA HOW SIGNIFICANT SHE IS.
GUILE MAY BE DEAD, BUT I'LL ENSURE MY FATHER'S LIFE'S WORK SEES FRUITION.
YOU WILL BOTH BE REMUNERATED VERY WELL.

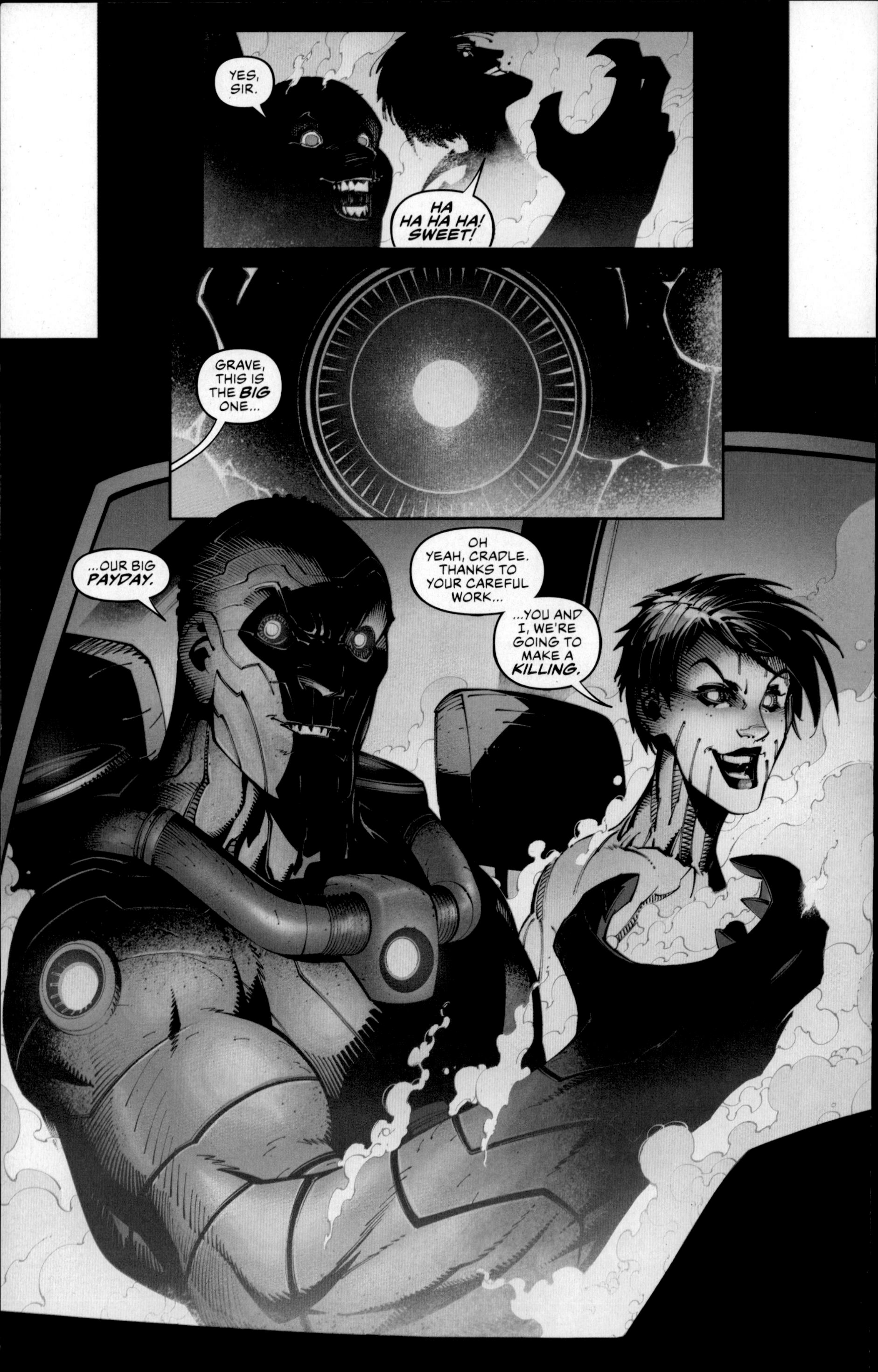

YES, SIR.
HA HA HA HA! SWEET!
GRAVE, THIS IS THE BIG ONE...
...OUR BIG PAYDAY.
OH YEAH, CRADLE. THANKS TO YOUR CAREFUL WORK...
...YOU AND I, WE'RE GOING TO MAKE A KILLING.

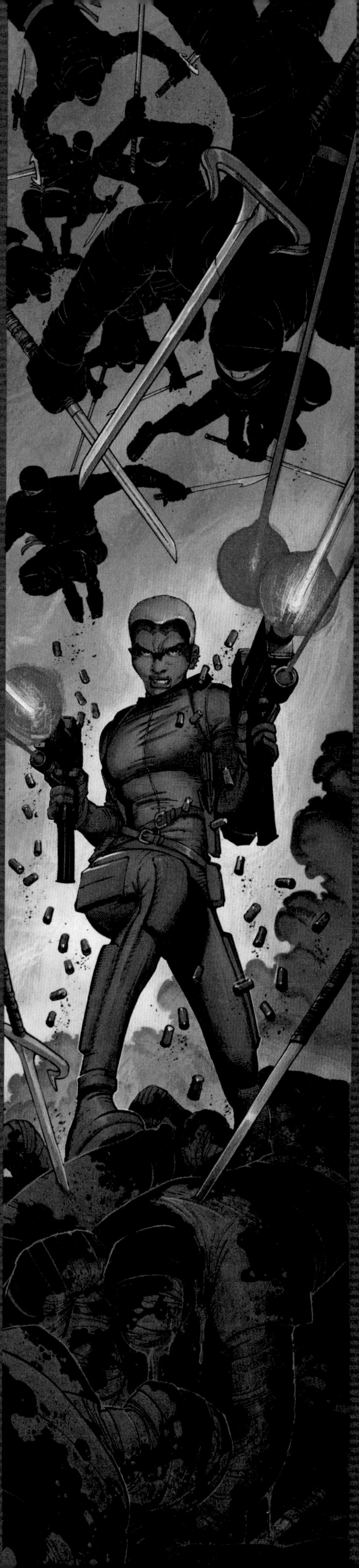

THE SILENCER #1 full triptych cover

by John Romita Jr., Sandra Hope & Dean White

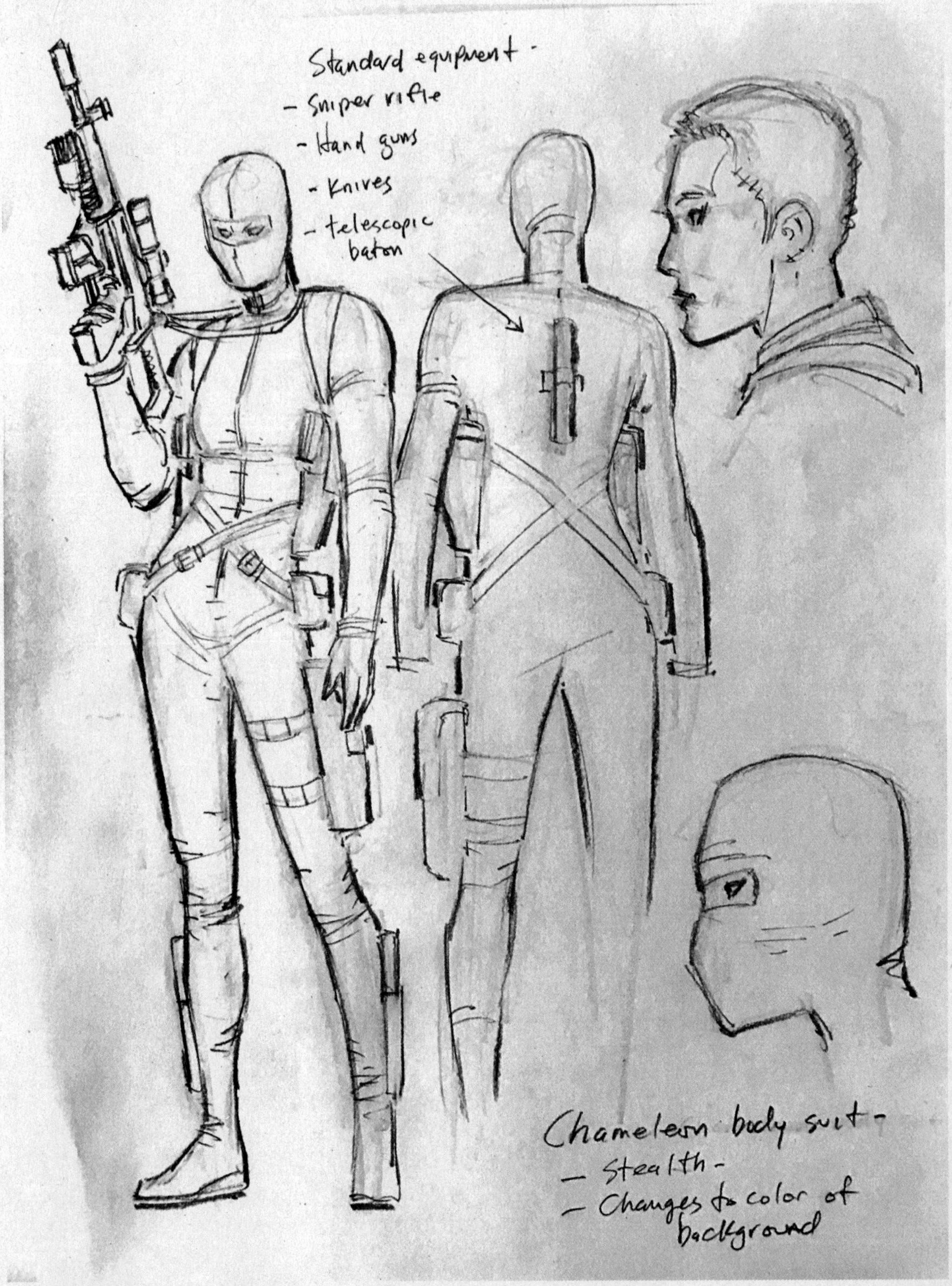

Standard equipment -
- Sniper rifle
- Hand guns
- Knives
- telescopic baton
Chameleon body suit -
- stealth -
- Changes to color of background

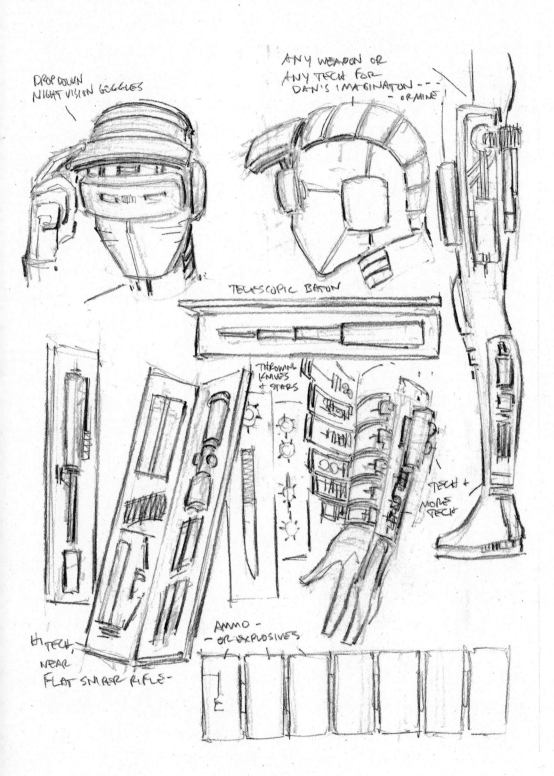

DROP DOWN
NIGHT VISION GOGGLES

ANY WEAPON OR
ANY TECH FOR
DAN'S IMAGINATION---
---OR MINE

TELESCOPIC BATON

THROWING
KNIVES
+ STARS

TECH +
MORE
TECH

HI TECH,
NEAR
FLAT SNIPER RIFLE-

AMMO -
-OR EXPLOSIVES

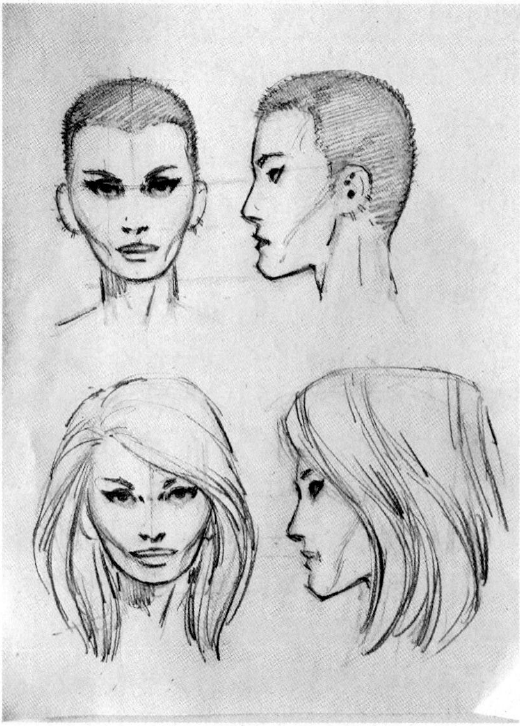

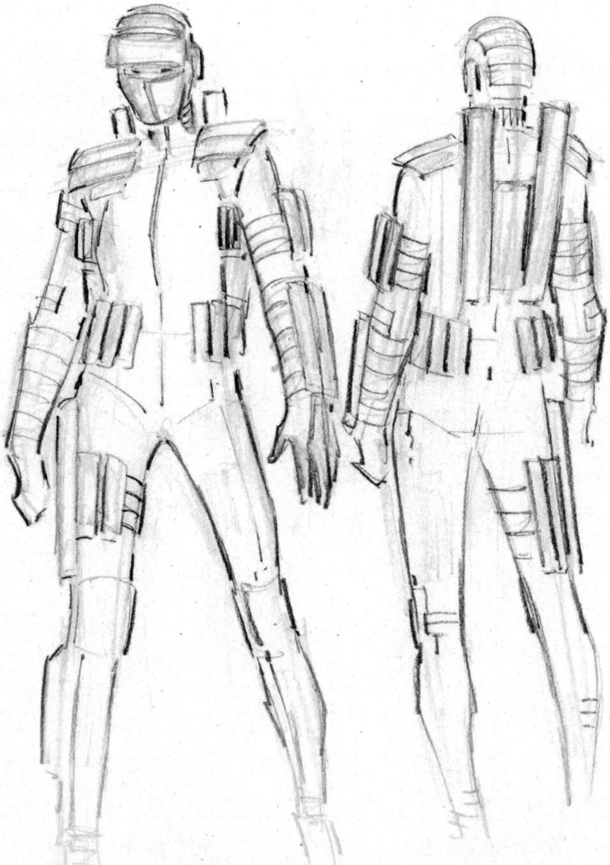

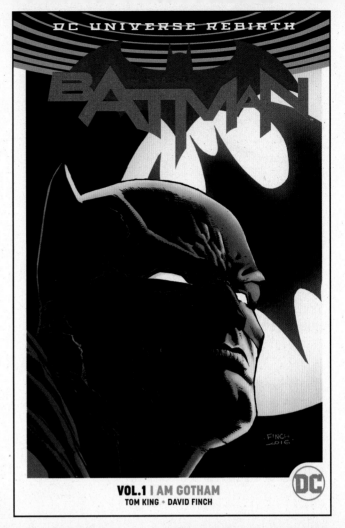

"Batman is getting a brand-new voice."
– USA TODAY

"A great showcase for the new team as well as offering a taste of the new flavor they'll be bringing to Gotham City." **– IGN**

DC UNIVERSE REBIRTH

BATMAN

VOL. 1: I AM GOTHAM

TOM KING
with DAVID FINCH

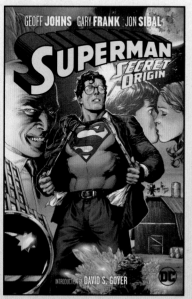
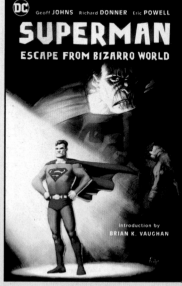

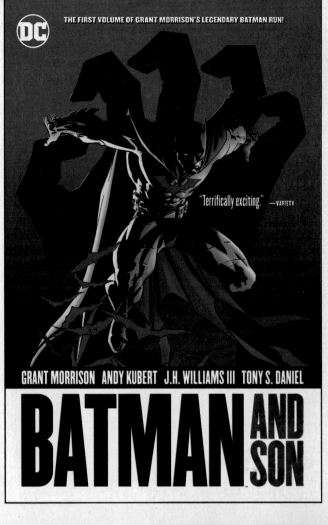

DC UNIVERSE REBIRTH

THE FLASH

VOL. 1: LIGHTNING STRIKES TWICE

JOSHUA WILLIAMSON

with CARMINE DI GIANDOMENICO
and IVAN PLASCENCIA

VOL. 1 LIGHTNING STRIKES TWICE
JOSHUA WILLIAMSON ∗ CARMINE DI GIANDOMENICO ∗ IVAN PLASCENCIA

JUSTICE LEAGUE VOL. 1:
THE EXTINCTION MACHINES

TITANS VOL. 1:
THE RETURN OF WALLY WEST

HAL JORDAN AND
THE GREEN LANTERN CORPS VOL. 1:
SINESTRO'S LAW